COLONIALISM AND ITS FORMS OF KNOWLEDGE

E D I T O R S

Sherry B. Ortner, Nicholas B. Dirks, Geoff Eley

A LIST OF TITLES

IN THIS SERIES APPEARS

AT THE BACK OF

THE BOOK

PRINCETON STUDIES IN
CULTURE / POWER / HISTORY

COLONIALISM AND ITS FORMS
OF KNOWLEDGE

THE BRITISH IN INDIA

Bernard S. Cohn

PRINCETON UNIVERSITY PRESS

PRINCETON, NEW JERSEY

PUBLISHED BY PRINCETON UNIVERSITY PRESS, 41 WILLIAM STREET,
PRINCETON, NEW JERSEY 08540
IN THE UNITED KINGDOM: PRINCETON UNIVERSITY PRESS, CHICESTER, WEST SUSSEX

LIBRARY OF CONGRESS CATALOGING-IN-PUBLICATION DATA

COHN, BERNARD S., 1928–
COLONIALISM AND ITS FORMS OF KNOWLEDGE :
THE BRITISH IN INDIA / BERNARD S. COHN.
P. CM. — (PRINCETON STUDIES IN CULTURE/POWER/HISTORY)
INCLUDES BIBLIOGRAPHICAL REFERENCES AND INDEX.
ISBN 0-691-03293-9 (CL : ALK. PAPER). — ISBN 0-691-00043-3 (PB : ALK. PAPER)
1. INDIA—HISTORY—BRITISH OCCUPATION, 1765–1947.   2. INDIA—CIVILIZATION—
BRITISH INFLUENCES.   3. INDIA—POLITICS AND GOVERNMENT—1765–1947.
I. TITLE.   II. SERIES.
DS436.C65   1996   954—DC20   96-6448   CIP

THIS BOOK HAS BEEN COMPOSED IN CALEDONIA

PRINCETON UNIVERSITY PRESS BOOKS ARE PRINTED ON ACID-FREE PAPER
AND MEET THE GUIDELINES FOR PERMANENCE AND DURABILITY OF THE
COMMITTEE ON PRODUCTION GUIDELINES FOR BOOK LONGEVITY OF THE
COUNCIL ON LIBRARY RESOURCES

HTTP:// PUP.PRINCETON.EDU

PRINTED IN THE UNITED STATES OF AMERICA

1   3   5   7   9   10   8   6   4   2

5   7   9   10   8   6   4
(PBK)

To the other doctor in the house

CONTENTS

FOREWORD

Nicholas B. Dirks

COLONIAL conquest was not just the result of the power of superior arms, military organization, political power, or economic wealth—as important as these things were. Colonialism was made possible, and then sustained and strengthened, as much by cultural technologies of rule as it was by the more obvious and brutal modes of conquest that first established power on foreign shores. The cultural effects of colonialism have too often been ignored or displaced into the inevitable logic of modernization and world capitalism; but more than this, it has not been sufficiently recognized that colonialism was itself a cultural project of control. Colonial knowledge both enabled conquest and was produced by it; in certain important ways, knowledge was what colonialism was all about. Cultural forms in societies newly classified as "traditional" were reconstructed and transformed by and through this knowledge, which created new categories and oppositions between colonizers and colonized, European and Asian, modern and traditional, West and East. Ruling India through the delineation and reconstitution of systematic grammars for vernacular languages, representing India through the mastery and display of archaeological memories and religious texts, Britain set in motion transformations every bit as powerful as the better-known consequences of military and economic imperialism.

Bernard Cohn has played a critical role in identifying and exploring these relations between colonialism and cultural transformation in the last three hundred years of South Asian history. Long before the powerful theoretical proposals of Michel Foucault made "knowledge" a term that seemed irrevocably linked to power, and before Edward Said so provocatively opened up discussion of the relations between power and knowledge in colonial discourses and Orientalist scholarship, Bernard Cohn had begun to apply an anthropological perspective to the history of colonialism and its forms of knowledge. In a series of essays written between the mid-1950s and the early 1980s, and now published in *An Anthropologist among the Historians and Other Essays* (Delhi: Oxford University Press, 1986), Cohn wrote about the history of British colonial knowledge regarding India, about the specific careers of terms like "village," "tribe," and "caste," about the anthropology of the colonizers as well as the colonized, and more generally about the anthropology of

British rule itself in India, ranging in example from the massively orchestrated darbars in Delhi to the enumerative technologies of power deployed by the census. The present collection of essays, which brings together in a single volume work largely written during the 1980s, demonstrates Cohn's continuing exploration of these themes, further elaborating and documenting his sense of what an anthropology of colonial knowledge should be.

In this collection of essays, Cohn has moved beyond the kind of explicit methodological and disciplinary evaluations that led him to chart the potential relations of history and anthropology in earlier programmatic essays. Nevertheless, these essays reveal more than ever his critical sense of how to renegotiate the normal assumptions and procedures of both his home disciplines. Cohn's anthropological agenda is firmly harnessed to a commitment to historicize the analytical schemas and institutional arenas of colonial knowledge and practice. And Cohn's historical sensibility is demonstrated in rich ethnographic explorations of the varieties of colonial mentalities and ways of life. In this volume, history and anthropology have been so firmly wedded in Cohn's writing that it is virtually impossible to tell them apart.

There are several substantive shifts in Cohn's newest writing. Whereas in the earlier volume there are detailed explorations of the way in which new and dramatic British innovations in India, including revenue and legal systems, led to certain fundamental structural changes in Indian social relations, we now read about areas in which the colonial impact was previously assumed to be either minimal or epiphenomenal. We read that the painstaking efforts by British Orientalists to study Indian languages was not part of a collaborative enterprise responsible for a new renaissance, but rather was an important part of the colonial project of control and command. We read that the very Orientalist imagination that led to brilliant antiquarian collections, archaeological finds, and photographic forays were in fact forms of constructing an India that could be better packaged, subsumed, and ruled. We read that concerns about appropriate forms of dress expressed the colonial imagination of domination, and worked later to demonstrate the colonial domination of imagination in the arena of nationalist resistance and appropriation. And we read that one of the sites of colonial power that seemed simultaneously most benign and most susceptible to indigenous influences—namely, law—in fact became responsible for institutionalizing peculiarly British notions about how to regulate a colonial society made up of "others" rather than settlers, leaving extremely problematic legacies for contemporary Indian society.

This volume not only goes into much greater detail than the first about the range of institutional contexts in which colonial knowledge

and colonial power were imbricated, it also makes clear that the historical anthropology of the colonial state must not be separated from the
historical anthropology of the modern nation state in general. The colonial state is seen as a theater for state experimentation, where historiography, documentation, certification, and representation were all
state modalities that transformed knowledge into power. Cohn now directs his interpretive gaze on the reports, investigations, commissions,
and data of colonial regulation, which he sees as part of a "documentation project" that is "both totalizing and individualizing." Not only are
subjects ruled by the state; the position of the subjects are constituted
by classifying and naturalizing such categories and identities as educated
or uneducated, rich or poor, male or female, young or old, Hindu or
Muslim, Welsh or Scottish, and so on. The classificatory rules that Durk-
heim and Mauss had seen as so fundamental to societal formations can
now be seen not as part of some elemental structure or internal social
logic but rather as incidents of state power. Cohn has brought the colonial state back into the anthropology of South Asia.

Although Cohn is interested in both the metropolitan and the colonial
state, he is obviously most interested in the colonial character of the
state, and indeed in the specific historical experience of British colonial
rule in India. Although he has traveled a long way from his early days
doing ethnography among the Chamars of Senapur, he maintains his initial interest in the cultures of domination, in the cultural and historical
construction of lived experience in India, in the implications of anthropology (and indeed of all American and European social science) in the
history of colonialism, as also in the ways in which colonial knowledge
continues to live on in the historiographic sources and anthropological
assumptions we depend upon in our study of the pasts of Indian society.

.   .   .   .   .   .

Cohn's early career and work have been admirably summarized and analyzed by Ranajit Guha in the introduction to Cohn's first volume of
essays. Guha makes the point that even though Cohn was trained in the
first (post-war) generation of American anthropologists to do sustained
fieldwork in Indian villages, at a time when anthropology was constituting itself yet again as a synchronic discipline capable of working best in
face-to-face field situations, Cohn resisted the prevalent functionalism of
the times. Sustained in part by Redfield's insistence that villages were
not isolates but rather components of large civilizations, Cohn went further than any of his anthropological colleagues in attending to the dis-
ruptions of decolonization as well as to the echoes of earlier periods of
rapid social change, in particular the years of initial colonial rule. Within

a few years Cohn had begun to investigate the structural changes associated with early revenue policies in the region of Uttar Pradesh in which he had done fieldwork, the political character of late pre-colonial regimes around Banaras, the ways the past lived on in the present of the village, and the impact of colonial legal systems on local life and legal practice in northern India.

If Cohn's early work was part of an effort to investigate the historical dimensions of Indian social relations, it led him also to reconceptualize the disciplines of anthropology and history as well as to rethink the relations between "culture," "society," and the "state." Cohn's early ethnohistorical research led him to argue that Indian tradition was neither fixed nor static, and increasingly it focused on the role of colonial institutions in radically transforming state and society. At the same time, Cohn became interested in the historical anthropology of colonial society itself, spending many years, for example, investigating the recruitment and training of East India Company officials in the late eighteenth and early nineteenth centuries. In constructing his research agendas, as also in training his students at the University of Chicago, Cohn actively subverted the usual divisions between history and anthropology, and more specifically between the history of colonial rule in India and the anthropology of Indian society.

While engaged in research during the 1970s on the history of colonial knowledge about India and on the development and use of this knowledge in official projects (such as a series of darbars planned by the British to replicate and appropriate Mughal sovereignty after 1858) Cohn actively supported the research of colleagues and students in a new kind of cultural analysis, labeled by McKim Marriott and Ronald Inden as the "ethnosociology" of India. The emphasis in ethnosociology was on collecting and representing indigenous categories and forms of thought concerning social relations, the person, the village, ritual, medicine, and so on. For Cohn, this emphasis converged with his own concerns about the distorting influence of colonial history and Western social scientific categories, as well as with his interest in the reconstruction of the forms and logic of Indian society. He engaged with the ethnosociological project insofar as he continued to demonstrate the epistemological violence of British rule, as well as the active and dynamic basis of Indian tradition. But during these same years Cohn increasingly concentrated on the capacity of the colonial state not only to misperceive but also to reconstruct fundamental aspects of Indian society. Colonialism was not just about the colonizers any more.

Indeed, as the early enthusiasm for ethnosociology gave way to worries about the epistemological difficulties concerning both the coherence and the certainty of any given cultural account, Cohn became steadily more interested in the role played by the colonial state in cultural construction. Although Cohn has not written explicitly about the ways in which any attempt to characterize something as specifically "Indian" might participate in the history of colonial forms of knowledge, or to examine how his own work seems systematically to subvert "cultural" analysis itself, his writings have certainly suggested that the colonial state has had extraordinary effects on the basic structures of contemporary Indian life. And in the essays presented in this volume, we confront in new and complex examples Cohn's insights into the ways in which colonial power was deployed and how the exercise of power and accumulation of knowledge were both parts of a single project.

. . . . .

In Cohn's introduction, we are told that he has organized his research around the identification and explication of "investigative modalities." Some of these modalities were general, some more specific, but all of them took shape in relationship to a governing sense of relevance and an ordering mode of organization. "Investigative modalities," in Cohn's usage, were made official through the production of usable knowledge in the form of published reports, statistical returns, official proceedings, administrative histories, and legal codes. All of these Cohn treats as "texts" that can be deconstructed in relation to the way in which they were written as part of specific colonial projects. In his outline, Cohn lists the following types of modalities: historiography, observation and travel, survey, enumeration, museology, and surveillance.

The present volume focuses on some but not all of these modalities. Elsewhere Cohn has documented how the British moved from virtually total misconception of their position in the eyes of the Indian rulers to virtually total acceptance of their role within the system. Ironically, this role, negotiated over time, drew them into seeking territorial control so that they would have the financial resources to support that role.[1] The initial misconceptions of the colonial rulers were fueled in part because the British were ignorant of any Indian language. Cohn demonstrates in the first essay that in the late years of the eighteenth century, general British incompetence in Indian languages yielded to a concerted effort to produce a set of texts—grammars, dictionaries, teaching aids—which were to make the acquisition of a working knowledge of the languages of India available to those British who were to be part of the ruling groups in India. In the process, Cohn argues, even grammar could be converted from an Indian form of knowledge into a European object. Language was to be mastered to issue commands and to collect information. Information was required in order to assess and collect taxes, maintain law and order, and identify and classify groups within Indian society. Thus Cohn surveys the history of such projects as Sir William Jones' Persian grammar and Halhed's Bengali grammar, suggesting some of the subtle ways in which the Orientalist project, even at the moment of its most spectacular successes, was always part of the colonial project of rule.

The connection between knowledge and power became even clearer in the concerns of men such as Carey and Gilchrist to order and teach the vernacular languages of Bengali and Hindustani. Much of Gilchrist's effort went into teaching the imperative forms and lexicons relevant to daily intercourse with servants and other inferiors. Representative of a new generation of British officials suspicious of the classicism of much Orientalist scholarship, Gilchrist was actively prejudiced against the Brahmans and native elites whose motives were seen as insufficiently harnessed to the simple structures of command upon which colonial rule was to be based. But even the great philologists Jones and Halhed, as well as their nineteenth-century successors—among them Ellis, Campbell, Brown, Caldwell—believed that the comparative methods of European scholarship rendered scientific, universal, and practical the knowledge that was held by natives only in an unformed and empirical sense. As the nineteenth century progressed, the local Indian scholars who provided all the tools of language learning were increasingly disparaged and ignored. Cohn ends the essay by arguing that the comparative philological method involved a use of history that was both foreign and violent, and that British disregard for different cultural procedures of language classification and analysis was sustained by the truth regime of colonial power.

The objectification of India, like the subtle and sinuous relations of knowledge and power, is perhaps most directly visible in the institutional domains of revenue policy and legal practice; Cohn has previously written extensively about both. In this volume Cohn offers another essay on "Law and the Colonial State in India," developing and expanding earlier arguments. He rehearses the story of Sir William Jones' attempt to recover an "ancient Indian constitution," suggesting (as he has earlier) that the learning of language, in this case Persian and then Sanskrit, was deemed critical in the effort to rule India properly (and profitably). Jones believed that the Manu *Dharmashastras* were the most authoritative Indian law books, reifying Indian conceptions of revelation and textual authority in the context of his own European philological sense that he could find the oldest and most original sources of legal theory in Indian tradition. Colebrooke carried on Jones' attempts to understand and organize Indian law, developing a philological model of legal schools that was intended to reveal the structural relations between different laws and their textual traditions. Jones, Halhed, Colebrooke, and other British

legal scholars all shared a suspicion about the integrity of Indian scho-
ars, and wished to develop an unmediated relationship to the canon of
authoritative texts. But, Cohn argues, in the obsessive attempts to re-
constitute genuine Indian law, Indian legal traditions and principles
were systematically refigured. British convictions that all Indian traditions were based on texts, and that different commentaries and interpretations could be systematically sorted out by school and region, led
to the refashioning of a system of law that increasingly resembled the
precedent-based case law of British tradition. Colonialism produced a
level of institutional self-mimesis in India that was completely at odds
with its own self-representation and rhetoric.

This process can be generally understood as the "objectification" of
India. For Cohn, objectification has different forms and meanings, but
always involved the coding of India in ways that rendered it increasingly
available for colonization. By the late nineteenth century, the formation
of official ethnography seemed to involve little more than the addition of
endless new categories to the array of castes and customs that became
part of the compendia of information Cohn refers to as the "documentation project." India, now as ever static, timeless, and exotic, was increasingly available not only for plunder but for science, as photography and
statistics replaced and at the same time reified older forms of representation.

The collection of artifacts for museums, and more generally for the
historiographical modality of providing India with a history, is discussed
in the next essay, "The Transformation of Objects into Artifacts, Antiquities, and Art in Nineteenth-Century India." From the early seventeenth
century, India was looked upon as a major source of commodities for
Europe, chief among which were textiles and spices. The consolidation
of British rule in India in the late eighteenth and early nineteenth centuries opened up new opportunities for the exploitation and appropriation of these and other commodities. But the commodities of interest to
the British, Cohn reminds us, were not only goods with market value.
In addition to the many objects that were profitably bought, sold, and
generally extracted, including land—which became a commodity
through the concentration on land revenue as a principal source of government income—India provided a whole host of wares that could symbolize and display an imperial archaeology with Britain at the helm.
These were the commodities of colonial history and anthropology.

Cohn recounts the outlines of the career of Colin Mackenzie, first
surveyor general of India, who managed the first surveys of the Deccan
in the late eighteenth and early nineteenth centuries after the cession of
land from, first, the Nizam of Hyderabad and then, after Britain's 1799
triumph at Seringapatam, from Tipu Sultan. Mackenzie not only
mapped the newly possessed land, doing triangulated maps and topo-

graphical surveys; he collected every historical artifact and document he could find. Extravagantly exceeding his brief from the East India Company, he employed and trained a group of Brahman research assistants, and identified the Amaravati ruins as containing important documentation of a much earlier Buddhist history in southern India.

The subsequent history of the Amaravati "marbles" provides a way for Cohn to sketch out the early history of archaeology in colonial India: the simultaneous neglect and exploitation of extraordinary artifacts, as well as the launching of a number of significant careers. James Fergusson, for example, used the marbles to help him establish the importance of studying Indian architecture to facilitate a genuine understanding of the ethnology and religions of India. Fergusson's curious comparative approach to architecture aligned his critique of nineteenth-century British architecture with his sense that architecture alone could convey the scientific principles of India's historical past. But Fergusson's career also reveals, as did the later history of Mackenzie's collection, the way in which colonial officials increasingly disparaged the scholarly participation of Indians in favor of consolidating scientific capital by a select, if often seriously deficient, European elite. The antiquarian and archaeological collection of India followed the general exclusionary principles of profit and glory that characterized earlier forms of imperial plunder.

The final essay, "Cloth, Clothes, and Colonialism," suggests various ways in which clothes have been part of the history of colonialism. Here we learn that the famous Sikh turban, rather than being—as is commonly asserted today—a traditional insignia of Sikh religious identity, became a critical marker for Sikhs through its use in the British army to give the Sikh regiment a distinctive uniform. Clothing was an important component in the self-representation of the British, both in establishing the credentials of a new imperial rule and in protecting themselves from the dangers of the tropical climate. Clothing was contested and regulated during the breast-cloth controversy, initiated by missionaries, which raged in Travancore in the late nineteenth century. And Gandhi used cloth, in both his adoption of simple peasant dress and his advocacy of undyed homespun khadi, as a sign of nationalist fervor, to symbolize and sustain resistance to British rule. Colonialism, nationalism, and even missionary zeal were thus deeply implicated in representational strategies and politics.

Any attempt to make a systematic statement about the "colonial project" in India runs the risk of conflating cause with effect, or ascribing intention as well as system to a congeries of activities and a conjunction of outcomes which, though related and at times coordinated, were usually diffuse, disorganized, and even contradictory. It could be argued that the power of colonialism as a system of rule was predicated at least in part on the ill-coordinated nature of power, that colonial power was

British in India
power dependant upon Knowledge

never so omniscient or secure as to be thought total, and that although
the British in India were always aware that their power was dependent
on their knowledge, they were never aware of all the ways in which
knowledge was, in any direct or strategic sense, power. Ever aware of
the contradictory character of colonial power, Cohn has moved from
limb to limb of the colonial "elephant," never finding closure or seeking
the last word. This volume makes available fragments of Cohn's own
project, mirroring the fragments of colonial institutions and practices he
so carefully documents and analyzes.

Programmatic statements of the kind I make here run the risk of missing what is altogether distinctive about Cohn's writing. In essay after
essay Cohn exercises a profound scholarly curiosity about the character
of colonial societies in India. Whereas much of the writing about colonialism today looks only at colonial exploitation, through the relentlessly
instrumentalist but little contextualized unmasking of colonial discourses,
Cohn trains his ethnographer's eye on the details of colonial life and
thought. Thus in the pages that follow we read about the medical genealogies of cummerbunds and solar topis, the manic efforts to excavate
and collect relics and rocks of variable significance, and the extraordinary encounters between early British Orientalists and the texts and
languages of India.

Cohn's inventive sense of how to study different aspects of colonial
history not only anticipated many recent theoretical developments; it
has also directly inspired a great deal of recent historical and anthropological work.[2] In Cohn's work, colonialism is no longer an historical
irruption that has to be stripped away to get down to the real subject of
anthropology, but rather the focus of the study of social transformation
in all societies touched by world systems of colonial rule. For Cohn,
colonialism played a critical role in the constitution of the metropole—
in the formation of the state and in the development of its basic forms of
knowledge—even as it shaped, through its cultural technologies of domination, much of the modern history of colonized places and peoples. In
recharting the possibilities for historicizing anthropology, and at the
same time anthropologizing colonialism, Cohn has blurred old genres
and created new ones. Cohn helped pioneer the critique of anthropology
as a colonial form of knowledge, and has played a major role in remaking
anthropology (and imperial history) into a critical practice that has the
historical and reflexive self-consciousness to engage both its colonial genealogies and its postcolonial predicament.

This volume provides a few recent examples of the work of a scholar
who has charted out the contours of an anthropology of the colonial
state. For those of us who seek to continue this project, it is inconceiv-
able of doing so without the influence of Bernard Cohn.

ACKNOWLEDGMENTS

THE papers reprinted in this collection reflect ongoing intellectual projects. In addition to the colleagues, libraries, and archives acknowledged in the original publications, there have been a number of friends and colleagues who have provided continuing intellectual and scholarly stimulation and have helped shape the arguments that are represented in these papers. During the period in which these papers were written, I benefited from continuing conversations with a number of colleagues at the University of Chicago and other academic institutions, including Ronald Inden, Ranajit Guha, Nicholas Dirks, George Stocking, Marshall Sahlins, Michael Taussig, Arjun Appadurai, and Carol Breckinridge. In recent years I have also benefited from being able to work with a number of younger colleagues who have provided me with continuing stimulation and support, including Piya Chatterjee, Nick De Genova, Teri Silvio, Susan Seizer, and Steve Hughes.

Slightly different versions of the papers have appeared before; I thank each of the original publishers for permission to use them again here:

"The Command of Language and the Language of Command" appeared in an earlier version in Ranajit Guha, ed., *Subaltern Studies IV: Writings on South Asian History and Society* (Delhi: Oxford University Press, 1985), pp. 276–329.

"Law and the Colonial State in India" is reprinted from June Starr and Jane F. Collier, eds., *History and Power in the Study of Law*, New Directions in Legal Anthropology (Ithaca, N.Y.: Cornell University Press, 1989), pp. 131–52. Capitalization and footnote style have been altered to conform to this volume's style.

"The Transformation of Objects into Artifacts, Antiquities, and Art in Nineteenth-Century India" first appeared in Barbara Stoler Miller, ed., *The Powers of Art: Patronage in Indian Culture* (Delhi: Oxford University Press, 1982), pp. 301–29. The mechanics have again been adjusted to the style of this volume.

A shorter version of "Cloth, Clothes, and Colonialism: India in the Nineteenth Century," appeared in Annette Weiner and Jane Schneider, eds., *Cloth and Human Experience* (Washington, D.C.: Smithsonian Institute Press, 1989), pp. 303–54.

COLONIALISM AND ITS FORMS OF KNOWLEDGE

ONE

INTRODUCTION

IN THE PREMODERN STATE, in Europe as elsewhere, power was made visible through theatrical displays, in the form of processions, progresses, royal entries, coronations, funerals, and other rituals that guaranteed the well-being and continued power of the rulers over the ruled.[1] The theater of power was managed by specialists (priests and ritual preceptors, historians and bards, artists and artisans) who maintained the various forms of knowledge required.

From the eighteenth century onward, European states increasingly made their power visible not only through ritual performance and dramatic display, but through the gradual extension of "officializing" procedures that established and extended their capacity in many areas. They took control by defining and classifying space, making separations between public and private spheres; by recording transactions such as the sale of property; by counting and classifying their populations, replacing religious institutions as the registrar of births, marriages, and deaths; and by standardizing languages and scripts. The state licensed some activities as legitimate and suppressed others as immoral or unlawful. With the growth of public education and its rituals, it fostered official beliefs in how things are and how they ought to be. The schools became the crucial civilizing institutions and sought to produce moral and productive citizens. Finally, nation states came to be seen as the natural embodiments of history, territory, and society.[2]

The establishment and maintenance of these nation states depended upon determining, codifying, controlling, and representing the past. The documentation that was involved created and normalized a vast amount of information that formed the basis of their capacity to govern. The reports and investigations of commissions, the compilation, storage, and publication of statistical data on finance, trade, health, demography, crime, education, transportation, agriculture, and industry—these created data requiring as much exegetical and hermeneutical skill to interpret as an arcane Sanskrit text.[3]

The process of state building in Great Britain, seen as a cultural project, was closely linked with its emergence as an imperial power, and India was its largest and most important colony. It is not just that the personnel who governed Indian were British, but the projects of state building in both countries—documentation, legitimation, classification, and bounding, and the institutions therewith—often reflected theories, experiences, and practices worked out originally in India and then applied in Great Britain, as well as vice versa. Many aspects of metropolitan documentation projects were first developed in India. For example, the Indian civil service provided some of the models for the development of the Home services. Conversely, the universities and public schools in Victorian Great Britain were the factories in which the old aristocracy was associated with the new middle class, and new governing classes for the empire were produced. These models were exported to India and the other colonies to produce loyal governing elites.[4] And the central symbol of the British state and the focus of national loyalty, the Crown, was reworked in the second half of the nineteenth century in relation to India and the rest of the empire.[5] A guiding assumption in my research on the British conquest of India in the eighteenth and nineteenth centuries has been that metropole and colony have to be seen in a unitary field of analysis. In India the British entered a new world that they tried to comprehend using their own forms of knowing and thinking. There was widespread agreement that this society, like others they were governing, could be known and represented as a series of facts. The form of these facts was taken to be self-evident, as was the idea "that administrative power stemmed from the efficient use of these facts."[6]

What were these "facts" whose collection lay at the foundation of the modern nation state? To the educated Englishman of the late eighteenth and early nineteenth centuries, the world was knowable through the senses, which could record the experience of a natural world. This world was generally believed to be divinely created, knowable in an empirical fashion, and constitutive of the sciences through which would be revealed the laws of Nature that governed the world and all that was in it. In coming to India, they unknowingly and unwittingly invaded and conquered not only a territory but an epistemological space as well. The "facts" of this space did not exactly correspond to those of the invaders. Nevertheless, the British believed they could explore and conquer this space through translation: establishing correspondence could make the unknown and the strange knowable.

The first step was evidently to learn the local languages. "Classical" Persian, Arabic, and Sanskrit as well as the currently spoken "vernacular" languages were understood to be the prerequisite form of knowledge for all others, and the first educational institutions that the British established in India were to teach their own officials Indian languages. The knowledge of languages was necessary to issue commands, collect taxes, maintain law and order—and to create other forms of knowledge about the people they were ruling. This knowledge was to enable the

British to classify, categorize, and bound the vast social world that was India so that it could be controlled. These imperatives, elements in the larger colonial project, shaped the "investigative modalities" devised by the British to collect the facts.

An investigative modality includes the definition of a body of information that is needed, the procedures by which appropriate knowledge is gathered, its ordering and classification, and then how it is transformed into usable forms such as published reports, statistical returns, histories, gazetteers, legal codes, and encyclopedias. Some of the investigative modalities of the colonial project are quite general, such as historiography and museology, although they might include very specific practices such as the location and description of archaeological sites. Other modalities, such as the survey and the census, were more highly defined and clearly related to administrative questions. Most investigative modalities were constructed in relation to institutions and administrative sites with fixed routines. Some were transformed into "sciences" such as economics, ethnology, tropical medicine, comparative law, or cartography, and their practitioners became professionals. A brief discussion of a few of these modalities will illustrate my approach.

The Historiographic Modality

In British India, this modality is the most complex, pervasive, and powerful, underlying a number of the other more specific modalities. History, for the British, has an ontological power in providing the assumptions about how the real social and natural worlds are constituted. History in its broadest sense was a zone of debate over the ends and means of their rulership in India. From the beginning of their large-scale acquisition of territorial control and sovereignty, the British conceived of governing India by codifying and reinstituting the ruling practices that had been developed by previous states and rulers. They sought to incorporate, as much as possible, the administrative personnel employed by previous regimes. Thus knowledge of the history and practices of Indian states was seen as the most valuable form of knowledge on which to build the colonial state.

Starting in the 1770s in Bengal, the British began to investigate, through what they called "enquiries," a list of specific questions to which they sought answers about how revenue was assessed and collected. Out of this grew the most extensive and continuous administrative activity of the British, which they termed the land-settlement process. Entailed in this enterprise was the collection of "customs and local histories," which in the British discourse related to land tenure. The process culminated in the production of settlement reports, which were produced on a district-by-district basis.

A second strand of the historiographic modality involved the ideological construction of the nature of Indian civilizations, as typified in the major historical writings of Alexander Dow, Robert Orme, Charles Grant, Mark Wilks, James Mill, and James Tod. The historiographic practices and narrative genres of these writers can obviously be subjected to critical analysis, but beyond this they can be seen to have begun the formation of a legitimizing discourse about Britain's civilizing mission in India. *critical analysing*

A third historiographic strand involves histories of the British in India. This entails what might be thought of as "popular" history—the study of representations, whether in England or in India, of specific events. Thus stories of the Black Hole of Calcutta, the defeat of Tipu Sultan, or the siege of Lucknow involved the creation of emblematic heroes and villains, as individuals and types, who took shape in illustrations, various popular performances, and poetry; their "history" was made concrete through the construction of memorials and sacred spaces in India.

The Observational / Travel Modality

The questions that arise in examining this modality are related to the creation of a repertoire of images and typifactions that determined what was significant to the European eye. It was a matter of finding themselves in a place that could be made to seem familiar by following predetermined itineraries and seeing the sights in predictable ways. Two itineraries seem to have provided the narrative structure for many of the early travel accounts, and reflect the routes that brought Europeans to India. The earlier accounts follow the seventeenth-century trade pattern that brought merchants to the west coast of India, usually to Gujarat. The traveler then proceeded down the west coast to Ceylon, and up the east coast. By the eighteenth century much of British traffic to and from England went directly to Madras or Calcutta, and in the second half of the eighteenth century through the nineteenth century, arrival in Calcutta was followed by what became the standard traveler / tourist route—by boat up the Ganges, then to Delhi and either further north into the Punjab or southwest through Rajasthan and Gujarat to Bombay, then down to Malabar, Ceylon, and up the east coast to Madras. Although the travel routes were conceived as linear and continuous, there were particular things that had to be included: the river front in Banaras, the fort at Allahabad, a visit with the Nawab of Oudh, sightseeing

how to make familiar

in Agra and Delhi. In addition, travel accounts included set pieces, such as the description of Indian holy men and their austerities, encounters with traveling entertainers, and a sati seen or heard about. Increasingly in the nineteenth century, these accounts included discussions of historical sites—Hindu, Muslim, and British.

Although the itineraries and the particular sites, social types, practices, and encounters with India and Indians that are reported show considerable consistency through a two-hundred-year period, their representation changed through time. What is observed and reported is mediated by particular socio-political contexts as well as historically specific aesthetic principles, such as the "sublime," the "picturesque," the "romantic," and the "realistic."

The Survey Modality

The word "survey" in English evokes a wide range of activities: to look over or examine something; to measure land for the purpose of establishing boundaries; to inspect; and to supervise or keep a watch over persons or place. In other contexts it can mean to establish the monetary value of goods and objects. For the British in India in the late eighteenth century, it also meant a form of exploration of the natural and social landscape. The survey as an investigative modality encompasses a wide range of practices, from the mapping of India to collecting botanical specimens, to the recording of architectural and archaeological sites of historic significance, or the most minute measuring of a peasant's fields.

Although the mapping and establishment of routes were part of the mercantile history of India, the beginning of a systematic survey of India can be dated to 1765, when Robert Clive assigned James Rennell, a naval officer turned surveyor, the task of making a general survey of the newly acquired Bengal territories. In the context of colonial India, the concept of the "survey" came to cover any systematic and official investigation of the natural and social features of the Indian empire.

The result was the vast official documentation project that included the Survey of India, under the direction of George Lambton, which eventually covered India with an imaginary grid on which the government could locate any site in India. Upon the acquisition of each new territory, a new survey was launched, which went far beyond mapping and bounding to describe and classify the territory's zoology, geology, botany, ethnography, economic products, history, and sociology. The history of this documentation project has tended to be written in terms of the "genius" and / or obsessions of great surveyors—James Rennall, William Lambton, Colin Mackenzie, Alexander Cunningham, and Francis

Buchanan Hamilton. But this "great man" theory of surveying can be enriched by a study of the structure of the practices by which such knowledge was compiled, the underlying theories of classification and their implications for the governing of India, and the process by which these vast amounts of knowledge were transformed into textual forms such as encyclopedias and extensive archives that were deployed by the colonial state in fixing, bounding, and settling India.

The Enumerative Modality

For many British officials, India was a vast collection of numbers. This mentality began in the early seventeenth century with the arrival of British merchants who compiled and transmitted lists of products, prices, customs and duties, weights and measures, and the values of various coins. A number was, for the British, a particular form of certainty to be held on to in a strange world. But when they turned to early attempts to enumerate the population of India in various localities, as part of early surveys, they found that even the simplest of enumerative projects raised problems of classification.

As part of the imperial settlement project after the repression of the Indian uprising of 1857–1858, the Government of India carried out a series of censuses which they hoped would provide a cross-sectional picture of the "progress" of their rule. By 1881 they had worked out a set of practices that enabled them not just to list the names of what they hoped would be every person in India but also to collect basic information about age, occupation, caste, religion, literacy, place of birth, and current residence. Upwards of 500,000 people, most of whom were volunteers, were engaged in carrying out the census. The published census reports not only summarized the statistical information thus compiled but also included extensive narratives about the caste system, the religions of India, fertility and morbidity, domestic organization, and the economic structure of India. The census represents a model of the Victorian encyclopedic quest for total knowledge.

It is my hypothesis that what was entailed in the construction of the census operations was the creation of social categories by which India was ordered for administrative purposes.[7] The British assumed that the census reflected the basic sociological facts of India. This it did, but through the enumerative modality, the project also objectified social, cultural, and linguistic differences among the peoples of India. The panoptical view that the British were constructing led to the reification of India as polity in which conflict, from the point of view of the rulers, could only be controlled by the strong hand of the British.

The Museological Modality

For many Europeans India was a vast museum, its countryside filled with ruins, its people representing past ages—biblical, classical, and feudal; it was a source of collectibles and curiosities to fill European museums, botanical gardens, zoos, and country houses.

Until the 1860s the generation and transmission of knowledge of the antiquities of India—its art, architecture, scripts, and textual traditions—were largely left to individuals and scholarly societies, and were the by-products of other investigative modalities. In the late eighteenth century artists who traveled in India in pursuit of commissions and patronage, such as the Daniells brothers, William Hodges, and George Chinnery, sketched and painted not only landscapes and portraits of opulent princes and British officials but also created a visual record of the monuments of past dynasties. There was a large market in Great Britain for illustrated books, portfolios, prints, and drawings of oriental scenes and depictions of the people of India.

As a byproduct of the revenue surveys and the settlement proceedings, many archaeological sites were identified and mapped. The first large-scale excavation of an Indian archaeological site was directed by Colin Mackenzie who, in addition to his official duties, carried on a twenty-year project in south India which involved the collection of archaeological specimens, texts, manuscripts, and oral histories. James Fergusson, who had gone to India as an indigo planter, traveled widely in India in 1837–1842, and wrote a series of accounts of its art and architecture, which established a hegemonic history and evaluation of Indian art and architecture. He was active in the planning of the Crystal Palace exhibition, and became the "official" connoisseur of India's artistic achievements.

An army engineer, Alexander Cunningham, who had developed an interest in Indian archaeology, successfully lobbied Lord Canning in 1859 to establish the Archaeological Survey of India, of which he was to become the first director. The primary concern of the ASI was to record important sites on the basis of topographical research. In addition, the Survey became responsible for the preservation of historical sites, and began to develop on-site museums as well as to build a national collection of archaeological specimens. The first large-scale museum in India was built in Calcutta in the 1840s by private initiative, under the aegis of the Asiatic Society of Bengal. The museum developed into the India Museum, which is the largest general museum in India today with large collections and displays of archaeological, natural historical, and ethnographic specimens.

Representations of India bulked large in the international exhibitions and world's fairs of the second half of the nineteenth century, which in turn provided the basis of private and public collections of India arts and crafts, paintings, and antiquities. The power to define the nature of the past and establish priorities in the creation of a monumental record of a civilization, and to propound canons of taste, are among the most significant instrumentalities of rulership.

The Surveillance Modality

The British appear in the nineteenth century to have felt most comfortable surveying India from above and at a distance—from a horse, an elephant, a boat, a carriage, or a train. They were uncomfortable in the narrow confines of a city street, a bazaar, a *mela*—anywhere they were surrounded by their Indian subjects. In their narratives of their lives and travels in India, few Indians are named other than royalty and personal servants. Indians who came under the imperial gaze were frequently made to appear in dress and demeanor as players in the British-constructed theater of power, their roles signaled by prescribed dress, their parts authored by varied forms of knowledge codified by rulers who sought to determine how loyal Indian subjects were to act in the scenes that the rulers had constructed. Everyone—rulers and ruled—had proper roles to play in the colonial sociological theater.

There were, however, groups and categories of people whose practices threatened the prescribed sociological order. These were people who appeared by their nature to wander beyond the boundaries of settled civil society: sannyasis, sadhus, fakirs, dacoits, goondas, thags, pastoralists, herders, and entertainers. The British constructed special instrumentalities to control those defined as beyond civil bounds, and carried out special investigations to provide the criteria by which whole groups would be stigmatized as criminal.

Starting in the late eighteenth century, certain clans, castes, and villages were accused of practicing female infanticide, a crime that was difficult to prove in British courts, in which only an individual and not a group could be proven guilty. Female infanticide became a "statistical crime" for which corporal punishment could be administered. In 1835 a Thagi and Dacoity Department was created to investigate and punish gang robberies and murders. The first task was to devise means for gathering information on the practices of those the government accused of committing a ritual form of murder, particularly of travelers. This involved primarily the use of informers who turned state's evidence, and acted not only as witnesses but also as informants on the "culture" of the

Thags. The work of the Thagi and Dacoity Department led to the formation of an archive of criminal ethnography and the designation of increasing numbers of people as members of "criminal tribes and castes."

The British in India (like the police in urbanizing western Europe) faced a problem identifying those who were suspected of antisocial, political, and criminal activities that the state sought to control or eliminate. The ideal was to create a systematic means of recording and classifying a set of permanent features that distinguished an individual. Although photography offered some possibilities for recording a physiognomy, India's large scale required a schema by which one could recover each of thousands from among potentially millions of images. Toward this end, in Paris in the late nineteenth century, Alphonse Bertillon, prefect of police, devised an anthropometric system that was believed to have the potential of providing the descriptive as well as classificatory power to identify individuals accurately.

At much the same time as Bertillon was carrying out his investigations, William Herschel, a civil servant in India, was experimenting with the use of fingerprints to individualize documents, as a means of preventing fraud and forgery. Herschel continued his explorations even after he left India and later Sir Francis Galton, in cooperation with Herschel and a number of Indian police officers, devised a system of classification that made possible fingerprinting as a means of identifying individuals.

Investigative Modalities in the Post-Colonial World

Both historians and anthropologists—though the latter might not have labeled themselves as such—were always directly involved in the colonial situation. The origins of anthropology as a distinctive form of knowledge lay, in fact, in the internal and external colonies of the Europeans. Throughout the colonial period, some anthropologists argued, in a highly ambivalent fashion, that they had a particular role to play in mediating between the colonial subjects and rulers. In the colonial history of India, there were explicit efforts made to construct an "official ethnography" at the moment that anthropology was beginning to be defined as a distinctive form of knowledge. Anthropologists developed practices through which they sought to erase the colonial influence by describing what they took to be authentic indigenous cultures. Their epistemological universe, however, was part of the European world of social theories and classifacatory schema that were formed, in part, by state projects to reshape the lives of their subjects at home and abroad.

Since the early twentieth century, there have been internal professional discussions among anthropologists about their responsibilities for their chosen subjects, who were frequently defined as "native" or "tribal" or "wild men," in relation to state policies and practices which sought to control them. With the end of political colonialism, anthropologists have translated their colonial past into history, and into a site for the critical and epistemological exploration of their own construction of knowledge. The anthropologists' characteristic investigative modality was and is ethnographic fieldwork; the essays in this volume expand the anthropologists' epistemological explorations into other investigative modalities that were also part of the cultural project of colonialism.

But ruling the colonies of an empire was not the only state enterprise that shaped the investigative modalities of Western social scientists. In the middle and late twentieth century, for example, as the United States replaced Great Britain as what came to be termed a "superpower," the study of "others" (whether Native American or Japanese) required collecting and interpreting data within the framework of dominant theoretical paradigms of the times. Social scientists first became heavily involved in government projects during the Depression; economists and sociologists, for example, were the most important architects of the New Deal's social welfare projects. In the 1930s, anthropologists were called upon to involve themselves directly with Native American affairs. Most notable was the effort of the Bureau of Indian Affairs to establish self-government / self-rule on Indian reservations. Anthropologists were called upon to develop histories and sociologies—through the interpretation of histories and sociologies from Indian interlocutors—which would then constitute the basis of the institutions of these tribal federations. There were also large numbers of anthropologists employed in planning economic development programs of Indian reservations, through the Department of Agriculture. The deployment of agricultural economists on the reservations provides a parallel to the general systemic analysis of the American economy at large in its recovery from the Depression. In keeping with that experience, the New Deal for Indians was to be effected by bringing them into the "mainstream" economy—and culture—thereby hastening the process of assimilation.

During the Second World War, and America's ascendence as a major player in that epochal crisis, academia increasingly became the site within which the struggles to understand the American place in the world was institutionalized within disciplinary arrangements, as well as deployed for more pragmatic contributions to what became more transparently imperial rule. The onset of the Second World War saw the beginnings of multi-disciplinary social science research, most notably at Yale University, where an interdisciplinary program was established through what was called the Institute of Human Relations. The Institute brought together sociologists, anthropologists, psychoanalysis and psychologists, and the dominant intellectual mode was positivism. positivism

Out of the Institute of Human Relations emerged several research projects. For anthropology the creation of the Human Relations Area File (HRAF) was a significant development. The HRAF was, and continues to be, at its core a taxonomy of "world cultures" that followed and elaborated on the models of the Cross-Cultural Survey at Yale, and its related undertakings such as the Plains Indians Survey at the University of Nebraska. One objective of the HRAF was to incorporate into a precise and "accessible" analytic framework a vast descriptive literature, the "descriptive data which no other social science can even remotely compare in quantity with in wealth of ethnographic detail available." The HRAF continues to be a "cooperative enterprise of fifteen universities, operating with the aid of foundation and government grants, for the assembly, translations and classification of the descriptive material of anthropology."[8]

The first task of the HRAF was to set universal criteria for delineating cultural units. Which social groups would be treated as cultural units? What were the criteria for separation of social groups from each other? The logic of this global cultural patterning, the creation of an elaborate mosaic connecting the smallest units with larger social wholes was expressed through a biological metaphor. Thus, the smallest group to carry essentially a total culture was the parallel to a "subvariety" in biology. A cultural system carried by a community could be called a "local cultural variant." Terms of biological evolution were grafted into this cross-cultural mapping in a transparent fashion: "In the realm of culture, the equivalent of inbreeding is diffusion, and barriers to diffusion may be used to separate cultural species."[9] The underlying logic of the HRAF was the need to define universals, to "discriminate between superficial and fundamental differences in ways of life. It was then necessary to define and classify that which is comparable from one society to another."[10]

The HRAF became directly involved with the war effort of the United States. It was quickly recognized that cross-cultural knowledge could very pragmatically assist the U.S. government in its strategic maneuvers. For example, when the U.S. Navy was getting ready to liberate Micronesia and Melanesia from Japanese control, it found itself in charge of civil government in these territories as well as being responsible for setting up such infrastructure as airfields with "native" labor. The importance for naval officers and policy makers to learn quickly about "customs and practices" was clear, and the HRAF stepped in to assist. A positivist social science, dependent on a notion of universals, which was based on an understanding of human society as comparable to a biological system—this "practical knowledge" created a taxonomy of cultures that was deployed well beyond the boundaries of the academy, and assisted in important ways the business of realpolitik.

There were, or course, other ways in which social science training assisted in the allied effort. A psychoanalytic approach to social analysis was dominant during the period of the war. For example, Karen Horney and Erich Fromm directed their attention to the German situation, which they viewed in terms of a distinct social pathology. Well-known "national character" studies were conducted by anthropologists Margaret Mead and Ruth Benedict, and exemplified in texts such as *The Chrysanthemum and the Sword*, which influenced U.S. policy toward the emperor of Japan. Historians found their skills useful in managing a variety of large-scale sources, and participated directly in military policy. Many were involved in the OSS. Furthermore, linguists were put to work to implement language-training programs for work in occupied, or newly liberated, territories. In order to do this, linguists rapidly had to analyze hitherto unknown languages for the purpose of teaching. The first small group of linguists worked in German and French linguistics, and branched into other languages.

At the end of the war, what happened to the academic institutes by which American scholars were inserted into the global arena? A number of scholars emerged from the war with a wide variety of "field" experiences, knowledge of languages derived from first-hand contact with other societies. It is they who founded the "area studies" programs as we know them in the American academic world. These programs emerged out of wartime experience in which the prime concern was to make sense of "imperfect information," in an important way to create "systems" out of scraps of knowledge that were trickling in as the war progressed. Interdisciplinary pooling was the method arrived at when social scientists and policy makers had imperfect access to the site, and couldn't conduct surveys, or use the other "investigative modalities" of their predecessors.

The social science paradigms of the postwar years, particularly in political science, rested on an explicitly evolutionary perspective. This was most apparent in the development policies that became one cornerstone of American foreign policy and whose overall agenda was articulated in the theories of Walt Rostow, Daniel Lerner and such. In anthropology, this was exemplified in important cultural studies such as *Contemporary Change in Traditional Societies*, edited by Julian Steward.[11] These studies were primarily interested in the "problems of modernization" in cross-cultural contexts, "to develop and test a systematic approach to the problems of modernity." The global scenario, which included newly independent states, had now to be understood within a telos of "modernity," where national development was graded against a model of Western development. Methodologically, members of this cross-cultural research project had a "specialized knowledge of different world areas which would ensure a cross-cultural selection of cases for field research."[12] As in direct lineal descent from HRAF's epistemological position, the research procedures were aimed at creating "a possible taxonomy of contemporary societies [through] the process of social change . . . in an effort to understand cross-cultural differences and similarities." Most significantly, the research study was to trace a "trajectory of social change" as societies moved from "tradition" to "modernity."[13]

Stasis was assumed, and history, including the effects of colonial processes, was erased. The clearly evolutionary model for social change that emerged had a shadow side—a Durkheimian notion of social *anomie*, the threat of possible disequilibria in the evolving system. The central preoccupation of these cultural analysts, defined within theoretical language, still manages to reflect the fears of powerful American political ideologies, the imperative for smoothly functional social change in societies moving from inert "traditional" ways into the light of "modernity."

TWO

THE COMMAND OF LANGUAGE AND THE

LANGUAGE OF COMMAND

THE RECORDS generated by the East India Company—in their published form found in series such as *The Letters Received from Its Servants in the East* and *The Fort William-India House Correspondence*, and in manuscript records stored in the National Archives of India and the India Office Library and Records—are the primary sources utilized by all historians to reconstruct the facts of the British conquest of India and the construction of the institutions of colonial rule. These archival publications are a tribute to the extraordinary labors of thousands of employees of the Company who produced this seemingly endless store of information. These records are tribute in another sense of the word, as well. To quote *Webster's Collegiate Dictionary* (1948), tribute is "a payment paid by one ruler or nation to another, either as an acknowledgment of submission, or of the price of protection."

In this essay I argue that the tribute represented in print and manuscript is that of complicated and complex forms of knowledge created by Indians, but codified and transmitted by Europeans. The conquest of India was a conquest of knowledge. In these official sources we can trace the changes in forms of knowledge which the conquerors defined as useful for their own ends. The records of the seventeenth and eighteenth centuries reflect the Company's central concerns with trade and commerce; one finds long lists of products, prices, information about trade routes, descriptions of coastal and inland marts, and political information about the Mughal empire, and especially local officials and their actions in relation to the Company. Scattered through these records are mentions of names and functions of Indians who were employed by the Company or with whom it was associated, on whom the British were dependent for the information and knowledge to carry out their commercial ventures.

The anglicized titles of some of these functionaries include akhund, banian, dalal, dubashi, gomastah, pandit, shroff, and vakil. The titles varied with the location of the Company's factories, but the Indians bearing these titles all had specialized forms of knowledge, some about prices and values of currencies, the sources of specialized products, locations of markets, and the networks along which trade goods flowed; others knew about local and imperial governments, diplomatic and political rules, and the personalities of the rulers on whom the British were dependent for protection. All of these specialists were multilingual and had command of specialized languages necessary for the various levels of communication between foreigners and Indians. The dubashi of the Coromandel coast had his function embodied in his title, which means "two languages." In Bengal, the akhund, sometimes referred to as "Muhammadan school teacher," was employed in "composeing, writing and interpreting all letters and writings in the Persian language."[1] The akhund was frequently trusted with diplomatic missions as well as with delivering letters and various documents to Mughal officials. Vakils were confidential agents who, like the akhunds, were frequently involved in negotiations with Indian officials and were not only Persian-using but had to be familiar with court formalities and personalities. They frequently advised the Company officials on courses of action in relation to the Company's continuing need to negotiate various legal and commercial matters with the Mughal state.

During the decade of the 1670s in Surat, the Company carried on repeated diplomatic negotiations with the Maratha ruler, Shivaji, seeking reparations for property lost in his attack on the Company's factory at Rajapur, and seeking to establish trading rights in Shivaji's territories. The Company was well served during this period by a number of Indians, especially two brothers, Rama Shenvi, Portuguese writer, and Narayan Shenvi, the Company's linguist.[2]

Almost from the inception of their trading efforts in India, the British had sought legitimacy and protection from Indian rulers, primarily the Mughal emperor. To this end in 1615 Sir Thomas Roe was dispatched to the Mughal's court jointly by the Company and James I, to obtain a treaty or pact that would guarantee "constant love and pease" between the two monarchs.[3] Roe read the political world in which he found himself in terms of his own system of meanings; it was one which he thought compelled him to undergo a "thousand indignities unfit for a quality that represents a Kings Person," and in which he could not accomplish his ends "without base creeping and bribing." Roe was plagued by a lack of knowledge of Persian, the court language, and did not have anyone whom he thought he could trust to translate properly the letters he had brought from his king, which were to be presented to Jahangir. Roe complained to his employers: "Another terrible inconvenience that I suffer: want of an interpreter. For the Broker's here will not speak but what shall please; yea they would alter the Kings letter because his name was before the Mughals, which I would not allow."[4]

Roe employed as interpreters at various times during his stay at the court of Jahangir a Greek, an Armenian, an eccentric Englishman, and on at least one occasion an Italian who knew Turkish but no Persian. Roe spoke to this interpreter in Spanish, a language he had learned in the Caribbean; the Italian then would translate this into Turkish for an officer of Jahangir's court who knew both Turkish and Persian.[5]

The British realized that in seventeenth-century India Persian was the crucial language for them to learn. They approached Persian as a kind of functional language, a pragmatic vehicle of communication with Indian officials and rulers through which, in a denotative fashion, they could express their requests, queries, and thoughts, and through which they could get things done. To use Persian well required highly specialized forms of knowledge, particularly to draft the many forms of documents that were the basis of official communication throughout much of India. Persian as a language was part of a much larger system of meanings, which was in turn based on cultural premises that were the basis of action. The meanings and the premises on which the Indians constructed actions were far different from those of the British.

Europeans of the seventeenth century lived in a world of signs and correspondences, whereas Indians lived in a world of substances. Roe interpreted the court ritual of the Mughals in which he was required to participate as a sign of debasement rather than an act of incorporation in a substantive fashion, which made him a companion of the ruler. Relations between persons, groups, "nations" (qaum), and between ruler and ruled were constituted differently in Europe and India. The British in seventeenth-century India operated on the idea that everything and everyone had a "price." The presents through which relationships were constituted were seen as a form of exchange to which a quantitative value could be attached, and which could be translated into a price. Hence, the cloth which was the staple of their trade was seen as a utilitarian object whose value was set in a market. They never seemed to realize that certain kinds of cloth and clothes, jewels, arms, and animals had values that were not established in terms of a market-determined price, but were objects in a culturally constructed system by which authority and social relations were literally constituted and transmitted.

Hindus and Muslims operated with an unbounded substantive theory of objects and persons. The body of the ruler was literally his authority, the substance of which could be transmitted in what Europeans thought of as objects. Clothes, weapons, jewels, and paper were the means by which a ruler could transmit the substance of his authority to a chosen companion. To be in the gaze or sight of one who is powerful, to receive food from or hear sounds emitted by a superior, was to be affected by that person.

Meaning for the English was something attributed to a word, a phrase, or an object, which could be determined and translated, at best with a synonym that had a direct referent to something in what the English thought of as a "natural" world. Everything had a more or less specific referent for the English. With the Indians, meaning was not necessarily construed in the same fashion. The effect and affect of hearing a Brahman chant in Sanskrit at a sacrifice did not entail meaning in the European sense; it was to have one's substance literally affected by the sound. When a Mughal ruler issued a farman or a parvana, it was more than an order or an entitlement. These were more than messages or, as the British construed them, a contract or right. Rather, they were a sharing in the authority and substance of the originator, through the act of creating the document. Hence, in drawing up a document, a letter, or a treaty, everything about it was charged with a significance that transcended what might be thought of as its practical purpose. The paper, the forms of address, the preliminary phrases of invocation, the type of script, the elaboration of the terminology, the grammar, the seals used, the particular status of the composer and writer of the document, its mode of transportation, and the form of delivery—all were meaningful.[6]

The British mode of living in India provided cultural blocks to their acquisition of knowledge beyond their problem with language. From the middle of the seventeenth to the middle of the eighteenth centuries there were comparatively few covenanted servants of the Company. In 1665 there were 100 Company officials in India,[7] in 1740 approximately 170,[8] in 1756, on the eve of the Battle of Plassey, there were 224.[9] The majority of the Company's servants lived in the cosmopolitan port cities, generally within the confines of their factories. Most of their social contacts were with other Europeans. The Indians who worked for them as domestic and commercial servants appear to have known some English or Portuguese, the coastal trade language of India. Most British found they could manage their affairs with these languages and with some knowledge of a pidgin version of "Moors," the lingua franca of India. Most of the Company servants lived for a limited time in India, some succumbing to disease or serving, as was the practice in the Company, for five years and then returning to Great Britain. The Europeans most likely to have known Indian languages well were the Portuguese, and "country-born" Europeans, many of whom were engaged in small-scale trading activities or found employment with the East India Company in subordinate positions. The directors looked with suspicion on this latter category, as they felt they were untrustworthy and likely to put their own interests ahead of those of the Company.

In 1713, when the Company wished to obtain a *farman* (royal order) from the Mughal empire to reduce taxes on their internal trade in India and to make permanent a whole series of grants they had received at various times from the Mughal, they had no one in their Bengal establishment who knew sufficient Persian to carry out the negotiations, and had to depend upon an Armenian merchant for that vital function. John Surman, head of the embassy, eventually learned Persian, but not before their interpreter had led them into a number of difficulties. Their embassy was successful, but Surman died soon after his return to Calcutta, and knowledge of Persian went with him.

It was not until the 1740s and 1750s that any significant number of officials of the Company knew any of the Indian languages, a result of more and more of them serving up-country in Company stations and having longer and longer careers in India. James Fraser, who was in the Surat establishment for nineteen years, learned Persian well enough to write a contemporary history of the court of Nadir Shah, based on a Persian account and "constant correspondence" with Persians and Mughals. He had learned his Persian from a Parsi, and had studied with a scholar who was famous for his knowledge of Muslim law in Cambay.[10]

In mid-century there were increasing numbers of British officials with knowledge of Persian and what the British termed Indostan or Moors, as well as other "vulgar" languages of India. Warren Hastings had learned Persian and Moors while serving in Kassimbazar in commercial and diplomatic positions.[11] J. Z. Howell knew enough Bengali or "Indostan" to serve as judge of the zamindar's court in Calcutta and, at the time of the capture of Calcutta by Siraj-ud-daula, was translating into English an Indostan version of a "shastra." Those British immediately involved in the negotiations that led to the overthrow of the nawab of Bengal— William Watts, Henry Vansittart, and Luke Scrafton—were linguistically well enough equipped to outwit even such a canny political operator as Omichand. The architect of the Bengal revolution, Robert Clive, however, appears not to have known any Indian language except the Portuguese trade language, and he was dependent on his banian, Nubkissen, for translating and interpreting in his dealings with Indian rulers.[12] The British success at Plassey and the subsequent appropriation of the revenues of Bengal were to provide the impetus for more and more British civilians and military officers to learn one or more of the Indian languages.

Indian Languages and the Creation of a Discursive Formation

The years 1770 to 1785 may be looked upon as the formative period during which the British successfully began the program of appropriating Indian languages to serve as a crucial component in their construction of the system of rule. More and more British officials were learning the "classical" languages of India (Sanskrit, Persian, and Arabic), as well as many of the "vulgar" languages. More importantly, this was the period in which the British were beginning to produce an apparatus: grammars, dictionaries, treatises, class books, and translations about and from the languages of India.[13] The argument of this essay is that the production of these texts and others that followed them began the establishment of discursive formation, defined an epistemological space, created a discourse (Orientalism), and had the effect of converting Indian forms of knowledge into European objects. The subjects of these texts were first and foremost the Indian languages themselves, re-presented in European terms as grammars, dictionaries, and teaching aids in a project to make the acquisition of a working knowledge of the languages available to those British who were to be part of the ruling groups of India.

Some of these texts, such as Balfour's *Herkern* and Gladwin's *Ayeen*, were to be guidebooks—the one to the epistolary practice of professional scribes, the other to the administrative practices of the Mughal empire. The translations of Dow and Davy of Persian chronicles were intended to be expositions of the political practices and the failures of the imperial predecessors of the British conquerors. Halhed's *Gentoo Laws* and Wilkins's *Geeta* were translations thought to be keys with which to unlock, and hence make available, knowledge of Indian law and religion held tightly by the "mysterious" Brahmans.

Seen as a corpus, these texts signal the invasion of an epistemological space occupied by a great number of diverse Indian scholars, intellectuals, teachers, scribes, priests, lawyers, officials, merchants, and bankers, whose knowledge as well as they themselves were to be converted into instruments of colonial rule. They were now to become part of the army of babus, clerks, interpreters, sub-inspectors, munshis, pandits, qazis, vakils, schoolmasters, amins, sharistadars, tahsildars, deshmukhs, darogahs, and mamlatdars who, under the scrutiny and supervision of the white sahibs, ran the everyday affairs of the Raj.

The knowledge which this small group of British officials sought to control was to be the instrumentality through which they were to issue commands and collect ever-increasing amounts of information. This information was needed to create or locate cheap and effective means to assess and collect taxes, and maintain law and order; and it served as a way to identify and classify groups within Indian society. Elites had to be found within Indian society who could be made to see that they had an interest in the maintenance of British rule. Political strategies and tactics had to be created and codified into diplomacy through which the country powers could be converted into allied dependencies. The vast social world that was India had to be classified, categorized, and bounded before it could be ordered. As with many discursive formations and their discourses, many of its major effects were unintended, as those who were to be the objects produced by the formation often turned it to their own ends. Nonetheless, the languages that the Indians speak and read were to be transformed. The discursive formation was to participate in the creation and reification of social groups with their varied interests. It was to establish and regularize a discourse of differentiations that came to mark the social and political map of nineteenth-century India.

I have chosen to utilize a mode of exposition that is obviously influenced by the work of Michel Foucault. My effort will be to try to locate the kinds of questions his work directs us toward by rehearsing a history, much of which is familiar to students of India's past. It recounts some of the details of how the English, during the period from roughly 1770 to 1820, went about learning Indian languages, and how they developed a pedagogical and scholarly apparatus for this purpose. It does not aim to be complete, nor will it even deal with what might be thought of as its most important texts, its most famous leading figures, or its most important institutions, such as the College of Fort William and the College at Fort St. George.

Persian: The Language of Indian Politics

A knowledge of Persian was needed immediately after the Battle of Plassey to recruit and train an Indian army, and to develop a system of alliances and treaties with native independent princes and powers so as to protect "the rich and fertile territories" in Coromandel, upper India, and Bengal which the Company had conquered.[14] William Davy, who as a military officer in the Bengal army had found a knowledge of Persian highly lucrative, thought that the important job of translation could not be entrusted to Indian interpreters. In describing the talent needed for this important task, he wrote:

> A Persian interpreter should not only be able to speak fluently in the language, but to read all such letters as he may receive, . . . to answer them with his own hand, if the importance of the subject, of which they treat should render it necessary. Otherwise the secret negotiations and correspondence of government are liable to be made public through the medium of the native Munchees, or writers, whom he will be obliged to employ and trust.[15]

Davy appears to have learned his Persian from a munshi, and without the aid of a Persian-English dictionary or grammar. The only dictionary of Persian then known was one in Latin by Franciscus Meninski, which was so scarce in India that Davy paid one hundred guineas for a copy he found in Calcutta in 1773. This was not much use to him, as Meninski, Davy thought, did not know Persian but did have an extensive knowledge of Turkish, on which he based his Arabic, Turkish, and Persian lexicon. The result, Davy felt, was that "words in one language, bearing a variety of significations, are given through the medium of words in another, having also various meanings, and many directly contradictory, were translated by words in a third, which in many significations, differs totally from both."[16]

There had been a chair in Arabic established at Oxford in the late seventeenth century and there were on the Continent a few scholars of Persian who, according to Sir William Jones, "had confined their studies to minute researches of verbal criticism." Jones further complained that the learned "have no taste, and the men of taste, have no learning." There was no patronage for literary and scholarly research on oriental languages. Jones wrote that Meninski's work may have immortalized him as a savant but it ruined him financially. Jones thought the Persian language "rich, melodious and elegant," with important works in poetry and history, which was due for a great interest now that India had become "the source of incredible wealth to the merchants of Europe.[17] Jones wrote:

> The servants of the company received letters they could not read and were ambitious of gaining titles of which they could not comprehend the meaning; it was found highly dangerous to employ the natives as interpreters, upon whose fidelity they could not depend; and it was at last discovered that they must apply themselves to the study of the Persian language. . . .
> The languages of Asia will now perhaps be studied with uncommon ardour; they are known to be useful, and will soon be found to be instructive and entertaining.[18]

Sir William Jones' *Grammar of the Persian Language*, published in London in 1771, was very successful and went through six editions by 1804. Although it was recommended by the Court of Directors to their employees, they did not subsidize it, as they did many subsequent publications on Indian languages.

In constructing his *Grammar*, Jones was centrally interested in Persian poetry, and the descriptive statements on which the grammatical rules were based were "poetry composed in the Shiraz literary 'dialect' between the tenth and fifteenth centuries A.D."[19] The *Grammar* provided for its time a useful description of the phonology, morphology, and syntax of the language Jones was describing.[20]

Jones supplied his readers with advice on how to learn Persian, which was premised on the availability of a native speaker to Persian. The student should learn to read the characters with fluency and "learn the true pronunciation of every letter from the mouth of a native." Jones recommended using Meminski's dictionary but warned the learner that "he must not neglect to converse with his living instructor and to learn from him the phrases of common discourse."[21]

After six months, Jones recommended, the student should move on to reading "some elegant History or poem with an intelligent native." He should get his munshi to transcribe a section of the Gulistan or a fable of Cashefi, "in the common broken hand used in India." In a year's time, the reader was assured, if he worked according to Jones' plan, he would be able to "translate and to answer any letter from an Indian Prince, and to converse with the natives of India not only with fluency but with elegance." However, if he aspires to be "an eminent translator," he will have to learn Arabic as well, "which is blended with the Persian in so singular a manner." Another benefit for the would-be official of the East India Company would be a knowledge of "the jargon of Indostan, very improperly called the language of the Moors," which, Jones reports, "contains so great a number of Persian words that I was able, with little difficulty, to read the fables of Pilpai, which are translated into that idiom."[22]

The prestige of Persian as the best language for an ambitious cadet or junior writer continued into the early nineteenth century. Warren Hastings, who had lobbied unsuccessfully in 1765 for the establishment of a chair in Persian at Oxford,[23] vigorously argued that Persian and Arabic should be the keystone of the curriculum at the newly established College at Fort William:

> To the Persian language as being the medium of all Political intercourse the first place ought to be assigned in the studies of the Pupils; and as much of the Arabic as is necessary to shew the principles of its construction and the variations which the sense of the radical word derives from its inflections, to complete their knowledge of the Persian, which in its modern dialect consists in a great measure of the Arabic. . . . The Persian language ought to be studied to perfection, and is requisite to all the civil servants of the Company, as it may also prove of equal use to the Military Officers of all the Presidencies.[24]

Through the first fifteen years of the college, the Persian department was the most prestigious and best supported. Those young officials who did well in Persian were frequently slated for the best beginning jobs, which often led to lucrative and influential positions in the central secretariat in Calcutta. In addition, it would appear that, as Persian and Arabic were the "classical languages" of India, they were worthy to be studied by gentlemen whose English education stressed the learning of the European classical languages, Latin and Greek, as the emblem of an educated man fitted thereby to rulership.

Sanskrit: The Language of Indian Law and Lore

In India the other "classical" language, Sanskrit, was seen by the seventeenth- and eighteenth-century British as a secret language "invented by the Brahmins to be a mysterious repository for their religion and philosophy."[25] There was considerable curiosity about the religion of the Gentoos among the Europeans, and there had been scattered and discontinuous efforts to learn Sanskrit, particularly by Catholic missionaries in the seventeenth century, of which the British in the eighteenth century seemed unaware. James Fraser, J. Z. Howell, and Alexander Dow had all made unsuccessful efforts to learn Sanskrit. What knowledge the British had of the learning and religious thought of the Hindus came from discussions with Brahmans and other high-caste Indians, or from Persian or "Indostan" translations of Sanskrit texts.

John Z. Howell, who in his thirty years' experience in India had learned Persian, Bengali, and Indostan, wrote an extended account of the "religious Tenets of the Gentoos," published in 1767.[26] This account was based on an unidentified "Gentoo *Shastah*" (shastra), which he was translating at the time of Siraj-ud-daula's capture of Calcutta in 1756. At this time Howell lost "curious manuscripts" as well as a translation of a Hindustani version of a shastra. Howell also alluded to conferences with "many of the most learned and ingenious amongst the laity."[27]

Howell criticized all his predecessors' views that the Hindus were "a race of stupid and gross idolaters." Most of the more recent accounts of the Hindus, he argued, were by those of the "Romish communion," who had a vested interest in denigrating Hindus, as they wanted to convert them to Catholicism. Howell stigmatized Roman Catholic religious tenets as more idolatrous than those of the Hindus. He not only castigated "Popish authors" but also most others who had written only on "exterior manners and religion" of the Hindus. The casual observer or traveler, Howell suggested, had to get beyond "his own ignorance, superstition and partiality" and the provincialism involved in thinking that anything "beyond the limits of their native land" was greatly inferior to their own. Howell castigated a travel writer as superficial:

His telling us such and such a people, in the East or West-Indies, worship this stick, or that stone, or monstrous idol; only serves to reduce in our esteem, our fellow creatures, to the most abject and despicable point of light. Whereas, was he skilled in the language of the people he describes, sufficiently to trace the etymology of their words and phrases, and capable of diving into the mysteries of their theology; he would probably be able to evince us, that such seemingly preposterous worship, had the most sublime rational source and foundation.

The traveller, who without these essential requisites, (as well as industry and a clear understanding) pretends to describe and fix the religious tenets of any nation whatever, dishonestly imposes his own reveries on the world; and does the greatest injury and violence to letters, and the cause of humanity.[28]

The motivation for the British in India to learn Sanskrit had a dual basis: at one and the same time there was a scholarly curiosity to unlock the mysterious knowledge of the ancients, and an immediate practical necessity fueled by Warren Hastings' plan of 1772 for the better government of Bengal. In writing to the Court of Directors explaining this plan, he stated that it would establish the Company's system of governance on a "most equitable, solid and permanent footing." The plan was based on "principles of experience and common observation, without the advantages which an intimate knowledge of the theory of law might have afforded us: We have endeavoured to adapt our Regulations to the Manners and Understandings of the People, and the Exigencies of the Country, adhering as closely as we are able to their ancient uses and Institutions."[29]

In Hastings' plan the theory was clear: Indians should be governed by Indian principles, particularly in relation to law. The practical question arose as to how the British were to gain knowledge of the "ancient uses and institutions." The answer was easy enough to state. The Hindus, Hastings averred, "had been in possession of laws which continued unchanged, from remotest antiquity." These laws, he wrote, were in the hands of Brahmans, or "professors of law," found all over India, who were supported by "public endowments and benefactions from every and all people." The professor received a "degree of personal respect amounting almost to idolatry."[30] In each of the criminal courts established, the qazi, mufti, and two maulavis "were to expound the laws, and to determine how far the delinquents shall be guilty of a breach thereof." In the civil courts, "suits regarding inheritance, Marriage, caste and other religious usages and institutions, the Laws of the Koran with respect to Mahometans, and those of the Shaster with respect to the Gentoos shall be invariably adhered to."[31]

For officers of a commercial company it was clearly the laws that the civil courts were to administer which were most crucial, as they dealt with disputes "concerning property, whether real or personal, all cases of inheritance, marriage and caste; all claims of debt, disputed accounts, contracts, partnerships and demands of rent."[32] Through this plan, the Company's government was to become the guarantor of what Hastings and the other eighteenth-century British saw as the basic rights of Indians, oddly enough in a polity that was supposed to be despotic and hence without such rights.

In his discussion of his plans, Hastings was translating for a British audience theories and practices from one culture to another. India had an ancient constitution which was expressed in what came to be thought of as two codes, one Hindu and the other Muslim. Pandits were "professors," and some even came to be conceived of as "lawyers." For the demonstration of law there were also experts—qazis, "judges"—who knew the appropriate codes to apply to particular cases. Following the current practice in Bengal, which was ruled by Muslims, the British accepted Muslim criminal law as the law of the land, but civil law was to be Hindu for Hindus and Muslim for Muslims. The decision of Hastings and the Council at Fort William was to have profound effects on the course of the judicial system in India.[33]

If the British were to administer Hindu law with the guidance and assistance of Hindu "law officers" (pandits), they had to establish some fixed body of this law, one that they hoped could become authoritative and that could be translated into English, so that the judges would have some idea of the nature and content of this law.

In order to establish what the Hindu law was, Warren Hastings persuaded eleven of the "most respectable pandits in Bengal" to make a compilation of the relevant shastric literature. Hastings appointed N. B. Halhed to supervise this compilation and to translate the resulting text into English.[34] Halhed described the manner in which the text was compiled and translated:

> The professors of the ordinances here collected still speak and original language in which they were composed. . . . A set of the most experienced of these lawyers was selected from every part of Bengal for the purpose of compiling the present work, which they picked out sentence by sentence from various originals in the Shanscrit language, neither adding to, nor diminishing any part of the ancient text. The articles thus collected were next translated literally into Persian, under the inspection of one of their own body; and from that translation were rendered into English with an equal attention to the closeness and fidelity of the version.[35]

The compilation was known in Sanskrit as the *Vivadarnavasetu* (bridge across the sea of litigation). The manner in which the translation was made, and the authoritative nature of the compilation, came into question within the next fifteen years. Halhed had only a very limited knowledge of Sanskrit and depended on Bengali or Hindustani explanations of passages in the text by the pandits, which discussions were then abstracted into Persian by a munshi, and from this Halhed did the final translation into English.[36]

Sir William Jones, who had been appointed judge in the Supreme Court of Judicature in 1783, thought the *Gentoo Code* was like a Roman law digest, consisting of "authentic texts with short notes taken from commentaries of high authority." He praised the work as far as it went, but it was too diffuse, "rather curious than useful," and the section on the law of contracts was too "succinct and superficial." But if the Sanskrit text itself was faulted, the translation, he felt, was useless:

> But, whatever be the merit of the original, the translation of it has no authority, and is of no other use than to suggest inquiries on the many dark passages, which we find in it: properly speaking, indeed, we cannot call it a translation; for, though Mr. Halhed performed his part with fidelity, yet the Persian interpreter had supplied him only with a loose injudicious epitome of the original Sanscrit, in which abstract many essential passages are omitted. . . . All this I say with confidence, having already perused no small part of the original with a learned Pandit, comparing it, as I proceeded, with the English version.[37]

On his arrival in Calcutta, Jones had no plans to undertake the study of Sanskrit; he complained to Wilkins, "life is too short and my necessary business to long for me to think of acquiring a new language."[38] Jones' curiosity about Indian thought and his role as a judge of the Crown Court in Calcutta, however, led him to undertake the task of learning Sanskrit. After he had been in India less than a year, Jones journeyed to Banaras, where he met maulavis, pandits, and rajas, among whom were Ali Ibrahim Khan, long regarded by the British as a distinguished scholar and judge. Jones had hoped to obtain from Khan a Persian translation of the "Dherm Shastr Menu Smrety," which was considered to be the authentic source of Hindu law. Although Khan obtained a Sanskrit text, Manu's *Dharmashastra*, the pandits refused to assist Khan in translating it into Persian.[39]

Jones became increasingly frustrated in having to depend on defective Persian translations of Hindu law books. He reported to William Pitt the Younger in February 1785 that he was almost "tempted to learn Sanskrit, that I may check on the pandits in the Court."[40] A month later he was complaining to Wilkins that "it was of the utmost importance that the stream of Hindu law should be pure: for we are entirely at the devotion of the native lawyers, through our ignorance of Sanskrit."[41] In September 1785, Jones had gone to Nadiya, a center of Sanskrit learning sixty miles north of Calcutta on the Hugli river, where he hoped "to learn the rudiments of that venerable and interesting language."[42] In October he was back in Calcutta, with the "father of the University of Nadya" who, Jones explained, was not a Brahman but who had instructed young Brahman students in grammar and ethics. He would serve Jones' purpose as a teacher, as he lacked the "priestly pride" which marked his students.[43] A year later Jones could report that he was "tolerably strong in Sanskrit," and getting ready to translate a law tract ascribed to "Menu, the Minos of India."[44]

By October 1786, Jones had considerable confidence in his own knowledge of Sanskrit, for he was correcting his own court pandits' interpretations of legal texts by translating to his own satisfaction "the original tracts" on which they based their decisions.[45] Jones was now to go on to plan a much bigger project that he believed would free the British judges in India from dependence on what he thought was the venality and corruption of the Indian interpreters of Hindu and Muslim law. This was the exact counterpart of the effort a few decades earlier by the British to free themselves, through knowledge of Persian, from the akhunds, munshis, and kayasthas who translated and interpreted political documents. Jones now proposed to compile from the best available sources a digest of Hindu and Muslim law, which could then be translated into English and which would provide the European judges a "check upon the native interpreters." Jones wanted a means by which the "laws of the natives" could be preserved inviolate, and the decrees of the courts made to conform to "Hindu and Mahomedan law."[46]

If the system which Jones hoped to see implemented was to succeed, it would require that several forms of knowledge become codified and public. The English judges and other officials would require access to what Jones and others believed at the time was *the* Hindu and *the* Mahomedan law," which was locked up in the texts and the heads of pandits and maulavis. There had to be found a fixed body of knowledge that could be objectified into Hindu and Muslim law. This body of knowledge could be specified, set into hierarchies of knowledge, linearly ordered from the most "sacred" or compelling to the less powerful.

Jones and others had the idea that there was historically in India a fixed body of laws, codes, which had been set down or established by "law givers," which over time had become corrupted by accretions, interpretations, and commentaries, and it was this jungle of accretions and corruptions of the earlier pure codes which was controlled in the present by those Indians whom the British thought of as the Indian lawyers. An Ur-text had to be found or reconstituted, which at one and the same time would extablish *the* Hindu and Muslim law as well as free the English from dependency for interpretations and knowledge on fallible and seemingly overly susceptible pandits and maulavis. The task had also to be accomplished somehow by using the knowledge which their Indian guides, the mistrusted pandits and maulavis, seemed to monopolize. Jones, even before arriving in India, seemed to distrust Indian scholars' interpretations of their own legal traditions: a distrust that grew with experience in India. He wrote Cornwallis, the governor-general, in 1788, that he could not with "an easy conscience, concur in a decision, merely on the written opinion of native lawyers in any case, in which they could have the remotest interest in misleading the court."[47] Jones wanted to provide the English courts in India, Crown and Company, with a sure basis on which they could render decisions consonant with a "true" or "pure" version of Hindu law. Then the pandits, Brahmans, and Indian "lawyers," Jones believed, henceforth could not "deal out Hindoo law as they please, and make it at reasonable rates, when they cannot find it ready made."[48]

In advocating his ambitious plan for a digest of Hindu and Muslim law, Jones deployed a discourse that made a direct connection between the British future in India and the late classical Roman past. In discussing his plans, he explained that his mode of proceeding would be that of Tribonian, the compiler of the Justinian code, with only "original texts arranged in a scientific method."[49] The main subject of the digests would be the laws of contract and inheritance and, as Jones was again and again to reiterate, these subjects were at the heart of the establishment of rights in property, "real and personal."[50]

Jones did not live to see the completion of his ambition to become the Tribonian of India, but to this day he stands in stone in St. Paul's Cathedral, a statue commissioned by the Court of Directors, dressed in a toga, with pen in hand and leaning on two volumes which are "understood to mean the Institutes of Menu."[51] Visual reminders of the British as Romans can still be found in the gardens of the Victoria Memorial, where we find Warren Hastings in the toga of a Roman senator, standing above a Brahman pandit with a palm-leaf manuscript, and a Muslim maulavi poring over a Persian manuscript.

Classical Models and the Definition of the "Vulgar" Languages of India

N. B. Halhed, the translator of the *Gentoo Code* and author of the first English grammar of Bengali, drew heavily on analogies between the eighteenth-century English in India and the Romans. His grammar was part of a large project that would stabilize and perpetuate British rule in Bengal. The "English masters of Bengal," wrote Halhed in 1778, needed to add its language to their acquisitions, like the Romans, "people of

[handwritten margin notes: medium of intercourse btw. Govt and subjects, Europeans, Indians]

little learning and less taste," who applied themselves to the study of Greek once they had conquered Greece. So the British in Bengal needed to cultivate a language that would be the "medium of intercourse between the Government and its subjects, between the natives of Europe who are to rule, and the inhabitants of India who are to obey." In addition, the English needed to know the language to explain "the benevolent principles" of the legislation which they were "to enforce."[52]

The British in late eighteenth-century Bengal found what was for them a complex language situation. Few of the British knew Bengali; rather, they used "Moors" and Persian in many of their transactions. This reflected the language use of many of their Indian associates and subordinates.

H. P. Foster, who produced an English / Bengali and a Bengali / English dictionary between 1799 and 1802, provided a hypothetical example of the results of dependence on Persian in the courts of Bengal at the time. A Dom—who, he informed his readers, is from "the lowest and most illiterate classes"—goes to a darogah, a minor police official, to make a complaint. According to Foster, the darogah's knowledge of Persian was restricted to reading *Tales of the Parrot*, a popular class book of the time. The Dom delivers his complaint in the "vulgar" dialect of Bengali, and gets it written down by the police official in "bad Bongalee in Persian characters with here and there a mangled Persian phrase." This document may then get translated into Persian, and finally, if the case makes its way up to the Nizamat Adalat, the documents that have accumulated are translated into English.[53] If the British learned Bengali, says Foster, it was because it was the language spoken around the major cities, such as Murshidabad, Dacca, and Calcutta, which were the "seats of foreign governments and the rendezvous of all nations," where the language spoken was much influenced by "Hindostanee of Moors," and this was the language that the British adapted as their "medium of communication" with the people of Bengal.[54]

William Carey observed that the Indian servant, personal and official, in speaking Bengali with Europeans "generally intermixes his language with words derived from the Arabic or Persian and with some few corrupted English and Portuguese words."[55] Carey warned his countrymen that dependence on poor interpreters and the continued use of the "jargon of Moors" limited their ability to deal directly with "men of great respectability" as well as the common folk of Bengal, who could "provide information on local affairs."[56]

The *Grammar* of the Bengali language that Halhed produced was organized in terms of European grammatical categories, the various chapters dealing with: the parts of speech, elements and substantives, pronouns, verbs, words denoting attributes and relations, numerals, syntax, orthography, and versification. Halhed took pride in being the first European who related Bengali to Sanskrit: "The following work presents the Bengali language merely as derived from its parent Shanscrit," with all the words from the Persian and "Hindostanic" dialects expunged. He warned, though, that those who wanted to be accurate translators would have to study the Persian and "Hindostanic" dialects, "since in the occurrences of modern business, as managed by the present illiterate generation, he will find all his letters, representations and accounts interspersed with a variety of borrowed phrases or unauthorized expressions."[57] Halhed based his knowledge of Bengali grammar on "a pandit who imparted a small portion of his language to me" and readily "displayed the principles of his grammar."[58]

The speakers of pure "Hindostanic" are found in upper India and in western India, where they still use this language for purposes of commerce. Halhed drew an analogy between "Hindostanic" and Bengali:

> What the pure Hindostanic is to upper India, the language which I have here endeavoured to explain is to Bengal, intimately related to the Shanscrit both in expressions, construction and character. It is the sole channel of personal and epistolary communication among the Hindoos of every occupation and tribe. All their business is transacted, and all their accounts are kept in it; and as their system of education is in general very confined, there are few among them who can write or read any other idiom: the uneducated, or eight parts in ten of the whole nation are necessarily confined to the usage of their mother tongue.[59]

Halhed prefigured Jones' statement on the relation of Sanskrit to Latin and Greek. He was astonished "to find the similitude of Shanscrit words with those of Persian and Arabic, and even of Latin and Greek . . . in the main ground work of the language, in monosyllables, in the names of numbers, and the appellations of such things as would be discriminated at the immediate dawn of civilization."[60] He also commented that the "Hindostanic" dialect spoken over most of Hindostan proper was "indubitably derived from Shanscrit," with which it has exactly the same connection as the modern dialects of France and Italy with pure Latin.[61]

Another variety of "Hindostanic," wrote Halhed, was developed by the Muslim invaders of India, who could not learn the language spoken by the Hindus; the latter, in order to maintain the purity of their own tongue, introduced more and more abstruse terms from Sanskrit. The Muslims in turn introduced many "exotic" words from their own languages, which they superimposed on the "grammatical principles of the original Hindostanic." Halhed refers to this form of "Hindostanic" as a compound idiom which was spoken in Bengal by Hindus connected with Muslim courts. Those Brahmans and other well-educated Hindus "whose ambition has not overpowered their principles" continued to speak and write the pure form of "Hindostanic" and wrote it with Nagari characters rather than with the Arabic script.[62]

Halhed's introduction of the *Grammar* stands as a prime text that both summarizes and constitutes knowledge that the British were beginning to develop regarding Indian languages. It prefigures much that was to happen in the next thirty years. As a classically educated man he was concerned to find general principles about Indian languages, and these were to be found in Sanskrit, the treasury of knowledge about India. Languages for the English were to be learned for practical reasons, but this was best done through some knowledge of the "classical" languages that underlay the contemporary dialects, jargons, vernaculars, and idioms.

Halhed's view that the languages currently spoken in Bengal and upper India were fallen, broken, or corrupt versions of some pure, authentic, coherent, logically formed prior language was one shared, of course, by his Hindu and Muslim instructors, who frequently were contemptuous of the spoken languages and favored the sacred and literary languages of Sanskrit, Arabic, and Persian.

The Establishment of Hindustani
as the British Language of Command

Until the late part of the eighteenth century, the British in India had done little to study systematically the wide variety of languages spoken in India. Portuguese, German, and Danish missionaries, as well as the Company's Dutch and French trade rivals, had produced grammars and dictionaries of one or another of the Indian languages. The British appear to have been ignorant of these efforts. The classifications of the Indian languages used by the British were vague and shifting, reflecting both geography and function. "Malabar" referred to the language spoken by fishermen and boatmen on both the Malabar and Coromandel coasts, and was by extension used as a label for the language spoken in what is today Tamilnadu. "Gentu" or "Telinga" was found in what is Andhra, but was also widely diffused in south India, reflecting the presence as mercenaries of large numbers of Telingas in the south Indian armies. "Banian" was at times used to refer to Gujarati, reflecting the fact that many of the merchants on the west coast were Gujaratis. Calcutta, Bombay, and Madras were heterogeneous and polyglot cities. In the light of the political history of the seventeenth and eighteenth centuries, the British regarded Marathi, Persian, and "Moors" as important languages in south India.[63]

From their first exposure to the Mughal court, the British were aware of the central importance of the language spoken there and elsewhere in India. Reverend Terry, who accompanied Sir Thomas Roe, described the language thus:

> The language of this Empire, I mean the vulgar, bears the name of it, and is called Indostan; it hath much affinitie with the Persian and Arabian tongue . . . a language which is very significant, and speaks much in a few words. It is expressed by letters which are different than those alphabets by which the Persian and Arabic tongues are formed.[64]

For the next two hundred years this language or variants thereof carried a bewildering variety of labels: Moors, Indostan, Hindoostanic, Hindowee, Nagreeo, and Koota. Most generally the British labelled it "Moors," and pejoratively referred to it as a jargon.[65]

In the period immediately after the Battle of Plassey, even before there were published grammars for this language, notes and manuscripts were circulating as aids for the Company's officers, particularly military ones, to acquire a working knowledge of it. The first grammar of Moors published in England was that of Edward Hadley, an officer in the Bengal army who had found it "impossible to discharge my duties . . . without a knowledge of the corrupt dialect" spoken by those troops he was to command. Hadley rejected the prevalent idea of the "Eastern Literate" that Moors was so irregular that it did not have a grammar. He demonstrated that the verbs in Moors were not declined as they were in Persian, and that its grammar was derived from some other language which, he speculated, was derived from India's northern invaders, the Tartars.[66] Hadley's grammar, revised by a number of authors, was to go through seven editions by 1809, at which time it was superseded by a series of works by John Borthwick Gilchrist, who is generally regarded as the creator of what was to become the British language of command in India—Hindustani.

In 1782, at the age of twenty-three, after studying medicine in Edinburgh, John Gilchrist arrived in Bombay, where he obtained an appointment as an assistant surgeon and was attached to a regiment in the Bengal army.[67] Gilchrist wrote that on his arrival at Bombay in 1782,

> I instantly foresaw that my residence, in any capacity, would prove as unpleasant to myself, as unprofitable to my employers, until I acquired an adequate knowledge of the current language of the country, in which I was now to sojourn. I therefore sat resolutely down to acquire what was then termed as the *Moors.* . . . During the march with the Bengal troops under the command of Col. Charles Morgan from Surat to Futigurh, I had innumerable instances in every town and village we visited of the universal currency of the language I had been learning.[68]

Within two years Gilchrist had left the army and was settled in Faizabad, where he grew a beard and "assumed for a period the dress of the natives." Here he began an effort to prepare, with the assistance of several "learned Hindoostanees" (a term, he was careful to point out, that referred to Hindus and Muslims alike in upper India), a dictionary and grammar of their language.[69] His associates could not supply him with a dictionary of their language, so he began to extract from them *viva voce* every known word in their voluminous tongue. He did this by instructing his munshis to furnish him with every signification they could possibly attach to such words as *a, ab, abab, abach*, and so on. The syllables he wrote led the way to a "numerous tribe of words." He found this system of establishing a corpus for his dictionary too cumbersome and resorted to using Johnson's English dictionary. Gilchrist would explain the English term as best he could to the Hindustanis, who would then "furnish the synonymous vocables in their own speech."[70]

Gilchrist quickly discovered that his learned associates, rather than providing him with "the most easy, familiar and common words," would let their mind's eye roam for far-fetched expressions "from the deserts of Arabia, or they would be beating and scampering over the mountains of Persia." Others would search "in the dark intricate mines and caverns of Sanskrit lexicography." Not only did Gilchrist have difficulties with glossing, he kept insisting that there must be a written grammar of the language they were studying. His collaborators replied to his question with one of their own, asking "if it was ever yet known in any country that men had to consult vocabularies and rudiments for their own vernacular speech." Only after many enquiries did his colleagues produce a "Tom Thumb" performance, a *Khalig Baree*, which the Indians called a "vocabulary," but which Gilchrist slightingly referred to as "old meagre School vocabulary."[71]

What Gilchrist took to be the failure of his associates to take seriously their own vernacular speech, he attributed to the favorite British explanation of a conspiracy on the part of educated Indians to prevent the British from having access to the great mass of the Indian population. He theorized

> that it is not at all improbable, that the cormorant crew of Dewans, Mootsuddies, Sirkars, Nazirs, Pundits, Munshis and a tremendous roll call of harpies who encompass power here see with jealous solicitude every attempt in their masters to acquire the means of immediate communication with the great mass of the people who those locusts of the land conceive their lawful prey.[72]

Why was Hindustani so badly studied, even ignored, by Gilchrist's European predecessors? Throughout the preface, he builds a complicated argument to answer this question. At base the problem was that the British labeled the language a "jargon," and conflated what Gilchrist began to call "Hindostanee" with what the majority of Europeans in India referred to as "Moors." Moors today would be termed a pidgin. Gilchrist thought of Moors as a "barbarian gabble [which] exists nowhere else but among the dregs of our servants, in the snip snap dialogues with us only. Even they would not degrade themselves by chattering the gibberish of the savage while conversing with or addressing each other in the capacity of human beings."[73]

Gilchrist and the Definition of Hindustani

The Hindustani language has three levels or styles, which Gilchrist identified as the "High Court or Persian" style, the "Middle or Genuine Hindostanee" style, and the "vulgar of the Hinduwee."

The Court or Persian style is found in the elevated poems of Sauda, Vali, Mir Dard, and other poets. This is the "pompous and pedantic language of literature and politics," wrote Gilchrist, and it draws heavily on Arabic and Persian. The second level of Hindustani is what Gilchrist wanted to establish as the standard language, and it can be found in the elegy of "Miskeen, the satires of Sauda," and the translation of the articles of war. The third level, or the vulgar, is evidenced, Gilchrist wrote, "in Mr. Forster's translation of the Regulations of Government . . . in the greatest part of Hindostanee compositions written in the Nagaree character, in the dialect of the lower order of servants and Hindoos, as well as among the peasantry of Hindoostan."[74]

Gilchrist was very much aware that he was dealing with shadings, fluctuations, and a language that was evanescent. What made his task all the harder, he felt, was that those Indians, Hindu and Muslim, who professionally used languages and had a knowledge of them were dominated by what he felt was pedantry: "In a country where pedantry is esteemed [as] the touchstone of learning, the learned Moosulman glories in his Arabic and Persian. . . . The Hindoo is no less attached to Sunskrit and Hinduwee."[75]

Gilchrist explained the emergence and fixing of these language styles by constructing a history. He believed that before the "irruptions, and subsequent settlement of the Mossulmans there was a language spoken all over north India, referred to by Hindus as Brij Bhasa, a pure speech . . . the language of the Indian Arcadia." This language was referred to by the Muslims as "Hinduwee," the language of the Hindus. In his construction of a history of the Indian languages, Gilchrist compared Hinduwee to the language of the Saxons before their conquest by the French. Hinduwee, like Saxon, was then deluged by Arabic and Persian.

After repeated invasions of Muslims, this resulted in the creation of the language which Gilchrist termed "Hindostanee." Muslims referred to this language as "Oorduwee" in its military form, "Rekhtu" in its poetical form, and "Hindee" as the everyday language of the Hindus.[76]

As a cover term for this language Gilchrist chose the term "Hindostanee," which had a geographic referent, Hindustan. This could denote in the eighteenth century the whole of the South Asian peninsula or, in its more restricted sense, India north of the Vindhyas. Gilchrist intended through the use of the term "Hindostanee" to denote the contemporary spoken language of India, used by both Hindus and Muslims; he preferred it to labeling the language "Hindee," lest it be confused with Hinduwee, used exclusively by Hindus. For him it was a term like "British or European . . . a conciliating appellation for people in other matters very dissimilar, consequently the most applicable also to the grand popular connecting language of vast regions of the East."[77]

In Gilchrist's theory, Sanskrit, "the dead, sacred, mysterious tongue of the Hindoos," plays little part. He thought that Sanskrit was derived from Hinduwee, which was spoken over much of India before the Muslim invasions.[78] The other languages that he distinguished in north India were Bengalee, Rajpootee, and Poorbee (Bhoj Puri). He thought these languages were very different in both spoken and literary forms from the language he was classifying as Hindostanee. Other languages found in India included Dukhunee, the language spoken by Muslims in south India, Ooreea (Oriya), Mulwaree (Marwari), Goojaratee (Gujarati), Tilungee (Talinga, Telugu), and Kismeere (Kashmiri). These languages Gilchrist thought had been derived from Hinduwee, Brij Bhasha or Bhakha. Gilchrist noted that the subdivisions of Indian languages were almost endless, with many local names. Some of the variations he thought of as varieties. Dukhunee and Punjabee were varieties of Hindostanee, whereas others like Bungal Bhasa were specific dialects and, he implies, derived directly from the parent Hinduwee.[79]

Gilchrist theorized that there were "three grand indigenous languages which were to be found in India." Two were "orally current," Hinduwee and Hindostanee; the third was Sanskrit, "which really is the dead letter of civil and religious policy, is the consecrated palladium of science and the priestcraft among the Hindoos. The Hinduwee and Hindostanee have produced in the several kingdoms and states through which they range territorial varieties or dialects."[80]

The historical ordering of these three languages, Gilchrist speculated, was first Hinduwee, then Sanskrit, and most recently Hindostanee. Sanskrit was not a natural language but a "usurpation" on Hinduwee, a "cunning fabrication" of Hinduwee by "the insidious Bruhmans." The logic by which Gilchrist came to believe that Sanskrit was historically posterior to the Hinduwee was based on a general theory of language development. If Sanskrit was the original parent language of the other two, why is it so "inextricably perplexing" (by implication, to the Europeans), and why does its name imply that it is "polished or artificial"? He further wondered how such a language could be developed in "the earliest stages of civilization." The answer was that the cunning grammarians created Sanskrit out of a pre-existing language that was the language of the folk themselves. From this folk language they constructed "a mystical, but splendid factum factorum for the reception of the priest craft." The language of the priests was part of a conspiracy or plot, which resulted in the creation of a double yoke of "a mild despotism" and an "insatiable catholick religious persuasion." The language and its creators, the Brahmans, used their knowledge to enslave the Hindu population of India. The Brahmans he characterized as "a villainous priesthood" whose teachings are nothing but the "sonorous inarticulate bellowings of Brahmanical wolves."[81]

Gilchrist, with the publication of his *Dictionary* (which appeared in parts and with great difficulty), began to become more and more vociferous in his attacks on both Indian and British scholars of Indian languages, especially those who insisted that one or another of the Indian "classical" languages was the prerequisite for learning Hindustani. In 1799 Gilchrist wanted to establish an oriental seminary in Calcutta to teach the newly appointed Company servants Hindustani. This was to replace the then current practice of granting Company appointees a Rs 30 allowance to enable them to hire a munshi to teach them the country languages. This system he deemed ineffective since few of the munshis spoke English and there were no adequate teaching materials. Simultaneously with the establishment of Gilchrist's seminary, the governor-general, Lord Wellesley, had published a notification that starting on January 1, 1800, no civil servant "should be nominated to . . . offices of trust and responsibility until it shall be ascertained that he was sufficiently acquainted with the laws and regulations . . . and the several languages, the knowledge of which is required for the due discharge of the respective functions of such offices."[82]

The seminary was quickly replaced by Lord Wellesley's ambitious plan for the College at Fort William, established in 1800, at which Gilchrist was appointed professor of Hindustani.[83] Here he supervised a staff of Indian scholars who were engaged in an extraordinary burst of scholarly, literary, and pedagogical activities directed toward making available to students at the college a corpus of works from which they could learn to read, write, and speak Hindustani.[84] At the college there was a distinct split in the European faculty, with some stressing the study of classical languages and others emphasizing the spoken languages. Gilchrist and William Carey led the spoken languages group. Each published "Dialogues" or phrase books to convey to the neophyte something of the flavor of the languages, as well as to introduce the young officials to the "manners and customs" of the Indians among whom they were going to work.[85]

Carey's *Dialogues* begins with a khansaman or sirkar talking with a European. The dialect is one in which there are mixed Persian, Bengali, and English phrases. The topics covered in this dialogue include phrases necessary to set up and run a household. The sahib learns how to berate his servants for slovenly attire and behavior. He learns brief commands to obtain food, requisites while traveling, and to have a garden laid out for his home. The rest of the work presents dialogues between various types of Indians: a Brahman talks in an elevated dialect about rituals and the family, and the sahib learns something about kinship terminology and the religious practices of Indians. There are also examples of the common talk of lower orders, fishermen and lower-caste women, whose dialect is characterized by Carey as the "greatest instance of literal irregularity." Carey compiled his work "by employing sensible natives" who composed dialogues "dealing with subjects of domestic nature." Sisir Kumar Das identifies the Bengali associates of Carey in this work as probably being Ram Ram Basu and Mrityunjay Vidyalamkar.[86]

Gilchrist published his first set of Hindustani conversations in 1798 in the *Oriental Linguist*. These were reprinted and revised in 1809 and 1820. In the 1809 version of the *Dialogues*, Gilchrist provides the young Englishman in India specific rules on how to talk with Indians, all of whom in his work seem to be servants.[87] The European must begin by learning how to get the native's attention, and this is accomplished by the command, "sunno." This, Gilchrist tells the reader, serves the function of putting the servant "on his guard." The commands issued should be as simple as possible, he advised; do not say "give me a plate," just utter the command, "plate." The European should always use the imperative plural, "we want such and such." The asking of casual questions should be avoided since "the Hindostanee is too apt to conceive the most innocent of queries only so many traps set to catch him in some villainy or other."

Dialogues covers the following topics: eating and preparation of food (31 pages); personal service, such as dressing and preparing for bed (18 pages); traveling, both locally and long distance (43 pages); sports and leisure activities (27 pages); the "memsahib" and her dealings with servants (only 7 pages); studying (14 pages); commercial transactions (13 pages); expostulating and abusing servants and eliciting information (13 pages); time and weather (5 pages); polite enquiries (2 pages); necessary military activities (5 pages); health, medicine, and consulting local doctors (40 pages, perhaps reflecting Gilchrist's original profession as a surgeon). The tone of the dialogues are mainly declamatory: "bring me this or that," "take everything away," "get the breakfast ready." The sahib, following Gilchrist's instruction, would quickly learn a considerable range of admonitions: "let me see them every morning on my table without fail, or I shall turn you off, as a good-for-nothing fellow"; "take care! or the House of Corrections will be your lot." Food sellers have to be constantly warned about the quality of the provisions. We get phrases like "the bread has sand in it." In almost all the dialogues the mishap, mistake, or stupidity of the Indian servant is the theme: soup is served without a spoon, food is either too hot, cold, thick, or thin. "In the future," the servant is told, "do not dress these Hindustanee dishes with so much spice, this tastes of nothing but pepper." The wine is never properly cooled.

The real disasters seem to strike when the sahib ventures forth. Walking only needs 21 phrases, but riding or going about in a carriage or palanquin require 134. The sahib seems to get lost a lot, and servants are sent to make enquiries. While traveling everything seems to get misplaced, especially the wine. There are innumerable delays, people sleep when they should be working. But there are pleasures as well. The servant is sent off to find out from a local villager if there is game in the neighborhood; there is, but it turns out that it is dangerous to hunt there because of the large number of tigers. Orders have to be given to the local zamindar "to have his people beat up the game for us."

Language as command was not only a domestic or personal matter, but a matter of state. Lord Minto, in addressing the annual prize ceremony at Fort William College in 1808, explained to sixteen young officers that the nature of their relationship to Indians would be mediated by language:

> You are about to be employed in the administration of a great and extensive country in which . . . the English language is not known. You will have to deal with multitudes; who can communicate with you, can receive your commands, or render an account of their performance of them; whose testimonies can be delivered, whose engagements can be contracted; whose affairs, only in some one or another of the languages taught at the College of Fort William.[88]

The Englishman's honor and self-respect were also involved, as Minto echoed the statements of the Court of Directors and the governors-general and language teachers for the previous sixty years on the evils of interpreters. Without proper knowledge of the language of the people they were ruling, there would arise an "unlimited dependence on native and subordinate officers, which inevitably leads to oppressive vexation, extortion, and cruelty towards our native subjects." Without the knowledge of languages, the European is delivered into a "helpless and dependent thraldom" of a native assistant. The officers' "fair fame" would be threatened, there would be public loss and calamity and the officer would suffer individual shame and ruin.[89]

The Englishman needed not only to speak with grammatical precision, but had to learn to "manage his own language" in a manner most conducive to the execution of orders and the gratification of his own wishes on every occasion. Those who would follow Gilchrist's methods of teaching were assured that they would have the means to start their careers in India by making rapid progress in learning the vernacular and in doing so would acquire "local knowledge" and daily increase their "stock of general information." This Gilchrist contrasted with those who began with the study of the classical languages, who might find themselves diminishing "those intellectual powers, and that common sense which are frequently sunk under a heavy load of sheer pedantry and classical lore, very different indeed from real science and practical wisdom."[90] What emerges from reading Gilchrist is the image of the Englishman in India as the one who commands, who knows how to give orders and how to keep the natives in their proper place in the order of things through practical, not classical, knowledge.

The emphasis on the use of language as the key to understanding Indians, hence being able to control them, was stressed frequently in Lt. Col. John Briggs' *Letters Addressed to a Young Person in India*, a book written in the form of letters by an old hand in India to two brothers, the elder in the military, the younger a civil servant.[91] Briggs sets out to instruct the civil servant in proper behavior. The elder brother, who has already been in India for a few years, has made all the mistakes, which the younger brother is to avoid. He fails to learn languages, gets into debt, selects the wrong type of servant, beats and abuses his servants, and generally makes a mess of things. In the letters to the young civilian, not only are the failures of the elder brother a constant reminder of what may happen to shame the individual but, more importantly, to shake the foundations of British rule in India. Briggs instructs his younger readers in these principles, as laid down by Major General Sir John Malcolm.

Almost all who, from knowledge and experience, have been capable of forming any judgment upon the question, are agreed that our power in India rests on the general opinion of the natives of our comparative superiority in good faith, wisdom, and strength, to their own rulers. This important impression will be improved by the consideration we show to their habits, institutions, and religion—by the moderation, temper, and kindness, with

which we conduct ourselves towards them; and injured by every act that
offends their belief or superstition, that shows disregard of neglect of individuals or communities, or that evinces our having, with the arrogance of
conquerors, forgotten those maxims by which this great empire has been
established, and by which alone it can be preserved.[92]

The only way to gain the knowledge and sympathy that Malcolm's
instructions required was through the languages of the people. "The veil
which exists between us and the natives can only be removed by mutual
and kind intercourse." There might be kindly intercourse with the natives, but language was also the "channel of communicating your wants,
and of obtaining information," Briggs advised.[93] Knowledge of Indian
languages was the means of gaining a more complex knowledge of the
strange customs, codes, and rules of the Indians, who were in most
instances docile, cooperative, and quite willing to obey the orders and
commands of the sahibs, except when ignorance led the latter to offend
the prejudices of the natives. The newcomer seemingly had to be instructed in the simplest and most obvious of distinctions, that between
Hindus and Muslims. Gilchrist informed his readers that Muslims were
larger, bearded, and more fierce and robust in appearance than Hindus.
One had to learn how to distinguish the differences in dress by the way
they tied their garments, by the form of hair style and turban, and
above all by their names and their food habits.

Unlike Briggs and Malcolm, whose careers were amongst the peoples
of central and western India—and hence who were instructing their
juniors in proper behavior not only toward their Indian servants, domestic and civil, but toward learned men, chiefs, opulent bankers, and merchants and peasants—Gilchrist's image of Indian society seems to have
been largely restricted to domestic servants and lowly assistants. No
matter how one tried, apparently in Bengal there were occasions when
even the most knowledgeable and even-tempered European would be
driven "by the stupidity, perverseness, and chicanery" of natives to want
to beat his servants. But Gilchrist advises: "let the storm blow over"
with a volley of abusive words directed at the miscreant.[94] The normal
good manners of the European can be tested, according to Gilchrist, in
all sorts of situations, for example when invited to a wealthy Indian's
house for an entertainment. On such an occasion one should not con-
demn the music, dancing, and singing, or if a dramatic pantomime particularly offends the European's sense of modesty he should retire in
silence rather than offer vociferous exclamations such as "beastly stuff."
Quiet withdrawal in such situations, writes Gilchrist, "will do more to
establish our superiority in breeding and morality."[95]

The European has to learn to insist on proper performance of the

Indian's social and verbal codes in dealing with superiors. One should not let an Indian subordinate get away with behavior or speech that would be offensive not only to the European but to an Indian of superior quality. Gilchrist, like most Europeans in India, reduced what was and is an extremely sensitive, well-ordered, and complex system of deference and codes of demeanor that Indians follow to what for the Europeans were highly charged symbolic acts revolving around the wearing of various foot coverings.[96] Gilchrist explained that Europeans uncover their heads as a mark of respect, whereas Indians take off their slippers while performing worship in a mosque or temple or on entering a home of office. Yet he observes that natives

> intrude on the British inhabitants of Calcutta and environs, without the slightest attention to this act of politeness, most scrupulously observed amongst themselves, as if they were determined to trample us under the pride of Caste, by evincing, that to a Hindoo or Moosulman alone, it was necessary to pay the common marks of civility or respect.[97]

The wearing of shoes by Indians in the houses of Europeans was seen as part of a larger effort on the part of some Indians to establish equality or even superiority—not only in relation to Europeans but also with respect to other Indians, by appearing to be on a footing of equality with Europeans.

Indian languages, with their graded grammatical systems of polite forms and forms of various degrees of familiarity and respect, also could be a source of disrespect to the foreigners. For the unwitting Europeans in India, some servants and menials would use the singular pronoun in addressing the sahib. "It is rather surprising that servants and sipahees, etc., should be allowed to take such advantage of their master's ignorance of the language and customs of the country, as to *too* and *tera* them on every occasion: a liberty they dare not take with one another."[98] The insult of the use of familiar form by the servant to the sahib was not just a personal insult but had a much greater consequence for the loss of dignity for his country and nation. Gilchrist stressed that the necessary knowledge of indigenous language and custom was not one of just the sahib getting proper respect; it also entailed the sahib avoiding unwittingly acting in a disrespectful manner toward the Indian when he did not intend it.

Two issues arise related to Gilchrist's attempt to establish the British language of command. First, how well did the British learn this or any other Indian language? And second, how fixed did the standard that Gilchrist hoped to establish remain? Until the middle of the century there were recurrent complaints that the British lacked sophisticated knowledge of Hindustani, or Urdu as it became more generally called.

F. J. Shore, who had considerable empathy with Indians and who was continually critical of both the policies of the Company's government and the behavior of his fellow countrymen toward Indians, ridiculed the level of knowledge of Hindustani that most "judges, magistrates and military officers" had attained even after a number of years' service in India. He likened their speech to the broken English of Frenchmen or Italians who are made objects of fun or contempt on the stage. This lack of capacity to speak properly, he felt, encouraged Indians to be equally slovenly or mannerless in their dealings with the sahibs. He cited a hypothetical case:

> Two or three English are out hunting or shooting; one of them who speaks broken Hindustanee, asks a peasant some questions relative to the sport: the native answers him in a careless way, perhaps without stopping his work; and sometimes without even looking up from it, after the first glance; omitting, at the same time, the respectful terms of speech. Should another of the party, who can speak in a gentlemanlike manner, address the peasant, in an instant the latter will rise up, or stop his work, make a salaam, and reply in the most respectful language. Were the native asked by any one to whom he could speak freely, why he made such a difference in addressing the two gentlemen, his answer would be something to the following effect: "Two gentlemen! Do you call the first a gentleman; if so, why did he not speak like one? The second evidently was so, by his language, and I answered him as such."[99]

The Englishman with a limited grasp of Hindustani indeed received answers to his questions. The issue that Shore raises is not about communication of facts but about behavior and status, and I think this issue continued through much of the history of the British in India. There were obviously those British who spoke and understood the standard or even the literary registers of the varied languages of India, and hence could manage their official persona as F. J. Shore would have wished they did. I would speculate, however, that the majority knew only very restricted and specific codes, which were adequate to specified contexts such as running their households, dealing with their subordinates in the courts and offices, and in giving orders in the military.

The battle between the classicists and vernacularists in relation to Hindustani was to continue throughout the nineteenth century. Each new dictionary or grammar that would appear caused argumentation. The missionaries soon joined the officials of the Company, and questions of scripts and sources of borrowings for lexical items and for grammatical refinements became politically charged issues. In the 1860s Indians, some of whom had added a sophisticated knowledge of English to their own "classical" education, began to argue, organize, and eventually to demand in the name of history and religion that the government favor one or another script and associated literatures.[100]

British Power and Indian Knowledge

On the eve of the fiftieth anniversary of the founding of the Asiatic Society of Bengal, W. C. Taylor, in an address to the Royal Asiatic Society in London, declared that it was the British who in the last decades of the eighteenth century were responsible for the "literary treasures of Hindustan being opened up to the wonder and admiration of the world." He went on, like a twentieth-century counterpart in Great Britain or the United States, to appeal for funds to support continuing research and publication by linking the knowledge gained through the study of oriental literature to success in "the pursuit of Oriental commerce." He clinched his argument by citing the aphorism "KNOWLEDGE IS POWER."[101]

In 1784 Warren Hastings had explicated for Nathaniel Smith, chairman of the Court of Directors, the relation of knowledge to power in the establishment of British rule in India: *"lessons the weight of the chain"*

> Every accumulation of knowledge and especially such as is obtained by social communication with people over whom we exercise dominion founded on the right of conquest, is useful to the state . . . it attracts and conciliates distant affections; it lessens the weight of the chain by which the natives are held in subjection; and it imprints on the hearts of our countrymen the sense of obligation and benevolence. . . . Every instance which brings their real character [i.e., that of the Indians] home to observation will impress us with a more generous sense of feeling for their natural rights, and teach us to estimate them by the measure of our own. But such instances can only be obtained in their writings: and these will survive when the British dominion in India shall have long ceased to exist, and when the sources which once yielded of wealth and power are lost to remembrance.[102]

Hastings drew a contrast between the "benevolent and sympathetic interest" that the British had shown toward the Brahmans, the keepers "of the mysteries of their own learning," and the previous rulers, the Muslims, who had systematically derided the religion of the Hindus and who sought from their studies "arguments to support their own intolerant principles." Hastings believed that as a result of the conciliatory nature of British rule, the pandits were now "no less eager to impart their knowledge, than we are to receive it."[103]

Twenty years later Sir James Mackintosh, a Benthamite and legal reformer who was Recorder of Bombay, struck a somewhat harsher note in addressing the first meeting of the Bombay Literary Society. He urged his colleagues to "mine the knowledge of which we have become the masters." He went on to remind his listeners "that all Europeans who visit remote countries . . . are detachments from the main body of civilized men sent out to levy contributions and knowledge, as well as gain victories over barbarism."[104]

H. T. Colebrooke, in a letter to his father, described the ambivalence that characterized much of the British reaction to Indian culture:

> The further our literary enquiries are extended here, the more vast and stupendous the scene which opens to us; at the same time that the true and the false, the sublime and the puerile, wisdom and absurdity, are so intermixed, that at every step, we have to smile at folly, while we admire and acknowledge the philosophical truth, though couched in obscure allegory and puerile fable.[105]

British studies of Indian languages, literature, science, and thought produced three major projects. The first involved the objectification and use of Indian languages as instruments of rule to understand better the "peculiar" manners, customs, and prejudices of Indians, and to gather information necessary to conciliate and control the peoples of India. The second project entailed what the Europeans defined as "discoveries" of the wisdom of the ancients, the analogy being to the restoration of Greek and Roman thought and knowledge in the fifteenth and sixteenth centuries. This was a European project, the end being to construct a history of the relationship between India and the West, to classify and locate their civilizations on an evaluative scale of progress and decay. The third project involved the patronage of institutions and religious and literary specialists who maintained and transmitted—through texts, writing, recitations, performances, painting and sculptures, rituals, and performances—that which the British conquerors defined as the traditions of the conquered. To appear legitimate in the eyes of the Indians, the British thought they had to demonstrate respect and interest in those Indians and institutions that were the carriers of the traditions.

There were to be consistent differences in the valuation of the three projects between the two centers of decision making. One was in London, where the Court of Directors represented the "owners" of the East India Company, and the Board of Control had been established by Parliament to exercise political control over the Company's affairs. In India there was a theoretically subordinate group of officials headed by the Governor-General in Council and the governors of Bombay and Madras, which supervised the functioning of the instrumentalities of colonial rule. Given the distance and time that separated London and India, and the growing weight and power of senior civil servants, Calcutta, Madras, and Bombay frequently acted independently of the owners of the Company and the Home government.

London tended to put the question of language learning at the top of its priorities. The construction of "European" knowledge was increasingly left to semi-official bodies such as the Asiatic Society of Bengal, and to professional scholars in the colleges and universities. The issues entailed in the construction of the legitimacy of the Company's rule through the preservation and patronage of Indian knowledge caused a political and epistemological battle between London and Calcutta over the allocation of resources, and a financial and moral battle about the forms of knowledge and the shape of institutions that could most effectively preserve and transmit their own and European thought.

Education and the Preservation of the Past

In September 1780, a delegation of Muslims of "credit and learning" called upon Warren Hastings to urge him to establish a madrassa for the instruction of young students "in Mahamadan law and other sciences."[106] The visit had been occasioned by the arrival in Calcutta of a famous teacher and scholar, Muiz-ud-din, whom the petitioners hoped the government would employ to direct the madrassa.[107] Hastings, in justifying the expenditure of the Company's funds to support a madrassa in Calcutta, painted a bleak picture of decaying remains "of these schools which could be seen in every capital, town and city of Hindustan." The Calcutta Madrassa, Hastings hoped, would preserve and further knowledge, provide training for future law officers of the Company, contribute to the "credit" of the Company's name, and "help soften the prejudices excited by the growth of British dominions."[108]

The madrassa, under the direction of Muiz-ud-din, appeared to have gotten off to a good start, with ninety students pursuing a wide range of studies. Within a few years, however, the maulavi was accused of mishandling Company funds, favoritism in appointments, and losing control over the students. A committee of British officials was appointed to supervise the administration of the college, the maulavi was dismissed, and the college was reorganized along European lines, although the subject matter studied remained Islamic.[109]

The Sanskrit College in Banaras had a similar history. The college owed its inception to the initiative of Jonathan Duncan, Resident in Banaras. He recommended that surplus revenue, expected to accrue to the Company from the Permanent Settlement of the Banaras zamindari, be applied to the establishment of "a Hindoo College . . . for the preservation and cultivation of Laws, Literature and Religion of that nation, at this centre of their faith." Such an institution, Duncan felt, "would endear our Government to the Native Hindoos." There were, he observed, "many private seminaries" for the study of various forms of Hindu learning, but as the Company's college would be the only "public" institution dedicated to this purpose, the reputation of the Company would be enhanced. In addition to its teaching functions, Duncan noted that as an institution it could without too much expense build a "precious library of complete and correct treatises . . . dealing with Hindoo religion, laws, arts and sciences."[110]

Perhaps influenced by the history of the madrassa, Duncan drew up a set of rules that made the Resident, acting on behalf of the governor-general, responsible for the payment of stipends for those students being educated at government expense, hiring and firing of faculty, and the dismissal of students. Duncan was to attend the quarterly examinations, at least in those subjects that were not considered sacred; for these he would appoint a committee of Brahmans who would examine students in the "more secret branches of learning." Within ten years of its founding, accusations of financial mismanagement and favoritism similar to those that had plagued the madrassa led to a more intensive British supervision of the Sanskrit College.[111]

The history of the British experiments with the Calcutta Madrassa and the Sanskrit College in Banaras are symbolic of wider issues entailed in the establishing of educational institutions under the colonial state. The British conceived of education as taking place in institutions, meaning buildings with physically divided spaces marking off one class of students from another, as well as teachers from students. There were to be fixed positions of professors, teachers, and assistants, who taught regular classes in subjects. The students' progress had to be regularly examined to measure their acquisition of fixed bodies of knowledge. The end of the process was marked by prizes and certification that attested to the students' command of a specifiable body of knowledge. Even with the undoubted good will and best intentions on the part of Duncan, Hastings, and others, a British metalogic of regularity, uniformity, and above all fiscal responsibility could not help but participate in the erosion and transformation of what the British wanted to preserve, that is, Hindu and Muslim learning.

The political project of enhancing the credit of the Company and the British nation as the protector and preserver of indigenous knowledge was to lead them to become keepers of a vast museum which would, in turn, lead to providing definitions of what should be preserved, as well as to developing a program for locating and classifying the specimens to be maintained. The substance of Lord Minto's remarks on the decay of Indian science and literature was to echo throughout the nineteenth century:

It is a common remark that science and literature are in a progressive state of decay among the natives of India. From every inquiry which I have been enabled to make on this interesting subject that remark appears to me but too well founded. The number of the learned is not only diminished but the circle of learning even among those who still devote themselves to it appears to be considerably contracted. The abstract sciences are abandoned, polite literature neglected and no branch of learning cultivated but what is connected with the peculiar religious doctrines of the people. The immediate consequence of this state of things is the disuse and even actual loss of many valuable books; and it is to be apprehended that unless Government interpose with a fostering hand the revival of letters may shortly become hopeless from a want of books or of persons capable of explaining them.[112]

Lord Wellesley, who had a magisterial and imperial vision of the Company's rule in India, conceived in 1800 a plan for the education and training of the young men appointed to the Company's civil service. No longer should these appointees be thought of as agents of a commercial concern, he declared. They should be trained as "ministers and officers of a powerful sovereign." Wellesley, without the permission of the Court of Directors, established the College at Fort William to provide the education that he thought was required. He wrote to the Court of Directors that the education should impart a knowledge of "those branches of literature and science" such as was included in the education of persons "destined for high office in Europe." In addition, the young men required special instruction in the codes and regulations of the Company, as well as in the "true and sound principles of the British constitution." As they were to be the rulers of an alien race, they had to obtain "an intimate acquaintance with the history, languages, customs, laws and religions of India." As if this wasn't enough for a group of sixteen- and seventeen-year-olds, the college had to shape their moral character so they would be armed with the virtues of "industry, prudence, integrity, and religious sensibility" which would help them guard against the "temptations and corruptions" they would be exposed to because of the Indian climate and the "peculiar depravity" of the people of India. Their education, Wellesley claimed, had to form a natural barrier "against habitual indolence, dissipation, licentiousness and indulgence" which had marked the behavior of most of the employees of the Company.[113]

To accomplish this awesome educational project Wellesley planned a residential college where the young men's lives could be properly supervised. It was to be staffed by a European faculty of eight to ten who could teach Indian languages as well as the European curriculum. To set the proper tone, the vice-provost was to be a clergyman of the Anglican faith. To teach the oriental subjects fifty munshis were employed and divided into four departments: Sanskrit-Bengali, Arabic, Persian, and

Hindustani. Each department had a European professor, a chief munshi, a second munshi, as well as subordinate munshis. The pay of the European faculty ranged from Rs 1,600 to Rs 500; for the Indian staff, the range was Rs 200 for the four chief munshis, Rs 100 for the second munshis, and Rs 60 for the subordinate munshis.[114] The duties of the munshis involved providing individual tutorials, preparing (in collaboration with the European professors) teaching materials, preparing and publishing grammars and dictionaries, as well as undertaking extensive projects in publishing "classic" works of Indian literature.

The Court of Directors, when they learned of the very ambitious plans, quickly cut back on the European part of the curriculum and barred the building of a residential college. Their central concern was with the college as a language-teaching institution. They did, however, establish in England the East India Company's Training College at Haileybury for the education of their appointees to the civil service in India. Here the young men received an education in European subjects and some Indian language work.[115]

The College Council, which was the governing body of the College at Fort William, was estimated by the Court of Directors to have spent upwards of £40,000 to subsidize the editing, writing, and publishing of eighty-eight "oriental works" in the period 1801 to 1812. The vast bulk of the funds was spent on works in or about Persian (Rs 110,000), Arabic (Rs 52,000), and Sanskrit (Rs 44,000). The Company informed their servants in Calcutta that any subsidized work should show "value and merit" in the teaching of languages. The Court complained of "the very heavy expense to which you have subjected us by the encouragement, which seems to have been indiscriminately afforded to publications, several of which are very ill executed, or of no use as class books, nor are they in any other way objects which call for the patronage of your government."[116]

The Indian staff recruited for the college included a number of distinguished scholars such as Mrityunjay Vidyalamkar from Midnapur and Maulavi Allah Daud from Lucknow. In addition several, such as Ram Ram Basu, Mir Amin, and Lalljilal from Gujarat, made major contributions to the prose literature of Bengali, Urdu, and Hindi. Some made a major scholarly and intellectual impact on their European counterparts. Mathew Lumsden, whose Persian *Grammar* was published in 1810, described Maulavi Allah Daud as "the great master under whom I have studied," and acknowledged his great debt to "his knowledge and industry." Lumsden assured his European readers that though he was the author of the *Grammar*, "the more arduous task of supplying the information devolved . . . onto Daud."[117]

Lumsden's remark, I think, typifies the relations between Indian and

British scholars who were engaged not only at the college but in other settings as well, transforming Indian knowledge into European information. The Indians were sources or "native informants" who supplied information, *viva voce*, in English or Indian languages; who collected, translated, and discussed texts and documents; and who wrote exegeses of various kinds that were classified, processed, and analyzed into knowledge *of* or *about* India.

As Das points out, in the college there were two separate categories, sahibs and munshis. There was indeed mutual learning going on, there was respect and some amicability in the relations between the two categories of persons, but it was the British who set the agenda and who had the authoritative voice in determining what was useful knowledge to be processed for the European projects: "The Indian scholar knew he was superior to his European Master in respect of Indian languages, [but] he was primarily an informant, a mere tool in the exercise of language teaching to be handled by others."[118]

The differences between the Indian scholars and their British counterparts were based on more than the social and political relations which had made the British dominant; there was a major epistemological gulf between the two cultures as well. Those British who sought to produce grammars, dictionaries, or translations of literary or "practical" works, such as law codes, frequently complained about the way in which Indian scholars worked and thought. C. P. Brown, who spent forty years working on Telugu, writes of working with Brahmans who nearly "shipwrecked" him with their pedantry. He complained that the Brahmans valued only the abstract and abstruse and despised "all that is natural and in daily use."[119] He rebelled against their instructions to "learn by rote long vocabularies, framed in meter" while he was trying to construct his dictionary of Telugu. The Reverend Robert Caldwell claimed that the learning of "versified enigmas and harmonious platitudes" resulted in Indians developing a great capacity for patient labor and an accurate knowledge of details, but also prevented the development of a "zeal for historical truth" and the "power of generalization and discrimination."[120]

Developing a capacity for memorizing was part of the education which the British received as well. Brown complained of his pandits' demands to memorize, but also took pride in the fact that they thought he knew the Bible, Shakespeare, and Milton by heart. What baffled the British most about the Indians' prodigious feats of memorization was that it appeared to them that the Indians did not know the meaning of what they had internalized so effectively.

A. D. Campbell found in Bellary district in 1823 that great attention was being paid in the schools to proper pronunciation of syllables of a "poetical" language but not to the meaning or construction of words in this language. He found that the teachers themselves could not "understand the purport of the numerous books which they had learn[ed] from memory." The result was that the students had a "parrot-like capacity to repeat, but not to understand what they had learned, they gained little from their education, as they did not have the means" to expand their general stock of useful knowledge.[121]

William Adam, in his reports on vernacular education in Bengal and Bihar, believed that the education in the local schools was "superficial and deficitive [sic]." Even at the Sanskrit colleges at which grammar, law, rhetoric, literature, and logic were taught, following William Ward's assessment, few attained very high levels of knowledge and only five out of one thousand students in the colleges knew anything of the philosophical systems of the Veda, even though they could chant from memory long passages in Sanskrit.[122]

One of the few Europeans of the early nineteenth century who was not dismissive of the Indian form of education based on memorization was Francis W. Ellis of the Madras civil service. Ellis, who had a career as judge and collector in south India, was one of the most accomplished and sensitive of the early Orientalists.[123] Ellis was one of the founders of the Company's College at Fort St. George in 1812, which differed significantly in its purpose from the College at Fort William, since, in addition to training the British in south Indian languages, it also included the training of Indians in Hindu and Muslim law as part of its responsibilities. As in north India, the Company's courts administered Hindu and Muslim personal law, but in Madras they found that few of the south Indian Brahmans appeared to know the Dharmashastric literature. Ellis had drawn up a list of what he thought were the most useful and important compilations of Sanskrit works for the purpose of forming a "practical guide" for the administration of Hindu law in the Madras presidency. He recommended that these works be translated into Tamil verse for the use of the Hindu students in the college. He explained that only if they were translated into Tamil would they have any authority for the Indians. Ellis argued that "the mode of study prevalent among the natives of India [was] the best means of conveying the law." He went on to state that all knowledge and science in India "from the lowest to the highest form of logic and theology" were acquired by "committing to memory technical verses." These memorized verses were like a tap root which the scholar or pandit could draw upon to "explain, illustrate or enforce dicta."[124]

What Ellis was pointing to was that the Indian mode of knowing and thinking was radically different from what the British assumed was the natural or normal form, and which they used as a standard by which they could adjudge Indian forms of knowledge as marred or inadequate, rather than different. Indian reasoning was based, Ellis wrote, on "the habit of their education," which rested on the memorization of "concentrated not diffuse knowledge," which was easier to comprehend in verse form. The use of Tamil in its verse form also would diminish the influence of the Brahmans, who were regarded with "jealousy" by the shudras in south India; the latter could now study law in their own language. It would also enable the pleaders in their courts to read the law, and would serve a more impartial administration of justice. In addition, as the English judges were required to learn Tamil in Madras, they could discuss issues directly in a language common to themselves and their law officers.[125]

Conclusion: The Reordering of the Nature of Indian Knowledge

The British conquest of India brought them into a new world which they tried to comprehend using their own forms of knowing and thinking. To the educated Englishman of the late eighteenth and early nineteenth centuries, the world was knowable through the senses, which could record the experience of a natural world. This world was generally believed to be divinely created, knowable in an empirical fashion, and constitutive of the sciences through which would be revealed the laws of Nature that governed the world and all that was in it. Unknowingly and unwittingly they had not only invaded and conquered a territory but, through their scholarship, had invaded an epistemological space as well. The British believed that they could explore and conquer this space through translation: establishing correspondences could make the unknown and the strange knowable.

At one level they found this could be done relatively easily and quickly through labels that served to locate the strange in a frame of reference with which they were familiar. Brahmans became "priests," and the *Kosha* of Amarasinha was a "Dictionary of the Sanskrit Language." Since all languages had a grammar, the commentaries on Indian languages could be turned into tools to enable the sahibs to communicate their commands and gather information. They found and utilized extraordinarily able guides, aides, and assistants who knew highly specialized forms of Indian knowledge and could be interpreters, sources, and transmitters of this knowledge to the new rulers. The Victorian successors to the first generation of scholars were more likely to describe their goals as "scientific and historical"; the wonders that had excited Jones, Wilkins, Halhed, and Ellis now had to be normalized and located in a discourse that would make India into a "case" of an earlier civilization, or a museum of ancient practices, from which earlier stages of universal world history could be recovered.

Sir William Jones, in his declaration of the relationship of Latin, Greek, and Sanskrit in 1785, provided the impetus for the development, largely by German scholars, of comparative philology, which in turn supplied the "scientific" model for the comparative study of law, religion, and society. The comparative method, as it became formalized in the middle of the nineteenth century, drew together many strands of eighteenth-century thought and scholarly practice. It promised answers to the persistent European quest for the origins of things. In its linguistic and literary forms it utilized techniques of the collation of texts in order to construct the original and pure versions which could then be used to establish a linear chronology. Europeans had utilized these critical methods of textual reconstruction to establish the documents, records, and texts by which they constituted their own "true" history. They were now prepared to give to the Indian the greatest gift they could give anyone—the Indians would receive a *history*.

The theory of language implicit in the comparative method is that there are "genetic" or "genealogical" relations among languages that have been determined to belong to a "family." It is posited that there was once a single, original language from which all the languages in the family descend. The establishment of the membership in the language family was based on the comparison of formal features, displayed lexically, syntactically, morphologically, and phonetically, in the language. The goal of the method was to establish a history; those features which appear from formal comparison as the most common in the family of languages were thought to be the most "authentic." The end of the exercise was the reconstruction of "the unrecorded languages of the past."[126]

The Reverend Robert Caldwell, a Church of England missionary in Tinnevelly, applied the methods that had been so successful in reconstructing the history of the Indo-European family of languages to the south Indian languages, which he labeled the Dravidian language family. Caldwell had two goals, the first being to add to European knowledge of the languages of the world and, in particular, to establish the significance of Dravidian in relation to other Indian language families. The other was to stimulate the "native literate" of south India "to an intelligent interest in the comparative study of their own languages." He noted, as had many British before, that Indians had long studied grammar, but in a regressive and unscientific way. They were more interested in mystifying the knowledge of languages than contributing to the "progressive refinement" of it, making it the means of clear communication. By studying the Dravidian languages comparatively the native literate would come to realize that "language has a history of its own which, throwing light upon all other history," would thereby be capable of "rendering ethnology and archaeology possible."[127]

The power of the comparative method was that it enabled the practitioner to classify, bound, and control variety and difference. At a phenomenological level the British discovered hundreds of languages and dialects, and these could be arranged into neat diagrams and tables that showed the relationship of languages to each other. As with genealogies, which could represent all the members of a family or descent group visually as a tree with a root, trunk, branches, and even twigs, so could dialects and languages be similarly represented and grouped. Significantly, the trees always seemed to be northern European ones, like oaks and maples, and the British never seemed to think of using the most typical South Asian tree, the banyan, which grows up, out, and down at the same time.

The comparative method implied linear directionality: things, ideas, institutions could be seen as progressing through stages to some end or goal. It could also be used to establish regression, decay, and decadence, the movement through time away from some pristine, authentic, original starting point, a golden age in the past. The decline rather than the progress model came increasingly to be applied by the Europeans and some Indians to the textual traditions of India. In this view the present, because of the conquest, was seen as a period of dissolution and retrogression. This could be reversed by the re-establishment of "authentic" and pure versions of the great sacred works of the ancient Hindus.

C. P. Brown, in constructing a Telugu dictionary, after several false starts decided to establish his corpus of lexical items by standardizing several texts, one of which was *Manu Charitra*. He assembled a group of learned assistants and collected upward of a dozen manuscript versions of the texts. These manuscripts, he wrote, "swarmed with errors," which his assistants "adjusted by guess as they went along." Brown had copies made of each manuscript, leaving alternate pages blank with the verses numbered. He had a number of clerks with several copies of the manuscript in front of them, as well as three "professors," masters of grammar and prosody, both Sanskrit and Telugu. The verses were then read out, discussed by the pandits, with Brown deciding which version was correct, "just as a judge frames a decree out of conflicting evidence."[128]

Through this procedure, Brown was creating what he thought of as an authentic text. With the advent of printing in India, which was now developing along with the European ideas about how texts were constituted and transmitted, this was to have a powerful effect in standardizing the Telugu language and its literature. Implicit in this process were several European assumptions about literature. In European theory texts have authors who create or record what had previously been transmitted orally or through writing. Before the advent of printing it was assumed that texts "swarmed with errors" because of the unreliability of the scribes, leading to the corruption of the original and pure version created by the author.

Europeans in the nineteenth century saw literature as being conditioned by history, with an author knowing and building on great works of thought that he or she, through an act of genius and originality, could affect. Kamil Zvelbil has argued that Indians do not order their literature in a temporal linear fashion, but rather by structure and type. Literature in India "has a simultaneous existence and composes a simultaneous order."[129] He has also pointed out that persons are constituted differently in India than in the West. In India they are less unique individuals and more incumbents of positions in a social order that existed before they did and will continue to exist after their deaths. Poets or writers before the nineteenth century, Zvelbil states, did not invent or create a poem or a literary work, rather they could only express "an unchanging truth in a traditional form" and by following "traditional rules."[130]

The delineation of the cumulative effect of the results of the first half-century of the objectification and reordering through the application of European scholarly methods on Indian thought and culture is beyond the scope of this essay. The Indians who increasingly became drawn into the process of transformation of their own traditions and modes of thought were, however, far from passive. In the long run the authoritative control that the British tried to exercise over new social and material technologies was taken over by Indians and put to purposes which led to the ultimate erosion of British authority. The consciousness of Indians at all levels in society was transformed as they refused to become specimens in a European-controlled museum of an archaic stage in world history.

THREE

LAW AND THE COLONIAL STATE

IN INDIA

I N THE SECOND HALF of the eighteenth century, the East India Company had to create a state through which it could administer the rapidly expanding territories acquired by conquest or accession. The invention of such a state was without precedent in British constitutional history. The British colonies in North America and the Caribbean had from their inception forms of governance that were largely an extension of the basic political and legal institutions of Great Britain. The colonizing populations, even when drawn from dissident political and religious groups in Great Britain, still were thought of as English or British. The laws of these colonies were the laws of Great Britain.

The indigenous populations encountered in North America were quickly subjugated, relocated, or decimated, and even though there continued to be, from the colonial perspective, a "native" problem, it was a military and political one, requiring little in the way of legal or administrative innovation. In the Caribbean colonies, the indigenous population had all but been destroyed before British sovereignty was established, and the basic form of production through the plantations worked with enslaved labor was largely responsible for the maintenance of law and order. For the whites, the system of governance was much like that of the North American colonies. Only in Ireland, and to a lesser extent in Wales and Scotland, did the British face a colonial problem that required innovation. The solution in Ireland was the establishment of a Protestant landholding elite, with the virtual creation of plantations that a depressed Catholic peasantry provided with labor and rents.

Creating Instrumentalities of Rule in Colonial India

In all the British overseas colonies, at least until 1776, there was little debate concerning the role of the Crown and Parliament and about the basic jural and legal institutions of rule. Debates in Great Britain and raised overseas by white colonists shared a common discourse, were based on assumptions about the nature of the state and society, and could be encompassed within the existing institutions of rule. The constitutional and legal issues presented by the emergence of the East India Company, a major territorial power in India after the Battle of Plassey in 1757, could not simply be analogized to existing colonial experience. A whole new set of issues, for which there was no precedent, presented themselves. The issues included questions about the nature of sovereignty in India. Generally speaking, most of the British who were concerned with India agreed that India had a state system—which by the middle of the eighteenth century was in decline and disarray but which had recognizable institutions and functions of a state. They also agreed that the peoples of India, unlike the Indians and slaves of the New World, had an ancient civilization and forms of local self-governance that were stable and deeply entrenched. The sheer size of the eastern territories and the huge numbers of people becoming subjects of the East India Company were seen as signs that some of the existing state forms should be adopted. The key resources of India were the products of labor, not natural ones, and they involved a well-developed market system. In Bengal and parts of south India, the East India Company had succeeded in acquiring control of the financial resources of the state in the form of taxes, through which they could acquire commodities for export and support the buildup of military power to defend their territories from Indian and French adversaries. The East India Company had over time acquired many of the attributes of a state, in European terms. It could wage war, make peace, raise taxes, and administer justice to its own employees and to increasing numbers of Indians who inhabited the territories in which the company was acting as the sovereign.

Debate centered on the question of whether a private company that was exercising state functions could do so on the basis of royal grants and charters. What responsibilities did such a private company have for the well-being and prosperity of its subjects? These and many subsidiary issues were to be argued and to become central political issues from 1760 to 1790. By 1785, a dual principle of sovereignty had been established. The East India Company could administer its territories in its own name for the profit of its stockholders—but under regulations passed by Parliament, which would periodically review the adequacy of the company's system of governance in India. Although employees of the company owed allegiance to the British Crown, the natives of India—be they peasant or territorial rulers allied to the East India Company—did not. The company claimed its legitimacy in India from grants received or extracted from Indian rulers—for example, the grant of Dewani of Bengal in 1765, which made the Company the responsible agent for assessment and collection of the revenues of Bengal. Concerns with constitutional questions, at home and in India, and with the construction of legitimacy that would enable the Company to act as the state, were complex and difficult, but it was the pragmatics of building its administrative instrumentalities of rulership that were to engage those in India who were most directly concerned with the management of the company's territories.

In 1765 Clive wrote to his employers, the Court of Directors of the East India Company, informing them of the Mughal's grant of the Dewani of Bengal and claiming that the company "now became the Sovereigns of a rich and potent kingdom" and that they were not only the "collectors but the proprietors of the nawab's revenues." The directors' response to this news was less than enthusiastic, because they believed that Englishmen were "unfit to conduct the collection of revenues and to follow the subtle native through all his arts, to conceal the real value of his country, to perplex and elude the payments."[1] Instead, the directors envisioned their British servants supervising the collection and spending the revenues. There was a contradiction in what they were recommending, since the assessment and collection of land revenue was a complex and difficult job and in the hands of Indian specialists. If the British could not master the details of the revenue system, they would be dependent on those "subtle natives," who could "perplex" them at every turn. When in 1772 the British attempted to control their Indian subordinates by going into the "field," it was, as a modern historian has written, "a journey into the unknown. . . . At every step they came up against quasi feudal rights and obligations which defied any interpretation in familiar Western terms. The hieroglyphics of Persian estate accounts baffled them. . . . They could not easily master the language in which ancient and medieval texts relating to the laws of property were written; for tradition recorded only in memory and customs embedded in a variety of local usages wielded an authority equal to that of any written code."[2]

In the British cultural system, the capacity to assess taxes was inextricably linked with law. The courts established and protected property rights and were the instrument for enforcing payment of the "king's share of the revenue." The British in India initially tried to find who "owned" the land, so that person could be made responsible for payment of revenue. In theory this seemed simple, but in practice, as Guha suggests, it was fraught with difficulties. Forms of knowledge that would enable the foreign rulers to frame regulations that would guarantee their obtaining what they thought was the just share of the surplus of agricultural production had to be acquired or created. After 1765, the British so badly managed the task of assessing and collecting land revenue that within five years they found that their actions had caused a horrendous famine, in which they estimated that a third of the population of Bengal had died. The famine left in its wake large tracts of land that were uncultivated and rapidly turning into wasteland. Hence they added to their perplexing efforts to create information a theoretical set of questions about how best to revive agricultural production in Bengal. Both the famine and the revenue policies of the British also led to a breakdown in law and order; roving gangs (*dacoits*) began to prey on a helpless peasantry and to disrupt trade.

Hastings and the Redefinition of Traditional Forms of Authority and Rule

Warren Hastings, who had a successful career in India as a commercial and diplomatic agent for the East India Company, was appointed in 1772, under a new parliamentary act, to the newly created position of governor-general and was instructed by the Court of Directors to place the governance of the Bengal territories on a stable footing. Hastings had to contend both with Indian complexities and British venality. Since 1757, appointments to the East India Company's service in Bengal were viewed as means of quickly attaining a fortune and, on return to England, the life of a successful country gentleman. He was also constrained by a cumbersome form of government by a council of five, of which Hastings was in effect only first among equals.

The crucial actor in Hastings' plan for the better administration of Bengal was to be a British officer designated a "collector." The collector would have mixed executive and judicial powers in a defined area, a "district," whose boundaries followed preexisting Mughal revenue units termed *circars*, which were the constituent units of the *subas* (provinces). Hastings had invented the emblematic figure of British imperialism who was to appear in Africa, Southeast Asia, and the southwest Pacific, the man on the spot who knew "the natives," who was to represent the forces of "law and order."

The premise of Hastings' plan was the idea that during the seventeenth century the Mughals had an effective administrative structure, clearly not based on European principles, but nonetheless consonant with Indian theory and practice. He was also aware that during the previous fifty years in Bengal this system had all but crumbled under almost constant warfare, maladministration, the growth of local chieftains who had usurped imperial powers, and the privatization of public offices.

Having been a scholar at Westminster, Hastings brought to his task a good "classical" European education. Perhaps more important for the first fifteen years of his career, even though concerned with the East India Company's trading activities, he was stationed up-country near the court of the last of the effective nawabs of Bengal. There he acquired

.first-hand knowledge of how an Indian state functioned and could not totally share the prevalent British ideas that Indian rulers were despotic, corrupt, and extortionate. He believed that Indian knowledge and experience as embodied in the varied textual traditions of the Hindus and Muslims were relevant for developing British administrative institutions.

One of the first Persian works to be translated into English was the *Ain-i-Akbari*, by Abu'l Fazl, an "account of the mode of governing" under the most illustrious of the Mughal emperors, Akbar. The account is part prescriptive and part descriptive. It contains the rules and regulations by which the Mughal court governed, but it also offered detailed discussions of the properties of a good ruler, vivid accounts of the varieties of animals kept by the king, of how to lay out a camp, and of how jewels and other valuable items were classified. Also included were what the British thought of as more practical matters—the regulations of the judicial and executive departments, a survey of the lands, and a "rent roll" of the Mughal empire.[3]

Hastings encouraged a group of younger servants of the East India Company to study the "classical" languages of India—Sanskrit, Persian, and Arabic—as part of a scholarly and pragmatic project aimed a creating a body of knowledge that could be utilized in the effective control of Indian society. He was trying to help the British define what was "Indian" and to create a system of rule that would be congruent with what were thought to be indigenous institutions. Yet this system of rule was to be run by Englishmen and had to take into account British ideas of justice and the proper discipline, forms of deference, and demeanor that should mark the relations between rulers and ruled. According to one of his biographers, Hastings "had to modify and adapt the old to fit English ideas and standards. He had to produce a piece of machinery that English officials could operate and English opinion tolerate . . . to graft Western notions and methods on to the main stem of Eastern Institutions."[4]

However these tasks were to be accomplished, they had to pass the basic test applied by the owners of the East India Company—that the administration should produce a fixed and regular return in the form of revenue, which was to pay all the expenses of the colonial state as well as provide a profit for the investors. Throughout the history of the company and its successor, the imperial Government of India, the best indicator of efficiency of the administration was its capacity to collect 100 percent of the assessed revenues. The British logic of administration rested on the capacity to classify actions into prefixed domains. If payment were made in cash or in kind by an agriculturalist to a superior, who appeared to have "rights" to the land, these payments were "rent," the receiver was a "landlord," and the payer was a "tenant." If the receiver of payments appeared to have a political function, maintained an army, provided protection, supported religious institutions, and displayed emblems of sovereignty, then the payments were taxes and the relationship constituted that of ruler and subject.

Hasting's "collector," in addition to his executive functions as a tax collector, was to preside over two courts. One, which dealt with revenue and civil litigation and followed Hastings's understandings of Mughal practice, was called the court of Dewani; the other, which dealt with internal order and criminal law, was called the Faujdari court. The substantive law to be administered in the Dewani court was Hindu law for Hindu and Muslim law for Muslims. In the Faujdari courts the law to administer was "Muslim" criminal law; in the Dewani courts the collector was to preside along with his Indian assistant, the *dewan*. Sitting as a judge, the collector was to establish the "facts" in the case based on testimony, usually in the form of depositions from witnesses, and the documentary evidence was placed before the court. The dewan and a Hindu law officer (*pandit*) were to find the "law" that was applicable to the case. If the dispute to be adjudicated involved Muslims, the law that applied was to be determined by a Muslim law officer (*maulavi*). It was assumed that in both traditions there were legal texts that were in effect "codes," which were known and could be interpreted by legal specialists (usually referred to by the British as "law professors") who could provide authoritative decisions on the particular sections of the codes that applied. In stressing the importance of using "Indian law," as it could be objectified out of textual traditions, Hastings was rejecting the prevalent European theory that the Indian state was despotic.

India as Lawless: The Despotic Model

The word "despot" is derived from a Greek word applied to the head of a household, and from this point of view, to govern despotically was to rule "as a master over a slave." By extension, to the Greeks, despotism meant arbitrary rule, and Aristotle "made this extended meaning apply specifically to certain governments, in which legitimate royal power was intrinsically the same as master over slave."[5]

Alexander Dow, an East India Company servant, prefaced his translation of Ferishta's *History of Hindostan*, a history of the Muslim conquerors of India published in 1770–72, by writing:

> The history now given to the public, presents us with a striking picture of the deplorable condition of a people subjected to arbitrary sway; and of the

instability of empire itself, when it is founded neither on law, nor upon the opinions and attachments of mankind. . . . In a government like that of India, public spirit is never seen, and loyalty a thing unknown. The people permit themselves to be transferred from one tyrant to another, without murmuring; and individuals look with unconcern upon the miseries of others, if they are capable to screen themselves from the general misfortune. This, however, is a picture of Hindostan in bad times, and under the worst Kings. As arbitrary government can inflict the most sudden miseries, so, when in the hand of good men, it can administer the most expeditious relief to the subject. We accordingly find in this history, that the misfortunes of half an age of tyranny, are removed in a few years, under the mild administration of a virtuous prince.[6]

Dow, and other English historians as well, stressed that the arbitrariness of the political order caused the salient characteristic of despotism to become the insecurity of property. The British believed that the Mughal emperor "owned" all the land of Hindustan and could distribute in the form of grants and *jagirs* to support the military nobility (*omrah* or *amirs*) throughout their lifetime or during his lifetime. They also believed that at the death of the emperor or a noble the land escheated to the throne (but Dow recognized that in many cases such grants were renewed and given to a son of the holder). They understood that some of the Hindu kingdoms, such as those ruled by the Rajputs in western India, were in effect held in perpetuity by ruling families as subjects of the Mughals and were confirmed by payment of an annual tribute.

As with property, so also with honors. The Mughal emperor was thought to be the sole source of all honors in the state. These honors were not hereditary, as they usually were in England. They lasted only for the lifetime of the person to whom they were granted. The British believed that this prevented development of a status group in the polity that could check the arbitrary power of the emperor, as in European states. In the model of the Mughal empire created by the British, there was no primogeniture for inheriting the throne (*masnad*), and each succession of a Mughal was accompanied by a bloody war. "The power of disposing of the succession naturally belongs to a despot. During his life, his pleasure is the law. When he dies his authority ceases." The Mughal might nominate one of his sons, not necessarily the oldest, but the son must still fight for the throne. A "prince must die by clemency, or wade through the blood of his family to safety and Empire."[7]

Although it was recognized that there was "law" in India, that "law" was believed to be different from the European kind. Because the government was seen as based on "no other principle than the will of one [the Mughal]," the law was based upon his will, and hence, argued

Orme, there could not be "any absolute laws in its constitution; for these would often interfere with that will." Orme believed that in 1752 there were "no digests or codes of laws existing in Indostan: The Tartars who conquered this country could scarcely read or write; and when they found it impossible to convert them to Mohammedanism left the Hindus at liberty to follow their own religion. To both these peoples (the lords and slaves of this empire), custom and religion have given all the regulations at this time observed in Indostan. . . . Every province has fifty sects of Hindus; and every sect adheres to different observances."[8] The British realized that there were a large number of judicial officials in India, and a regular system of courts, with the Mughal's *darbar* (court) at the top, and that redress was always open to the subjects of the emperor by going to his court to seek justice. But the courts found in the country were thought to be "extremely venal." Orme described the process of the administration of justice thus:

> The plaintiff discovers himself by crying aloud, Justice! Justice! until attention is given to his importunate clamours. He is then ordered to be silent, and to advance before his judge; to whom, after having prostrated himself, and made his offering of a piece of money, he tells his story in the plainest manner, with great humility of voice and gesture, and without any of those oratorical embellishments which compose an art in freer nations.
>
> The wealth, the consequence, the interest, or the address of the party, become now the only consideration. . . . The friends who can influence, intercede; and, excepting where the case is so manifestly proved as to brand the failure of redress with glaring infamy (a restraint which human nature is born to reverence) the value of the bribe ascertains the justice of the cause.
>
> Still the forms of justice subsist; witnesses are heard; but brow-beaten and removed; proofs of writing produced; but deemed forgeries and rejected, until the way is cleared for a decision, which becomes totally or partially favourable, in proportion to the methods which have been used to render it such. . . .
>
> The quickness of decisions which prevails in Indostan, as well as in all other despotic governments, ought no longer to be admired. As soon as the judge is ready, everything that is necessary is ready: there are no tedious briefs or cases, no various interpretations of an infinity of laws, no methodized forms, and no harangues to keep the parties longer in suspense.
>
> Providence has, at particular seasons, blessed the miseries of these people with the presence of a righteous judge. The vast reverence and reputation which such have acquired, are but too melancholy a proof of the infrequency of such a character.[9]

In summary, the model of the Mughal-Indian political system was absolute and arbitrary power, unchecked by any institution, social or political, and resting in the person of the emperor, with property and honors derived solely from the will of the despotic ruler. There were no fixed rules of inheritance and, above all, no primogeniture; succession to the throne was based on an inevitable struggle among the sons of the emperor. Justice was dependent not on the rule of law but on the rule of men, who could be influenced by money, status, and connection in the exercise of their office of judge.

The idea that India had been ruled by "despots" was revalorized in the nineteenth and twentieth centuries as one of several ruling paradigms that formed the ideological infrastructure of British rule in India. In its cleaned-up version it was expressed thus: Indians are best ruled by a "strong hand," who could administer justice in a rough-and-ready fashion unfettered by rules and regulations. The courts, their procedures, their regulations, and the propensity of Indians to perjury and to the suborning of witnesses only served to delay justice and made the simple peasant folk of India the prey of the urban-based lawyers, merchants, and agitators. This would lead to the alienation of the "natural" loyalty the masses always felt for the strong, benevolent despot. As benevolent despots, the British were to appear in several forms—as "platonic guardians," as patriarchs habitually addressed by the simple folk as *ma-bap* (mother and father), as authoritarian rationalist utilitarians, and in times of crisis as the not-so-benevolent Old Testament avengers.[10]

India as a Theocracy: Classical Models of the Indian State

Simultaneously with the development of the despotic model, Hastings and some of his associates in Calcutta were elaborating a countermodel of India as a theocratic state. This model included established and highly detailed codes of conduct that had the power of law and had already been worked out in the ancient era (as far as Hindus were concerned) and since the time of the Prophet in the sacred law (for Muslims). For both Hindu and Muslim law there were extensive bodies of texts and commentaries and sophisticated legal specialists who were the maintainers, expositors, and interpreters of these legal traditions.

In 1772 and 1773 a parliamentary committee was investigating the affairs of the East India Company and trying to decide what institutions of governance were most appropriate for restoring law, order, and prosperity to the company's territories. In this context, influenced by the "India as despotic" theory, it was argued that because there was no law in India, British law and institutions should be introduced into the vacuum. On hearing these reports, Hastings lobbied influential members of the Court of Directors and Parliament to prevent this, arguing that British law was too technical, too complicated, and totally inappropriate for conditions in India. He declared that the "ancient constitution" of Bengal was very much intact.[11] Writing to the Lord Chief Justice in 1774, Hastings denied the validity of the idea that India was ruled by nothing more than "arbitrary wills, or uninstructed judgements, or their temporary rulers" and the notion that "written laws are totally unknown to the Hindoos, or original inhabitants of Hindostan." The Hindus, Hastings averred, "had been in possession of laws which continued unchanged, from remotest antiquity." These laws were known to the Brahmans ("professors of law," found all over India) and supported by "public endowments and benefactions." These professors received a "degree of personal respect amounting almost to idolatry."[12] This attitude of reverence for the Brahman specialists in law was so entrenched that it was left unmolested even by Muslim governments.

The logic of Hastings' model of Hindu law read as "an ancient constitution" required that it be made accessible to the British who now were sitting as judges in the civil courts and would have to pass judgment on disputes "concerning property, whether real or personal, all cases of inheritance, marriage and caste; all claims of debt, disputed accounts, contracts, partnerships and demands of rent."[13] Some way to authoritatively establish the content of Hindu law to be administered in the East India Company's district courts had to be found. To this end, Hastings persuaded "eleven of the most respectable pandits in Bengal" to compile from the shastric literature on Hindu law a code that could be translated into English for the newly appointed judges to use. Because at the time there was no European in Calcutta who knew Sanskrit, the compilation by the pandits was translated first into Persian and then from Persian into English. As if this chain of translations is not tortuous enough, the Persian translation was done by a Bengali Muslim, who would discuss in Bengali with one of the pandits the passages being translated and then gloss them into Persian. The English translation from the Persian was by a young civil servant, N. B. Halhed, and published in London in 1776 as *A Code of Gentoo Laws; or, Ordinations of the Pundits.*[14] In his preface, Halhed described how the work had been produced:

> The professors of the ordinances here collected still speak the original language in which they were composed, and which is entirely unknown to the bulk of the people, who have settled upon those professors several great endowments and benefactions in all parts of Hindostan, and pay them besides a degree of personal respect little short of idolatry, in return for the advantages supposed to be derived from their studies. A set of the most experienced of these lawyers was selected from every part of Bengal for the purpose of compiling the present work, which they picked out sentence by

sentence from various originals in the Sanscript (*sic*] language, neither adding to, nor diminishing any part of the ancient text. The articles thus collected were next translated literally into Persian, under the inspection of one of their own body; and from that translation were rendered into English with an equal attention to the closeness and fidelity of the version.[15]

The original compilation in Sanskrit was termed *Vivadarnavasetu*, "bridge across the sea of litigation," and was circulated in Persian, Sanskrit, and English versions and used in the East India Company's courts until the early nineteenth century. The two leading scholars of the code disagree about its relationship to the legal traditions of eighteenth-century Bengal. Derrett argues that the topics covered—"Debt, Inheritance, Civil Procedure, Deposits, Sales of Strangers' Property, Partnership, Gift, Slavery, Master and Servant, Rent and Hire, Sale, Boundaries, Shares in Cultivation of Lands, Cities, and Towns and Fines for Damaging Crops, Defamation, Assault, Theft, Violence, Adultery, Duties of Women"—were topics Hastings believed would be useful in the district courts. He also asserts that the order in which the sections appear "does not correspond with anything known to the usual Shastric texts," that the pandits were working on a list of topics supplied by Hastings.[16]

In a detailed study of Halhed's career, Rosane Rocher argues that the Sanskrit version of the code was a "traditional compilation of the *nibandha* type, i.e., excerpts from a variety of authoritative sources, and extensive commentary."[17] She attributes the difference between her interpretation and Derrett's to the fact that his was based on the English version of the code, which does not accurately reflect the Sanskrit original.[18] The enduring significance of Halhed's translation has much less to do with the further development of the East India Company's legal system than with its role in establishing indological studies in Europe, where the work was read in English, and in translation in French and German, for information about the "mysterious" Hindus.

In his preface to the translation of the Gentoo code, Halhed makes it clear that his interests were not primarily legal, but concerned more with explicating Hindu thought, religion, and customs in relation to establishing a policy of toleration on the part of the British toward the conquered Indians. Halhed held up the model of the Romans, "who not only allowed to their foreign subjects the free exercise of their own religion and the administration of their own civil jurisdiction, but sometimes, by a policy still more flattering, even naturalized parts of the mythology of the conquered, as were in any respect compatible with their own system."[19] Halhed's reference to Roman imperial policy adumbrates the next phase of British efforts to find a basis for their legal system with respect to Hindu personal law in the work of Sir William Jones.

Sir William Jones (1746–1794), a classical scholar who studied Persian and Arabic at Oxford and qualified as a barrister, had by the time of his appointment to the Crown Court in Calcutta, in 1783, published a number of translations of Arabic and Persian works and written one of the first modern Persian grammars. In addition, he had an active political career and was a major intellectual figure of the time.[20] Jones had long lobbied his political friends for an appointment as a judge in India, which he hoped would provide him with financial security and the opportunity to further his orientalist studies. He originally did not think he would learn Sanskrit because he was too old, but as he began his judicial career in India he found that Halhed's code was badly marred— "rather more curious than useful."[21] There were Persian translations of some Sanskrit legal texts, but Jones believed these were defective, too. He was therefore at the mercy of "native" lawyers, as were the other British judges, and he determined to learn the rudiments of that "venerable and interesting language," Sanskrit, in order that the "stream of Hindu law remain pure." By 1786, Jones felt his Sanskrit was good enough that he could decide between differing opinions of his pandits by reading the "original tracts" and pronouncing whose interpretation of the law was correct.[22]

Shortly after his arrival in India, Jones sent Edmund Burke, the leading critic of the administration of the East India Company in Bengal, his ideas for the "Best Practicable System of Judicature." British law, Jones wrote to Burke, could not become the law of India because that would be counter to the very nature of an established legal system. There was no doubt in Jones's mind that British law was superior to the law existing in India, but even "a system of *liberty*, forced upon a people invincibly attached to opposite *habits*, would in truth be a system of tyranny." The system of judicature "affecting the natives of Bengal" had to be based on the "Old Mogul constitution." The basis of the law to be administered in the company's court should be digests of "Hindu and Mahomedan laws" compiled by "*Conogos* [keepers of land records] and *Maulavis* and *Pandits*," whom Jones (and most of the British at the time) considered to be a combination of legal scholars and practicing lawyers. There should be attached to the East India Company's court "native interpreters of the respective laws," but the honesty and competence of these interpreters had to be guaranteed by careful selection and by pay adequate to place them above temptation. The British judges, however, had to be in a position to be able to "check upon the native interpreters." This was to be accomplished through the "learning and vigilance" of the British judges. "The laws of the natives must be preserved inviolate," and the decrees of the courts must be "conformable to Hindu or Mahomedan law."[23]

If the system Jones hoped to see implemented was to succeed, it would require that several forms of knowledge become codified and public. The British judges and other officials would require access to what Jones and others believed at the time was *the Hindu* and *the Mahomedan* law," locked up in the texts and the heads of pandits and maulavis. A fixed body of knowledge that could be objectified into Hindu and Muslim law had to be found. This body of knowledge could be specified, set into hierarchies of knowledge linearly ordered from the most "sacred" or compelling to the less powerful.

Jones and others believed there was historically in India a fixed body of laws, codes, that had been set down or established by "law givers" and that over time had become corrupted by accretions, interpretations, and commentaries. They also believed that this jungle of accretions and corruptions of the earlier pure codes was controlled in the present by the Indians the British thought of as the Indian lawyers. An Ur-text that would simultaneously establish *the* Hindu and Muslim law and free the British from depending on fallible and seemingly overly susceptible pandits and maulavis for interpretations and knowledge had to be found or reconstituted. The task also had to be accomplished somehow by using the knowledge that their Indian guides, the mistrusted pandits and maulavis, seemed to monopolize. Even before arriving in India, Jones seemed to distrust Indian scholars' interpretations of their own legal traditions, a distrust that grew in India. He wrote to Governor-General Cornwallis in 1788 that he could not with "an easy conscience concur in a decision, merely on the written opinion of native lawyers, in any case, in which they could have the remotest interest in misleading the court."[24] Jones wanted to provide the British courts in India, the Crown, and the East India Company with a sure basis on which to render decisions consonant with a true or pure version of Hindu law. Then the pandits, the Brahmans, and the Indian "lawyers" henceforth could not "deal out Hindoo law as they please, and make it at reasonable rates, when they cannot find it ready made."[25]

What began as a kind of personal effort to correct what he saw as the villainy or venality of some of the law officers of the court was to grow within a few years of Jones's arrival in India into a much more ambitious project to compile a "complete digest of Hindu and Mussulman law." In proposing this to the acting governor-general, Jones worried that if his plan were known to the officials in London he would be accused of "proposing to be made the Justinian of India."[26] By 1787, Jones had formulated a plan for the administration of justice in India that he believed would be in accord with the Indians' own principles of jurisprudence.

The goal was to develop "a complete check on the native interpreters of the several codes." Jones wanted a "complete digest of Hindu and Musliman Laws, on the great subjects of Contracts and Inheritances." He wanted to employ two pandits and two maulavis at 200 rupees a month, and two writers (one for Sanskrit and one for Arabic) at 100 rupees a month. The modus operandi would be that of Tribonian, compiler of the Justinian code, and the digest would consist of only "original texts arranged in a scientific method." Jones then went on to describe the texts he wanted to abstract and translate:

> I would begin with giving them a plan divided into Books, Chapters, and Sections; and would order them to collect the most approved texts under each head, with the names of the Authors, and their Works, and with the chapters and verses of them. When this compilation was fairly, and accurately transcribed, I would write the Translation on the opposite pages, and after all inspect the formation of a perfect index. The materials would be these; Six or Seven Law Books believed to be divine with a commentary on each of nearly equal authority; these are analogous to our Littleton, and Coke.[27]

In March 1788, Jones formally wrote to Cornwallis to request government support for this plan. He reiterated the argument that the compilation and its translation into English would establish a "standard of Justice" and that the English judges would have accessible to them the "principles" and "rules of law applicable to the cases before them." Thus Jones hoped Cornwallis would become "the Justinian of India," and Jones by implication would become the Tribonian. The British government would give to the natives of India "security for the due administration of justice among them, similar to that which Justinian gave to his Greek and Roman subjects," Jones wrote to Cornwallis.[28] Cornwallis was quick to agree to support Jones's efforts to assemble the pandits, maulavis, and munshis to carry out his ambitious plans.[29] From 1788 until his death in Calcutta in 1794, Jones continued to devote as much time as he could spare from his regular judicial duties to supervising the assembling and collating of the materials that were to become the *Digest*. At his death in 1794, the compilation in Sanskrit and Arabic texts was complete, and he had begun translating them into English.[30] By 1797 the English translation was completed by H. T. Colebrooke and published as *The Digest of Hindu Law on Contracts and Successions* in Calcutta in 1798.

The Court of Directors of the East India Company expressed their respect for Jones's achievements in India by commissioning a monument placed in St. Paul's Cathedral by the sculptor John Bacon (the Younger). Jones in the statue is depicted wearing a toga, with pen in hand and leaning on two volumes that "are understood to mean the Institutes of Menu."[31]

Jones, and especially his successor, Colebrooke, established a European conception of the nature of Hindu law that was to influence the whole course of British and Indo-British thought and institutions dealing with the administration of justice down to the present. There was an inversion and contradiction in Jones's efforts to fix and translate what he believed to be the crucial aspects of Hindu law. Jones was trained in English common law, which although it embodied principles, legislation, ideas of natural law, and the concept of equity and justice, was essentially seen as case law. Case law was a historically derived law based on the finding of precedent. It was flexible and above all subject to multiple interpretations by judges and lawyers. Jones and other jurisprudes of his time saw the English common law as responsive to historical change. Because the manners of a nation of people—or today we might say their culture—could change, legislation would be ineffective "unless it was congenial to the disposition, the habits, the religious prejudices, and approved immemorial usages of the people for whom it was enacted."[32] But it appears that Jones believed that even though manners, habits, dispositions, and prejudices were not fixed or immutable, the Hindus of India had usages that were fixed from time immemorial. Unlike the British with their case law, in which a lawyer could trace changes both in manners and in customs as well as in the law, the Hindus therefore lived a timeless existence, which in turn meant that differences in interpretations offered by pandits must have arisen from ignorance or venality.

Jones and the British believed that the original or earliest legal text was assumed to have the most authority. Jones's conception of Hindu law was that its authority was seen by Hindus to derive from its "sacredness" and its antiquity. The authoritativeness of Hindu law was compounded by the texts being written in Sanskrit, which as a language was unchanging, ancient in origin, and sacred. Colebrooke, translator of the *Digest*, believed that "the body of Indian law comprises a system of duties religious and civil."[33] This being the case, the portions of the texts dealing with what the British thought of as ethical and religious matters—instructions for rituals, incantations, speculative philosophy, and even rules of evidence—all had to be excised to produce what the British thought of as the rules determining "contracts" and "succession." The object was to find and fix a Hindu civil law concerned with the topics that Jones, a Whig in political and legal philosophy, was centrally concerned with—those rights, public and private, that affected the ownership and transmission of property.

Jones, like Hastings, rejected the idea that India's civic constitution was despotic. He believed that in antiquity in India there had been "legislators" and "law givers," of whom Manu was "not the oldest only, but the holiest."[34] What Manu and subsequent commentators had therefore created was "a spirit of sublime devotion, of benevolence to mankind, and of amiable tenderness to all sentient creatures . . . [that] pervades the whole work; the style of it has a certain austere majesty that sounds like the language of legislation and extorts a respectful awe." Jones wanted to restore to India its laws, which pre-dated the Islamic invasions. To be content and productive under British rule, the 30 million black subjects of the East India Company, "whose well directed industry would add largely to the wealth of Britain," needed no more "than protection for their persons, and places of abode, justice in their temporal concerns, indulgence to their prejudices of their own religion, and the benefit of those laws, which they have been taught to believe sacred."[35]

Colebrooke and the Discourse
on the Nature of Hindu Law

Colebrooke, who completed the translation of Jones's *Digest* after his death in 1794, had been appointed to the East India Company service in 1782. His father was a banker who had an active role in the management of the company. Educated at home, Colebrooke had a good knowledge of classical languages and a special interest in mathematics. The latter interest led him in India to study Sanskrit, as he wanted to acquire knowledge of the "ancient algebra of the Hindu."[36] In 1795 he was posted as a judge in Mirzapur, where he had access to the Hindu college in Banaras recently founded by the East India Company "to preserve and disseminate a knowledge of Hindoo law" and to "collect treatises on the Hindoo religion, laws, arts and science."[37]

With access to this collection and to pandits in Banaras, Colebrooke's interest shifted from mathematics to Hindu thought, culture, and law. He was a much better Sanskritist than Jones, and he developed a quite different conception of the nature and function of Hindu law. He also had much firmer grasp on the nature of shastric texts and their history. More than any Englishman, Colebrooke fixed an interpretation of variation in the legal texts that was to become standard in the British courts. "The *Dharma-sastra* or sacred code of law . . . is called *smriti*," Colebrooke wrote, "what was remembered, in contra distinction to *sruti*, what was heard." The Smriti or Dharma shastra, he wrote in a memorandum to Sir Thomas Strange, chief justice of Madras, is a form of knowledge concerned with "inculcating duty or the means of moral merit."[38] Colebrooke argued that Dharma shastras had less to do with what Europeans thought of as substantive law, legal norms, and more to do with what was forensic law, which was concerned with the nature of pleadings in court or evaluation of evidence and the logic of legal argument.

Law, to Jones, was a set of prescriptive norms, the breach of which would be the cause for judicial redress. Such norms could best be sought, Colebrooke pointed out, in collections called *sanhitas*, which Hindus attributed to holy sages or sacred personages. These collections were extensive in number. Colebrooke went on to explain that these ancient sages produced treatises on which subsequent Hindu lawyers or pandits commented; the whole, the original treatises and the numerous commentaries on them, formed the body of legal texts. In addition, a vast number of texts "were subject to the same rules of interpretation and collected in *Mimamasa*—disquisitions on the proof and authority of precepts, which Indians "considered as a branch of philosophy, and is properly the logic of the law."[39] Mimamasa was and is the method used to reconcile conflicting texts of equal authority by applying various rules for the interpretation of words, phrases, and sentences; it was also a style of argumentation.[40]

While English jurisprudence of Jones's time sought certainty in the law, through either "rationality" or an ultimate appeal to ideas of natural law, Hindu jurisprudence sought flexibility through fixed means to interpret what had been revealed to man in terms of principles of right action and proper duties. A British lawyer schooled in case law was skilled in finding precedent in the case record and by analogy relating this precedent to a particular case. The Hindu lawyer, a logician and dialectician, sought reconciliation of conflicting interpretations through analysis of meanings and intentions. It must be remembered that Colebrooke, unlike Jones, was not trained in English law and did not have knowledge of Roman law—aspects that marked Jones's intellectual approach to Hindu law. Colebrooke's solution to the problem of conflicting interpretations was to suggest that there were regional variations or differences that led to the "construing of the same text variously." Ultimately, Colebrooke attributed the variations to historical and cultural differences in India, "for the whole Hindu people comprise diverse tongues; and the manners and opinions prevalent among them differ no less than their language."[41]

Colebrooke organized the differences conceptually, in what he termed "schools" of Hindu law. Ludo Rocher has argued that the invention of the concept of schools of Hindu law "engrafted upon Hindu law an element which was foreign to it." The source of Colebrooke's conceptions, Rocher argues, was based on several misconstructions. Colebrooke viewed the commentaries on Hindu legal texts as the work of "lawyers, juriscouncils and lawgivers" reflecting "the actual law of the land."[42] This was analogous to early modern English jurisprudes who sought English law in the varied customs of different parts of Great Britain. The second misunderstanding was the analogy made between Hindu law and Muslim law. The British were familiar with Muslim law, with its relatively clear distinctions between Sunni and Shia, with the Sunni having four variations: Hanafi, Shafai, Maliki, and Hanbali. Colebrooke seems to have analogized this to Hindu law, yielding a symmetrical set for Hindu law to match what were thought of as the schools of Muslim law.

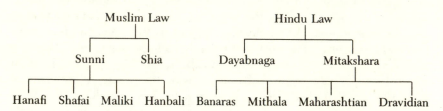

Colebrooke believed that the text, compiled by Jagannatha under Jones's direction, was defective because it did not order the "discordant opinions maintained by the lawyers of the several schools" of Hindu law.[43] In Colebrooke's view each school had fixed "doctrines," and English judges therefore needed access to "those authentic works in which the entire doctrine of each school, with the reasons and arguments by which it is supported, may be seen at one view and in a connected shape."[44]

If those Indian scholars who were cooperating with the British could not compile the texts that demonstrated the stability and completeness required for the administration of Hindu law in British courts, European methods must be used to achieve these ends. Colebrooke's solution was to supply a chronology to establish the authenticity the texts seemed to lack. The search for the oldest text was supposed to yield the most authoritative and authentic statement. If one could establish a chronological sequence of texts and trace them to a single original source, the tremendous variation added by subsequent commentators could also be controlled. Indian texts did have authors. Frequently one author cited another, and some texts appeared to contain bare facts about the relative chronological ordering of authors and commentators, but information on the history and age of authors was "very imperfect, as must ever be the case in regard to the biography of Hindu authors."[45] An agreed-on authoritative, fixed chronology was not established. Gradually over the next forty years, after Jones announced his intention to provide Hindus with their own laws through the mediation of English judges assisted by court-appointed pandits, a peculiar kind of case law came into being. At base there might be reference to a text of a particular author who was thought to represent the norm of a particular regional school, but it is the chain of interpretations of precedents by the English judges that became enshrined as Hindu law in such collections as Thomas Strange's *Elements of Hindu Law.*

After the reform of the judicial system in 1864, which abolished the Hindu and Muslim law officers of the various courts of India, and after the establishment of provincial high courts, publication of authoritative decisions in English had completely transformed "Hindu law" into a form of English case law. Today when one picks up a book on Hindu law, one is confronted with a forest of citations referring to previous judges' decisions—as in all Anglo-Saxon–derived legal systems—and it is left to the skills of the judges and lawyers, based on their time-honored abilities to find precedent, to make the law. What had started with Warren Hastings and Sir William Jones as a search for the "ancient Indian constitution" ended up with what they had so much wanted to avoid—with English law as the law of India.

FOUR

THE TRANSFORMATION OF OBJECTS INTO

ARTIFACTS, ANTIQUITIES, AND ART IN

NINETEENTH-CENTURY INDIA

THIS CHAPTER explores how things are fabricated and how they are transformed into objects that have value and meaning. The context is India and Great Britain in the nineteenth century. An object, be it a fired piece of clay, a bone, paper with colors applied to it, a lump of metal shaped into a sharp point, a shiny stone which is polished, a feather, everything that we think of as existing in nature, can be transformed through human labor into a product which has a meaning, use, and value.

A pot shard dug up and placed in a museum with a label identifying and dating it becomes a specimen along with thousands of others, which establish, for the archaeologist, a history. A bone found in a particular geological formation becomes a fossil for a palaentologist to read as part of an evolutionary sequence. For someone else this bone ground up becomes an aphrodisiac. The paper covered by paint is a god; in another time and place, it is a work of art. A piece of cloth fabricated for presentation marking the alliance between two families through a marriage becomes a bedspread. A piece of metal shaped and sharpened and used as a weapon by a great warrior becomes for his descendants an emblem of his power, and is carefully stored away in an armory, to be brought out in times of trouble to rally a failing army. In the hands of his enemies, it becomes a trophy. A piece of cloth worn by a religious leader at his moment of death has magical powers and for generations is revered as a relic.

The nominal subject of this volume (patronage in Indian culture) raises another set of questions about the production and meaning of objects, by shifting the focus from the fabricators of objects to those who commission, pay for, protect, support, and utilize the results of the labor and thought of the producers. In the language of the OED, a patron is "one who supports or protects, an institution, a cause, art or undertaking," and patronage, the OED goes on to define in its "commercial or colloquial usage," is "financial support given by customers in making use of anything established, opened or offered for the use of the public."

The examples of this usage given in the OED all date from the nineteenth century. In this chapter I will explore patronage in an extended sense, as a relationship located in a political context, in which the British increasingly impose on Indians their own conception of value. The objects through which this relationship was constructed were found, discovered, collected, and classified as part of a larger European project to decipher *the* history of India.

It was the British who, in the nineteenth century, defined in an authoritative and effective fashion how the value and meaning of the objects produced or found in India were determined. It was the patrons who created a system of classification which determined what was valuable, that which would be preserved as monuments of the past, that which was collected and placed in museums, that which could be bought and sold, that which would be taken from India as mementoes and souvenirs of their own relationship to India and Indians. The foreigners increasingly established markets which set the price of objects. By and large, until the early twentieth century, Indians were bystanders to discussions and polemics which established meaning and value for the Europeans. Even when increasing numbers of Indians entered into the discussion, the terms of the discourse and the agenda were set by European purposes and intentions.[1]

From the inception of direct trading relations between Great Britain and India in the early seventeenth century, India was looked upon as the source of commodities, the sale of which in Europe and Asia would produce profits for the owners and employees of the East India Company. Textiles in bulk and value came to be the primary Indian product imported and sold by the Company in Europe. Hence it was through these textiles that India was primarily known to the consuming classes in Britain and western Europe. The impact of Indian cloth was to play a major role in creating what Chandra Mukherji terms "modern materialism," and the development of industrial capitalism, in the efforts of eighteenth-century British entrepreneurs to find technological means by which British labor could organize to compete with Indian-made textiles. One gets a sense of how deeply embedded Indian goods are in Anglo-American culture through our language, in which so many terms relating to cloth have their origin in India.[2] In addition to those Indian products which were essentially seen as utilitarian goods, there was scattered interest in the sixteenth and seventeenth centuries in items thought of as curios and preciosities, or what today might be thought of as "collectibles." These include odd paintings, both by Indians and Lusho-Indians, inlaid ivory chests and other items of furniture, jewelry and precious stones, swords and weapons to be used as decorative items.[3]

European Interpretative Strategies for "Knowing" India: 1600–1750

The major interpretative strategy by which India was to become known to Europeans in the seventeenth and eighteenth centuries was through a construction of a history for India. India was seen by Europeans not only as exotic and bizarre but as a kind of living museum of the European past. In India could be found "all the characters who are found in the Bible" and the "books which tell of the Jews and other ancient nations."[4] The religion of the Gentoos was described as having been established at the time of Adam and Eve in the garden of Eden, and preserved by Noah; or the religion of "the seed of those who revolted against Moses" and the worshipers of the "molten calf."[5] The Brahmans were Levites or Nazarites; Jains, Rehabites. Indians were, for some Europeans, the direct descendants of one of the lost ten tribes, for others the manners and customs of Indians derived from the ancient Egyptians who were the descendants of Ham, the son of Noah.

The Bible and the medieval patristic literature offered another interpretation of the culture and religions of India for the European travelers: this was the home of traditional enemies of Christianity, Satan and his devils. One of the earliest of the British travelers in India knew what the religion of the Gentoos was all about.

> But above all, their horrid Idolatry to Fagods (or Images of deformed devils) is most observable: Placed in Chappels most commonly built under the Bannyan Trees. A tree of such repute amongst 'em, that they hold it impiety to abuse it, either in breaking a branch or otherwise, but contrarily adorne it with Streamers of silk and ribbons of all colours. The Pagods are of sundry sorts and resemblances, in such shape as Satan visibly appears unto them: ugly faced, long black haire, gogl'd eyes, wide mouth, a forked beard, hornes and stradling, mishapen and horrible, after the old filthy forme of Pan and Priapus.[6]

To have found the devil and Satan in India was not strange and unusual to the Europeans, as they knew they were there all along. Recent scholarship has tended to stress that European accounts of the peoples of the New World, Africa, and Asia, dwelt less on the strangeness of the "other" but rather on their familiarity. The "exotics," writes Michael Ryan, could be fitted into a familiar web of discourse, as they were after all heathens and pagans, and "no matter how bizarre and offbeat he appeared the unbaptised exotic was just that—a heathen."[7] When traveling in a strange land, even meeting an old enemy, the devil, is something of a comfort.

Europeans knew the world through its signs and correspondences to things known. The exploration of the terrestrial world was being carried out at the same time that Europeans were exploring their own origins in the pagan past of Greece and Rome. Hence another way of knowing Indians arose through looking for conformities between the living exotics of India and their ancient counterparts in Egypt, Greece, and Rome. The exotic and the antique were one and the same.[8] Brahmans, yogis, and sadhus were "gymnosophists," followers of creators of the Pythagorian ideas about the transmigration of souls. These holy men in their benign mode were naked philosophers who in some medieval European traditions were the symbols of natural goodness "who embodied the possibility of salvation without revelation . . . outside the established Church."[9] The Brahmans and yogis as "good" were to eventually lose out to another reading, and become the perpetuators of superstitions, which they created and manipulated to mystify and keep subordinated the rest of the Hindu population of India. The yogi, the sannyasi, the fakir, the sadhu had by the eighteenth century been converted into living devils and the followers of all that was lascivious and degenerate in Greek and Roman religion, the worship of Pan and Priapus.

The literature on India of the seventeenth and early eighteenth centuries varies in its content but it established an enduring structural relationship between India and the West: Europe was progressive and changing, India static. Here could be found a kind of living fossil bed of the European past, a museum which was to provide Europeans for the next two hundred years a vast field on which to impose their own visions of history. India was found to be the land of oriental despotism, with its cycles of strong but lawless rules, whose inability to create a political order based on anything but unbridled power led inevitably to its own destruction in a war of all against all, leading to anarchy and chaos.

The British, in their construction of the history of India, came into the Indic world at one of its periods of inevitable decay and degeneration into chaos. Through the development of their version of rational despotism, they were able to find and maintain a stable basis for ordering Indian society. Fortunately it turned out that there were enduring and unchanging institutions in India at the local level. The traditional Indian state was epiphenominal and it was found to have no political order, rather India turned out to be a land of unchanging institutions based on family, caste, and the village community. The "discovery" of the relationship between the classical languages of Europe, Latin, and Greek, and of Indian Sanskrit, led to refinement of comparative method. This enabled the Europeans to provide India with a macrohistory organized into developmental stages. Certain universal features were constructed as markers of progress; the presence or absence of communal or private property, of the centralized state and kingship, of pastoralism or settled agriculture, became markers of progress or the lack thereof.

The British found that some parts of India were still at the feudal stage of development. Indian modes of production were at a pre-industrial stage, whose products could be taken to represent what Europe had lost through industrialization.

India was to be provided with a linear history following a nineteenth-century positivist historiography as well. Ruins could be dated, inscriptions made to reveal king lists, texts could be converted into sources for the study of the past. Each phase of the European effort to unlock the secret of the Indian past called for more and more collecting, more and more systems of classification, more and more building of repositories for the study of the past and the representation of the European history of India to Indians as well as themselves.

The State and the Surveying of the Indian Past

The capture of Seringapatam in 1799 and the final defeat of Tipu Sultan begins the direct involvement of the Company's government in a systematic effort to explore and document India's past. The Company now controlled most of India south of the Vindhya mountains, completing a military and diplomatic conquest begun fifty years earlier. This victory, combined with Lord Lake's entry into Delhi in 1803, ended whatever doubts there were that the British were now the conquerors of India and had fulfilled Alexander's historical ambitions. The death of Tipu, the arch villain in the emergent British hagiography of India, provided the necessary counterpoint to construction of the British as valorous, virtuous, and above all, triumphant conquerors.

The Company had a governor-general, Lord Wellesley, who matched the times. Unlike the owners and managers of the Company, who rarely looked beyond the ledger sheets, Wellesley had an imperial vision of the future of India. His first move was to establish a college in Calcutta, where the young employees of the Company who were no longer just "agents of a commercial concern" were to be trained "as ministers and officers of a powerful sovereign."[10] In addition Wellesley recognized the need for the systematic collection of information about the natural resources, the arts and manufactures, and the social and economic conditions of the inhabitants of the newly acquired territories of south India. To this end Wellesley established several surveys, the model of which can be seen in John Sinclair's statistical surveys of the highlands of Scotland.

In the late eighteenth and early nineteenth centuries the term "statistical" did not imply as it does today the collection, aggregation, and presentation of numerical data, rather it implied collection of information thought necessary and useful to the state. Since the time of William Camden (1551–1623) information had been collected and published about current conditions, history, and antiquities of various localities in Great Britain. Central to this endeavor was the location and description of old buildings, ruins, sites of ancient settlements, collection of family histories and genealogies, as well as the description of local customs and laws, thought to be antique or unusual.

Wellesley established three separate surveys of the Mysore territories, one under the direction of colonel Colin Mackenzie, which was to embrace "two great leading objects, Mathematical and Physical."[11] Another was under the direction of Francis Buchanan (Hamilton), who was instructed by Wellesley that the primary object of his enquiries "should be the agriculture of the country," and Benjamin Heyne, who under Mackenzie's direction was to collect botanical and geological specimens.[12]

Little is known of the first twenty-eight years of Mackenzie's life. He was born and grew up in Stornoway on the Island of Lewis in the Hebrides, his father a merchant, and the family had connections with the owners of the island, the Seaforths. He had, early on, shown great talent in mathematics, and assisted Lord Napier of Merchiston in the writing of a biography of his ancestor John Napier, the inventor of English logarithms. It would appear it was in connection with an interest Merchiston had in Hindu mathematics that an appointment in the Madras Engineers was obtained for Mackenzie in 1783.[13]

For a short while after his arrival in India in 1782, Mackenzie worked with Lord Merchiston's daughter in Madurai, along with several brahmans employed to collect materials on Hindu mathematics. Soon, however, his official duties prevented his pursuing his interests in "collecting observations and notices of Hindoo manners geography and history." Mackenzie's military duties took him to most of the provinces south of the Kistna river, but frequent transfers, and the demands of his military profession, prevented him from learning any of the "native languages." Any opportunity for systematic study of "objects" and "traits of customs and institutions that could have been explained, had time and means admitted of the inquery" was lost."[14]

Mackenzie credited his meeting and subsequent association with Cavelli Venkata Boria, a Telugu brahman, in 1796 with enabling him to enter into "the portal of Indian knowledge."[15] Boria was twenty when he was employed by Mackenzie to act as his interpreter and more importantly to direct a growing staff of Indians, who were to be employed for the next twenty-one years by Mackenzie in traveling throughout south India, collecting texts, inscriptions, artifacts, and all kinds of historical and sociological information. Some of this vast amount of work was done with official patronage as an adjunct to Mackenzie's topographical surveying and mapmaking. Mackenzie was eventually to become the surveyor general of India. Boria at twenty had studied Sanskrit, Persian, Hindustani, and English, in addition to knowing Tamil and Telugu. At the age of sixteen he held his first job with the British as a writer and interpreter."[16] Until his death at the age of twenty-six in 1803 he accompanied Mackenzie, recording temple inscriptions, deciphering obsolete scripts, and translating books, manuscripts, and documents. In addition Boria, according to his brother Cavelly Venkata Ramaswami, wrote poems in Sanskrit and Telugu, including a poetical account of the fall of Seringapatam.

Mackenzie's ambition was to compile the source material necessary to write a history of south India. The Mysore Survey continued for almost ten years. Mackenzie summarized the results of this work:

1. The discovery of the *Jaina* religion and philosophy, and its distinction from that of Buddha.

2. The different ancient sects of religion in this country, and their subdivisions—the *Lingavanta*, the *Saivam* and *Pandaram Matts*, etc.

3. The nature and use of the *Sassanams*, and inscriptions on stone and copper, and their utility in throwing light on the important subject of Hindu tenures; confirmed by upwards of 3,000 authentic inscriptions collected since 1800, hitherto always overlooked.

4. The design and nature of the monumental stones and trophies found in various parts of the country from Cape Comorin to Delhi, called *Virakal* and *Maastikal*, which illustrate the ancient customs of the early inhabitants, and, perhaps, of the early western nations.

5. The sepulchral tumeli, mounds, and barrows of the early tribes, similar to those found throughout the continent of Asia and of Europe, illustrated by drawings, and various other notices of antiquities and institutions.[17]

The most active period of the Survey was from 1800 to 1810, when Mackenzie became chief engineer for the expedition sent to Java. Here had remained until 1813, where along with his military duties he initiated a survey similar to that being carried out in south India.[18] Mackenzie then returned to his post as surveyor of Madras, and in 1815, somewhat against his wishes, he was transferred to Calcutta and appointed surveyor general of India. This enabled him to travel widely and explore much of north India. Mackenzie brought with him to Calcutta much of the staff who had worked with him in Madras, who were to be engaged in trying to organize the vast amount of materials which they had collected during the previous twenty years. Subsequent to Mackenzie's death in 1821, this staff was to come under the charge of H. H. Wilson, who had been successful in having the Company establish an antiquarian department in Calcutta. This office was staffed by four translators, four pandits, a maulavi, and several copyists and peons. Wilson's primary interests were in the Sanskrit language and Persian, which he viewed as "the chief vehicle of the modern history of India." He had no knowledge of and little interest in the languages and history of south India.[19] Wilson had little interest in maintaining Mackenzie's staff, except as they were concerned with Sanskrit and Persian. The directors of the Company were long interested in Mackenzie's efforts to collect the materials to write a true history of south India. In 1810 they strongly expressed their admiration for the zeal with which he had carried out his statistical work and his "enquiries into the history, the religion and antiquities of the country."[20] They congratulated Mackenzie for providing the basis on which a real history and chronology of south India could be written, dispelling the idea that the "Hindoos possess few authentic records." They encouraged him to "digest and improve the materials" which he had collected and urged him to forward them for deposit in the Company's museum.[21] They also asked for an accounting of his own funds which he had expended so that he might be recompensed. It appears that Mackenzie never supplied the accounting.

In 1823 Palmer & Company, the executors of Mackenzie's estate, submitted a detailed accounting of his expenditures in assembling his collection, amounting to Rs 61,452. Palmer & Company pointed out that the accounting was based on scattered records and that the figure was undoubtedly an underestimate. They asked that the estate be paid Rs 100,000, a figure which the governor-general agreed to, but which the Court of Directors rejected.[22] Eventually, though, the court of Directors did agree to purchase the whole of the collection from Mackenzie's widow for £10,000.[23] Wilson, although he had little knowledge of the languages involved, and who seems to have dismissed most of Mackenzie's staff, undertook the task of organizing and publishing a catalogue of the papers, with excerpts, which appeared in two volumes of over eight hundred pages in Calcutta in 1828.

Wilson basically followed Mackenzie's own classification of the materials, which included 1,568 manuscripts in 13 languages in 19 scripts, which he described as dealing with "Literature." There were 264 volumes of what Mackenzie labeled "Local Tracts"; these were primarily based on oral accounts which Mackenzie's assistants had collected, and which related to the history of particular temples, kingdoms, families, and castes. There were also 77 volumes of copies of inscriptions recorded from temples, copper plates, and various grants, 75 volumes of translations, 79 plans, 2,630 drawings, 6,218 coins, 106 images, and 40 antiquities.[24]

Mackenzie, after Boria's death, established Boria's younger brother Cavelly Venkata Luchmiah as his chief assistant who trained and supervised the work of obtaining and collecting the vast array of materials in the collection. Luchmiah's original monthly reports for 1804 provide an excellent account of how the varied materials were obtained.[25] The reports are in Luchmiah's handwriting, in English, which although somewhat ungrammatical—he had difficulties with tenses—are quite clear and understandable. In the reports, he describes where he and the other collectors have gone, and who they talked with. Sometimes he provides brief summaries of the content of the conversations. There are frequent references to books bought and their prices. He also forwards to Mackenzie translations which were being done in various languages. He comments on sources of information which he is developing. He has heard about a history of a particular zamindari; he writes to the vakil who has the account, expressing his desire to meet him. Luchmiah reports that he is received with great respect by the vakil, who knows one of his relations. At his first meeting, which lasts three to four hours, the vakil learnedly discusses astrology, and Luchmiah does not raise the question of obtaining a copy of the history but assures Mackenzie that during his next visit he will undoubtedly obtain the copy which they are seeking. Luchmiah then follows up the discussion of astrology with a visit to the astrologer in Madras that the vakil thinks is such an expert. Luchmiah, having heard from his informant that the astrologer has a large collection of texts which have accounts of the lives of his clients, he decides to go see him "and try his skill."[26] Luchmiah day by day recounts for Mackenzie the letters received and sent to the various correspondents and assistants.

H. H. Wilson, as a means of illustrating the process by which the materials were collected, printed the "Report of Baboo Rao," Mackenzie's Maratha translator, of a trip along the Coromandel coast to collect historical information and coins. Day by day he reports where he has gone and who he has seen. Rao is asked by several English officials to take them to see a recently discovered temple at Mahabalipuram, and acts as their guide. He reports that he declined to accept four star pagodas for his trouble, "for fear of looseing my character with my master."[27] Wherever Rao goes he first checks in with the local British official and presents letters of introduction from Mackenzie. Most of Rao's efforts were devoted to collecting "ancient books," which he would either buy or copy. Failing to obtain texts and documents, he would question elderly people, pujaris, local chiefs, learned men, particularly about the Cholas and anything which dealt with "Bouddhas" and their conflicts with the Jainas.

Rao tracked down various stories about the discovery of hidden treasures, old pottery, ruins, and statuary. Rao was told that four months before, a cultivator while ploughing a field struck a gilded image of the Buddha. He informed the managers of the nearby temple, who secretly took it into the temple thinking it was all gold, but it turned out to be a brass image which was gilded. After rubbing off eight or ten pagodas worth of gold, the manager of the temple was preparing to melt the image down and to make brass pots out of it, "to save their character and to prevent its coming to knowledge of the Circar people."[28] On hearing this Rao went immediately to the managers, who at first denied any knowledge of the statue, but after more questioning they produced it. Rao offered to buy it for sixteen or twenty star pagodas. The head manager of the temple, having heard what had transpired, refused to go through with the bargain, saying he would never agree to sell the image even for thousands. A frustrated Rao "resolved to wait for my master's orders before I should apply to the Collector."[28] Rao then went to the site where the image was found with four coolies, where they dug, but after finding only "a stone image of *Bouddha* and two covered wells," he suspended further search and returned to his house.

In Kumbhakonam, Rao visited the chief priest of the "Sankar Archari Math," and after spending four rupees on "fruit etc." he asked the priest for a copy of the copper inscription that was in the Math. The priest was willing, but the managers of the Math (*Kyasthalu*) vociferously denied that there were any inscriptions to be found. They were afraid of "looseing their original documents," which, Rao suggests, had saved them from "the destruction of different wars."[29] Rao reassured them that he only wished to make a copy, to which the managers agreed on the condition that Rao recommend to Mackenzie that a jagir that they once possessed be restored to them. Rao agreed to this. The chief priest was so pleased by this that he promised to get Rao a particular account of the "*Cholen, Cheran,* and *Pandian*" together with the rajas of Bijanagur, as he was the "Guru of all the Rajas." He also promised to give him an account of all the "Rajas who had ruled since the commencement of the *Kaliyugam.*" Rao was then taken in to the chief priest's *agraram* and shown 125 copper *sasanams*. Rao was dismissed by the priest with a promise that he would give him these accounts along with several coins, if there was any assistance forthcoming in getting the return of the lost villages.[30]

Although the bulk of the Mackenzie collection was in Calcutta in 1823, when Wilson began to work on it, some of it already was known to be lost or missing. In 1808 Mackenzie had sent seven volumes described as "Memoirs of the Survey of Mysore to London" as well as two volumes of maps.[31] In 1827 Charles Wilkins, the librarian of the India Office, could not locate these. Wilson, as he finished sections of the catalogue, dispatched, in 1823 and 1825, portions of the collection to London. At the completion of his work in 1827, he sent all the works in Persian, Sanskrit, and Burmese, along with the plans, drawings, coins, and 106 images of Indian gods in silver, copper, and brass, to London. Some of these were displayed in the small museum which the Company had at its headquarters in Leadenhall Street. Also dispatched were five "large pieces of sculpture on stones from Amaravati," four smaller pieces and one "inscription on stone" from Amaracartu.[32] I will discuss what happened to these pieces subsequently.

Wilson also sent the materials classified as "local tracts," the accounts of the histories, stories, and descriptions taken down by Mackenzie's collectors from local priests, chiefs, and local scholars, to Madras, where they were placed under the charge of the Madras Literary Society. With their arrival in Madras, C. V. Luchmiah asked that he be placed at the head of an establishment which would complete Mackenzie's work. This fell on deaf ears.[33] Luchmiah persisted in lobbying for his plan, and the governor of Madras was sufficiently impressed that he forwarded the plan to the governor-general, who in turn sent it to the Asiatic Society of Bengal, for evaluation and to make recommendations on what should be done about Luchmiah's plan. Luchmiah wanted in effect to reestablish Mackenzie's program for collecting, under his own direction. For a start he wanted permission to be able to correspond with "gentlemen" of "literary endowments" to enable him to procure information on the subject of the history and antiquities of India.[34] In addition, he wanted to hire in each district in south India two "intelligent scholars," one versed in Sanskrit and the other in "Oriental Literature," who would continue to collect materials for the project. The plan was referred to the Committee on Papers of the Asiatic Society of Bengal, headed by James Prinsep— who took a dim view of Luchmiah's qualifications and his plan:

> Such an extensive scheme would need the control of a master head, accustomed to generalization, and capable of estimating the value and drift of inscription and legendary evidence. The qualifications of Cavelly Venkata for such an office, judging of them by his 'abstract', or indeed of any native, could hardly be pronounced equal to such a task, however useful they may prove as auxillaries in such a train of research.[35]

Prinsep and the committee did however make a strong argument for making knowledge of the collection more widely known and that efforts be made to preserve it, and make it available to scholars. To this end they recommended to the government that William Taylor, a missionary in Madras who had published some "oriental historical manuscripts," undertake the publishing of translations from the Mackenzie manuscripts. Taylor was more than willing to do this, and quickly submitted a budget to the Madras government of Rs 7,000 for eighteen months' work. He hired six pandits and munshis, as well as two "native writers." Over the next few years some excerpts appeared in the *Madras Literary Magazine*, and finally in 1857 the first three volumes of the excerpts appeared in Madras as *A Catalogue Raisonnée of Oriental Manuscripts in the Library of the (Late) College, Fort St George*. The corpus not only included the manuscripts sent by Wilson to Madras, but also some found in the library of East India Company by C. P. Brown in 1838. Brown also added some materials in Telugu and Tamil which he had himself collected. The Brown collection was shipped to Madras sometime after 1840. Taylor, who reprinted many of the excerpts already published in Wilson's catalogue, used the occasion to write an exegesis of his own theories about Hindu thought, religion, and what the true history of India had been. The materials in the collection on Indian architecture, wrote Taylor, were of little value as they contained too much on astrology. From the beginning of the work the reader is introduced to Taylor's overriding theory, that Indian culture is derived from Chaldean or Egyptian origins. There is in fact little or nothing in India which could be counted as their own; the Indians are merely poor imitators of an authentic antediluvian culture that existed in the Middle East. There is little to wonder at in the Indian mind, degenerate and debased. This is accounted for by the fact that "The Hindu skull is of a lower order than that of [even] the Celtic, and very inferior [to the] broad Saxon skull." The cerebellum of the Hindu brain is highly developed which accounts for the fact that their poetry runs rampant with "sexualities." The Indians have even outdone the licentiousness of Ovid in the way they "treat systematically on the *ars amoriis*."[36]

Taylor rejects the interpretation that the Indians have a theory of "moral action." This is easily seen to be wrong through his study of the *Bhagavad Gita*, in which Krishna advises Arjuna to kill without compunction or fear of moral retribution. He advises his readers that the proof of this assertion is to put the message of the *Gita* "into the mouth of any leading mutineer at Meerut." Then "the true character of the *Gita* will become instantly viseable." Because of the despotic nature of the Indian state, there is no chance for manly virtues to develop among Indians, as they are brought up to "cringe, fawn and flatter their rulers." Hence they have no sublime aspirations to pursue and under such circumstances the human mind becomes "naturally sordid, and wastes its time in puerile disputation."[37] The introduction to the materials in Volume Two is used as a platform to reiterate the major theme of the unoriginality of the Indians, this time with more attention to their romance-historical literature, which seems to be copied either from the ancient Jews or the Greeks.

The historical explanation put forward by Taylor is an account of the wanderings of the ancient Aryans, who brought this mishmash of "Hebrew Theology and Chaldean Sabism into India." There is a profound irony in the Mackenzie collection falling into the hands of an interpreter seemingly more familiar with the spurious and mystical Orientalism of the eighteenth century than with the post-Jones scholarship of the first half of the nineteenth century. The scholar to whom Taylor most frequently refers is Jacob Bryant, the eighteenth-century compiler and antiquarian. The members of the Asiatic Society doubted Cavelly Venkata Luchmiah's scholarly credentials, and instead they selected a crackpot to edit Mackenzie's papers.

Colonel Mackenzie's collection has not fared much better in the twentieth century. N. D. Sundatravivelu, vice chancellor of the University of Madras, states in the foreword of Volume I of the Mackenzie manuscripts, edited by T. V. Mahalingam, Professor of Ancient History and Archaeology (retired) at the University of Madras, published in 1972: "The keen interest evinced by Western Orientalists and Indian scholars testify to the importance of these documents." He seems, however, to be at some odds with the editor of the volume, who states:

> Scholars, who have hitherto attempted a critical study of the Mackenzie Manuscripts, have been sceptical of their historical value. 'The attempt to extract history from the confused chronicles in the Taylor Manuscripts seems a hopeless task', says K. A. Nilakanta Sastri, while discussing the views of S. K. Aiyangar on Malik Kafur's invasion of the Pandya country. Mackenzie has often been admired as a pioneer in the field of oriental research and his collections have found their way into several footnotes. Still, the authenticity of the information contained in them has been doubted, however not without reason. For his collections are generally based on secondhand traditions and unverified reports. But they have their own place in the field of historical research in India. Their testimony may be used as circumstantial evidence calculated to supplement the results arrived at from other sources and to furnish further details on the subject.
>
> It must be admitted that exaggerated notions on the value of the Mackenzie collection as containing original and authentic material are not justified.[38]

Colonel Mackenzie and the Amaravati Marbles

I have not yet finished with the results of Mackenzie's dedication and almost demonic urge to reveal to the West the history of south India. In 1797 Mackenzie was carrying out a topographic survey in Guntur district when he heard about the discovery of some antiquities in a small town, Amresvarem, on the Kistna river. He sent ahead his trusty guide Venkata Boria along with some brahmans and two sepoys. They were to make inquiries into the history of the place and to conciliate the inhabitants, particularly the Brahmans, "who are apt," wrote Mackenzie, "to be alarmed on these occasions."[39] On Mackenzie's arrival Boria reported that there was some apprehension at the approach of the British and their sepoys, but Mackenzie reassured the inhabitants that they had only come to look at the recently discovered ruins, which were being excavated by a local raja, who was using some of the materials in building a temple and his house. Mackenzie found a long circular trench 10 feet wide and 12 feet deep, which exposed a mass of masonry, and some slabs, some with bas reliefs on them. It was reported that some statuary had been uncovered and taken into the newly built temple.

One of Mackenzie's delineators, Mr. Sydenham, drew a number of the figures which were readily accessible. Mackenzie described seeing a number of lingams on the bas reliefs. In the mud wall of the temple he found a sculpture of "an attack or an escalade of a fortified place." The residents of the town believed that the remains were built by Jains. Mackenzie was generally mystified by the appearance of figures in the fragments that he saw:

> The legs of all the figures are more slender and gracefully disposed than I have observed in any other Hindu buildings. It would be rash to draw any conclusions until an opportunity offers of observing more sculptures."[40]

It was not until almost twenty years later, in 1816, that Mackenzie returned to investigate the Amaravati tope. This time he had a full team, including four or five specially trained delineators, presumably the "country born" graduates of the Madras Observatory and Surveying School established by Michael Topping in Madras in 1794.[41] Mackenzie spent four or five months at the site and his assistants worked through 1817, producing "careful plans of the buildings and maps of the surrounding country, together with eighty very carefully finished drawings of the sculptures." James Fergusson stated that these drawings were unsurpassed "for accuracy and beauty of finish."[42] Mackenzie was never to write up a full description of the site as he found it in 1816, integrating the plans and maps and drawings done by his assistants. After his death an article based on two letters to Mr. Buckingham appeared, first in the *Calcutta Journal* of 1822 and reprinted in the *Asiatic Journal* of 1823 under the title of "Ruins of Amravutty, Depauldina, and Durnacotta."[43]

In the twenty years between visits, the site was further destroyed, in the search for treasure (always assumed to be buried in ancient mounds), for building materials, and through firing of the marbles for lime. In addition the raja had decided to dig a large tank in the center of the mound. Nonetheless large numbers of fragments of sculpture remained, to be described and drawn. Mackenzie was impressed with the skill of the mysterious artists, who carved with taste and elegance. The human figures depicted "were well executed" and the proportions "correct."[44] The site, he believed, was dedicated to religious worship, but of what kind he did not know, except that it was clearly different from the brahmanical worship of the "present day" as none of the Hindu mythological figures was depicted.

Mackenzie speculated that, because of the circular nature of the larger outline of the enclosure, it perhaps was the same religion as the Druids and that the temple was devoted to sun worship. He was further mystified by the discovery on sculptured slabs of inscriptions in characters "entirely foreign to these countries," characters of a type that Mackenzie had never seen before.[45] Mackenzie appears to have sent copies of the drawings and plans to London, Calcutta, and Madras. In addition, and to the frustration of subsequent scholars, pieces of sculpture were sent to Musalapatam, Calcutta, Madras, and London, but how many there were, and their provenance, continues to be a mystery to this day.[46]

In 1830, Mr. Roberston, collector of Musalapatam, found some of the sculptures, and obtained others from the site, which he set up in the square of the new market place he had built in the town. These were seen five years later by the governor of Madras who was on tour, and he ordered them to be shipped to Madras, so that they could be better cared for by the Madras Literary Society. Some of these wound up in the garden of the master attendant.[47]

The first effort at deciphering the script found at the site was done by James Prinsep in collaboration with Pandit Madhoray, the aged librarian at the Sanskrit College who had been one of Mackenzie's associates. Prinsep identified the script as being the same type as found in the cave inscriptions from Mahabalipuram, and similar to the alphabets of Chattisgarh. He denominated the characters as Nadhra, and he decided they were transformations of the north India Devanagari. Prinsep declared that the inscription "refers in all probability to the foundation and endowment of some Buddhistic institution by the monarch of his day." However, he was disappointed as the monarch was not named, hence the date could not be established; "history will have gained nothing by the document," he declared.[48]

The largest collection of the sculptures and fragments, ninety in all, from the Amaravati site were made by Sir Walter Eliott, commissioner of Guntur, in 1840. These he shipped to Madras, where for fourteen years they were stored, unexamined and undescribed until 1854, when Dr. Balfour, who was in charge of the Central Museum, made a list of them. The description and analysis of these fragments was left to William Taylor, who again, as with the Mackenzie manuscripts, used the occasion to spin more hypothetical histories.

In 1857 the Madras collection, now dubbed the Eliott Marbles, was shipped to England, presumably for display in the Company's museum. They arrived in the winter of 1858, just at the moment when the Company's rule was being transformed into Crown rule. The marbles lay through the winter in open crates on a dock in Southwark. One of the better pieces was later affixed to an outer wall of the India Museum in Fife House on Whitehall, while the others dropped out of sight. In 1866, Henry Cole, who was organizing part of the British display to be shown the following year at the Paris International Exhibition, asked Fergusson to organize a display of archaeological and architectural photographs from India. Fergusson thought it would be a good idea to have some actual statuary on display as well. He remembered the Amaravati marbles, which he thought were "the principal ornaments of the Old Museum on Leadenhall Street." He tracked them down under piles of rubbish in the coach house of Fife House. Fergusson had a complete set of photographs, made by William Griggs of the India office, and by studying these, he sought to reconstruct the buildings of which they once were a part. [49]

As Fergusson studied the photographs he "perceived that they might be classified in three great groups." One, based on the analogy of Sanchi, formed an outer rail as an ornament, and belonged by the main building, as was seen in Mackenzie's drawings. Another set, smaller and finer, Fergusson believed belonged to the inner rail. What remained he declared "were to no architectural value" and could be placed anywhere. [50] Fergusson's interest in the Amaravati site and its fragments was to grow in the next few years into a major scholarly and intellectual project. He was determined to make the fragments tell part of the history of India. The representations of people, their clothes and ornaments, the animals, buildings and symbols, were to become for Fergusson a projective test.

Even before the Exhibition began, Fergusson was utilizing the photographs at a meeting of the Society of Arts, on 21 December 1866. With Sir Thomas Philips, under-secretary of state for India in the chair, and with a distinguished audience including Sir Henry Cole, the impresario of the Great Exhibition of 1851, he delivered a lecture "On the Study of Indian Architecture." [51] Rather than giving a scholarly and detailed exegesis of the principles and history of Indian architecture, he made an argument about the utility of the study of Indian architecture for an understanding of the ethnology and religions of India, and about the value of Indian architecture as a source of ideas for the improvement of architecture in England. He began his lecture by describing what he thought was the racial and ethnological history of India. He posited a distant past. Here was an aboriginal race in the Ganges valley, whose descendants were the hill tribes such as Bhils, Gonds, and Coles who had dominated north India. These people were conquered about 2,000 B.C. by the Aryans, a Sanskrit-speaking people to whom India owes its literary traditions, but they were not great builders, and like all outsiders to India, soon fell prey to the enervating climate and the degeneration which naturally followed, by their "intermingling with the aboriginal races." The Aryan's demise as effective rulers cleared the way for the rise of the great religious leader Buddha, who taught the people a new, pure religion, which following the iron law of decay in India, "gradually became idolatrous and corrupt" and perished beneath its own overgrown hierarchy. Simultaneously with the rise of Buddhism, there was yet another invasion of India, this time by the Dravidian peoples, who came also from the north, and who had crossed into India in the lower Indus valley. They traveled through Gujarat, and then spread southward through the Deccan. The Dravidians were a race of great builders, but "totally distinct from those in the North." A century or two before Christ, there was yet another invasion, the invaders unnamed by Fergusson, but settled in Rajputana and Gujarat. Some went as far south as Mysore and others went into the Agra–Delhi region in the north. The fourth invasion was that of the Muhammedan peoples. The fifth civilization to take over India "is our own."[52]

Architecture and its associated sculpture were for Fergusson the only reliable documents on which to build a "scientific history of India," a land where there "are no written annals which can be trusted." It is only when the annals of a king "can be authenticated by inscriptions and coins that we can feel sure of the existence of any king, and it is only when we can find his buildings that we can measure his greatness or ascertain . . . what the degrees of civilization to which either he or his people had attained."[53]

Fergusson summed up his brief arguments in the following terms:

I consider the study of Indian architecture important because it affords the readiest and most direct means of ascertaining the ethnological relations of the different races inhabiting India. It points out more clearly than can be done by other means how they succeeded each other, where they settled, how they mixed, or when they were absorbed.

In the next place, I consider it important, because it affords the best picture of the religious faiths of the country, showing how and when they arose, how they became corrupted, and when and by what steps they sank to their present level.

It is also, I believe, important because in a country which has no written histories it affords almost the only means that exist for steadying any conclusion we may arrive at, and is a measure of the greatness or decay of the dynasties that ruled that country in ancient times.

These considerations refer wholly to India, and to the importance of the study as bearing on Indian questions only; but I consider it as important also, because of its bearings on architectural art in our own country. First, because by widening the base of our observations and extending our views to a style wholly different from our own, we are able to look at architecture from a new and outside point of view, and by doing this to master principles which are wholly hidden from those whose study is confined to some style so mixed up with adventitious associations as our local styles inevitably are.

It is also important because architecture in India is still a living art. We can see there, at the present day, buildings as important in size as our mediaeval cathedrals erected by master masons on precisely the same principle and in the same manner that guided our mediaeval masons to such glorious results.

It also is, I conceive, important as offering many suggestions which, if adopted in a modified form, might tend considerably to the improvement of our own architectural designs.

Lastly, I consider the study worthy of attention from the light it may be expected to throw on some of our own archaeological problems.

Implicitly and explicitly, Fergusson in his 1866 lecture was enunciating a theory compounded out of seventy years of British Orientalist discourse. The primary components of this discourse revolved around India's double lack of a history. Since it has no documents, dateable records, chronicles, the kinds of materials out of which the West constructed a history of itself, the British were called upon to provide India with a history. In a second sense India has no history as it has not progressed. All the civilizations which had entered India, except the fifth one, displayed the same history, by succumbing to the inevitable effects of the climate, and their intermingling with the inhabitants, which in turn lead to enervation and the falling into the hands of overdeveloped hierarchies.

The European past can be seen in India as in a museum. Builders in India have been doing the same thing since time immemorial, which enables the British to understand how their own great religious buildings of the Middle Ages were constructed. Finally there are policy considerations the British should learn from the experiences of the other invaders. The only way to survive and flourish in India is to remain totally separated from the degenerate races who inhabit the country, and they should live in such a fashion as to minimize the effects of the climate.

Fergusson followed his pragmatic lecture with an analysis of the Amaravati Tope in Guntur,[54] which in turn led to the publication of Fergusson's magnum opus of his later years, *Tree and Serpent Worship: or Illustrations of Mythology and Art in India in the First and Fourth Centuries After Christ. From the Sculptures of the Buddhist Topes at Sanchi and Amaravati.* The work proclaims itself on the title page as being prepared under the authority of Secretary of State for India in Council.

In his 1868 paper, which was well illustrated with drawings based on the photographic collection, we find him reading an ethnology and a history into the sculptures, in which he finds three races; the Nagas, whose emblems associate them with snakes, are a handsome race, but are not the rulers of Amaravati. The Nagas were from Taxila "which seems to be the headquarters of snake worship in the early centuries of the Christian era." Also represented were Jats, and thirdly there are the autochthonous—"Gonds or some cognate Tamil race."[55] The paper ends with an announcement of his next project, the publication and explication of how the arts of Europe influenced those of the East, along with an essay on tree and serpent worship. As promised, the essay appeared five years later; in seventy-five folio pages the reader is taken on a world historical tour, demonstrating that there was a worldwide Ur-religion based on the worship of trees and snakes.

In Fergusson's history of religions, bits and pieces of this earlier nature worship get woven together along with the speculative thought of a great religious leader into one of the progressive religions. Once again the Indians turn out to be losers. They had their chance to be with the winners in the religious sweepstakes, but they turned their backs on the Buddha, and kept up the old snake and tree worship. Not only had the poor Indians, as represented by the Naga people and their snake worship, blown their chance for real salvation, but they also had in their grasp the beginnings of Western monumental architecture as worked out by the Greeks and Romans.

The buldings and their decorative motifs owed their fineness to "Greek or rather Bactrian art."[56] Fergusson faces a problem with his theory of Bactrian and Roman influence on the Amaravati site. He has to date it within A.D. 200 to 400. This he does, through developing a series of inferences, based on stylistic analogies found in the western Indian cave temples. This was counter to the inscriptional evidence, which made the site more recent than his argument for Greek and Roman influence would have sustained. Fergusson reserved his strongest argument for the relation of Amaravati to Rome to a footnote.

My impression, however, is that few who are familiar with the arts of Rome in Constantine's time, and who will take the trouble to master these Amaravati sculptures, can fail to perceive many points of affinity between them. The circular medallions of the arch of Constantine—such as belong to his time—and the general tone of the art of his age so closely resemble what we find here, that the coincidence can hardly be accidental. The conviction that the study of these sculptures has forced in my mind is, that there was much more intercommunication between the east and west during the whole period from Alexander to Justinian than is generally supposed, and that the intercourse was especially frequent and influential in the middle period, between Augustus and Constantine.[57]

Rajendralal Mitra, the first of India's Sanskritists and student of early Indian history who utilized European-based scholarship, took exception to Fergusson's theories on the origins of Indian architecture. In papers given before the Asiatic Society of Bengal, and then *The Antiquities of Orissa*, a two-volume work published in 1875 and 1880, and *Buddha Gaya: The Hermitage of Sakya Muni*, he mounted a full-scale attack on European assumptions, particularly those of Fergusson, of India's lack of originality and inventiveness in art and architecture, particularly the idea that there had been a strong influence of the Greeks and Romans in the development of monumental stone construction in India. Mitra approached the discussion of Indian antiquities and buildings from an historical standpoint, relating texts and inscriptions to his interpretation of the form and function and meaning of building, and the development of Indian artistic productions.[58]

Fergusson replied to what he thought was a cheeky and ill-trained Indian with a full-blooded defense of his own work, and by calling into question the capacity of any Indian to be able to master the methods which the understanding of Indian architecture required.[59] He began his defense by a statement of his love of India, recounting the delight "in visiting the various cities of Hindustaan, so picturesque in their decay, or so beautiful in their modern garb." He averred that all his "relations with the natives of India were of the most gratifying and satisfactory nature." He had enjoyed the hospitality of the rajas of central India, and he would never forget the "servants who served me so faithfully, so honestly, from the time I first landed till I left its shores."[60]

Fergusson had been in India from 1835 to 1842, a period he now looked back upon as a kind of golden age, before some of the natives were spoiled by contact with European civilization.[61] The agency of this change was the idea that Indians could become the equals of the British through education in the European fashion, which Fergusson stated they could not assimilate.

Bengalis—and for Fergusson, Babu Rajendralal Mitra was the typical case—had a marvelous facility for acquiring "our language, but only a superficial familiarity with the principal features of our arts and sciences."[62] The great skill of Indians was the capacity for memorizing vast amounts of materials and amassing a great many scientific facts. This was not the same thing as acquiring by "long study and careful reasoning, . . . the great truths of scientific knowledge." The Babu was accused of using a German technique to establish a reputation, something an Englishman would never stoop to, by attacking Fergusson only to enhance his own reputation. In addition he posed as a "patriot" by "defending the cause of India against the slanders of an ignorant and prejudiced foreigner."[63] Fergusson argued that in his refutation of the Babu there was more than just differences between two scholars about the history of Indian art and architecture. He related it to the then current attack by Europeans in India on the Ilbert Bill, which would have made them subject in criminal matters to Indian judges. It is easy to understand, wrote Fergusson,

> why Europeans resident in the country, and knowing the character of the people among whom they are living, should have shrunk instinctively, with purely patriotic motives, from the fatuity of the Ilbert Bill. It may, however, be useful to those who reside at a distance, and who have no local experience, to have it explained to them by a striking living example, wherein the strength and weakness of the cause resides, and for that purpose I do not know any example that can be more appropriate than that of Babu Rajendralala Mitra. If, after reading the following pages, any European feels that he would like to be subjected to his jurisdiction, in criminal cases, he must have a courage possessed by few; or if he thinks he could depend on his knowledge, or impartiality, to do him justice, as he could on one of his own countrymen, he must be strangely constituted in mind, body, and estate.[64]

Fergusson was certainly correct about the context in which what started as a scholarly debate about the effort to construct a history of India became centrally about politics, not just the issue of equality before the law but in all the questions entailed in the effort to represent to Indians there own traditions and pasts.

Thus far in this chapter I have been exploring one collection, that started by Colonel Colin Mackenzie and of the efforts at interpreting one archaeological site. It was not until 1942 that the Amaravati sculptures got the catalogue they deserved, when C. Sivaramamurti published his detailed descriptions of each piece along with a thorough iconographic and textually based commentary.[65] This was followed in 1954 by Douglas Barrett's discussion of the British Museum collection. Basil Grey, keeper of Oriental Antiquities there, commented that "the Amaravati sculptures are ranked with the Elgin Marbles and the As-syrian reliefs among the Great Possessions of the Museum."[66] Given the history of the collection, one might wonder what happens to those things in the British Museum which are not so ranked. The final irony, of course, is that the Amaravati sculptures are no longer on display.

Under the Company, official concern with the art, artifacts, and antiquities of India was haphazard, and filled with false starts. Efforts began through individual initiatives, but halted when the bookkeepers in Leadenhall Street became aware of the potential costs, and their ill effects on the balance sheet.

The most ambitious effort at providing a locus for the systematic study of Indian literature and history was the brainchild of Lord Wellesley, the first of the governors-general with an imperial vision, who founded, without the permission of the Court of Directors, the College at Fort William. This college had the purpose of providing a liberal education in western and Indian forms of knowledge to the young civilian appointees of the Company. Implicit in this was the necessity of the systematic study of Indian languages and literatures, by an accomplished body of Indian and British scholars.[67] Throughout the existence of the college there was to be constant friction about the costs of maintaining a faculty who were frequently more interested in scholarship than in producing useful textbooks and the daily grind of teaching young Englishmen.

The same conflicts plagued the East India Company's training college at Haileybury, established in 1805 as part of the effort to reduce the costs and significance of the College at Fort William.[68]

The most consistently important scholarly organization which concerned itself with the acquisition and dissemination of knowledge concerning India was the Asiatic Society of Bengal, founded in 1785. The society was a private body, with close official ties. Its membership always included the governor-general, who also frequently was the honorary president of the society. From time to time it received direct grants from the government, and had constantly referred to it matters which affected the study of Indian antiquities, and the development of the study of natural history in India.

In the eighteenth and early nineteenth centuries most of the significant collections of texts, paintings, sculptures, artifacts, and even botanical and zoological specimens which were later to show up in museums in Great Britain and India were the result of individual and personal efforts, which were later sold or presented to the government. James Fraser, a Company merchant in Surat in the 1730s and 1740s, and the author of a history of Nadir Shah, made what is probably the first extensive collection of Sanskrit manuscripts, which he brought back to Europe partially as a means of transferring some of his money from India.[69] After his death his collection was sold by his widow to the Radcliffe

Library in Oxford, and then in the latter part of the nineteenth century was transferred to the Bodleian, and is the basis of that library's Sanskrit collection.

Some of the British in India were attracted to Indian painting more, it would seem, for its documentary value than its intrinsic aesthetic qualities, and a number of important collections were made during the second half of the eighteenth century. Sir Elijah Impey and his wife collected Indian paintings and "commissioned Indian artists to paint natural history specimens."[70] The largest and most important collection made in the latter part of the eighteenth century still extant is the Richard Johnson collection of the India Office Library. Johnson collected, as well as commissioned, a wide range of albums from the time of Akbar to the end of the eighteenth century. Johnson had made a large collection of Oriental manuscripts as well, totaling 1,100 volumes. Charles Wilkins, the Sanskrit scholar and the Company's librarian, examined the collection in 1807, when Johnson had offered to sell it in its entirety to the Company, and in recommending its purchase for three thousand guineas, wrote to the chairman and deputy chairman of the Court of Directors:

> The books, as to the writing, illuminations, perfectness, preservation and binding are upon a par with any other collection which has come under my view. There are of course many in an indifferent state of preservation, a few works deficient in the number of vols and otherwise defective, and the binding, as is always the case, naturally bad and in a bad condition. On the contrary there is a great number of books of the first rank as to the beauty of the writing, and splendour of the decorations; and not a few exquisitely fine.
>
> As to the subjects, there is a good proportion of the best Histories, many very valuable Dictionaries of the Arabic and Persian languages, several useful treatises on Grammar, etc., with a great many specimens of fine penmanship in various oriental hands by the most celebrated masters. There are also a great many distinct treatises on Mathematics, Astronomy, Music, Medicine and other sciences and arts; a very ample and curious collection of Arabic and Persian Tales, perhaps unique, with the works of all the most celebrated Poets. There are many works on Law, Religion and ethics, some of them splendid copies; many valuable translations from the Sanskrit into Persian; some works in the original Sanskrit and Hindi—a few rare; with a miscellaneous division upon a great variety of useful and interesting subjects; particularly a choice collection of statistical works consisting of particular tables and statements of the lands and revenues of several of the provinces of India.[71]

Shortly after this Dr. John Flemming, who had been in the Company's medical service, presented the library with "eight miscellaneous paintings of religious subjects," but his massive collection of botanical drawings wound up in the collection of a Belgian nobleman. Francis Buchanan also presented his collection of official papers which included a large number of drawings done by Indian artists who had been employed by Hamilton during his Bihar Surveys.[72] These acquisitions marked the end of any purposeful acquisition of collections of Indian paintings by the India Office until the beginning of the twentieth century. Falk and Archer explain this lack of interest in Indian paintings in terms of the dominance of utilitarian and evangelical views of India, which saw its art as degraded, even obscene. What collecting was done for the India Office stressed the utility of books of reference and aids to language study, and increasingly from the middle of the nineteenth century, Indian handicrafts and texiles.

During the nineteenth century in England there were several important collections of paintings and at least one massive collection of Indian sculpture in private hands. In 1774, William Watson, a Company official, acquired a set of paintings during the Rohilla campaign, which in recent times has come to be known as *Manley Ragamala*, an album of illustrated musical modes. Robert Cran dates these as early seventeenth century. In 1815 Watson gave the album to his daughter, and wrote at the time that the album "gives you a perfect idea of the customs, manners and dress of the men and women in Bengal, Persia and most parts of the East Indies . . . also of their birds, trees and plants." He annotated the individual folios for his daughter.[73]

In a series of publications Mildred Archer has abundantly documented the patronage of the British, from the second half of the eighteenth century until the middle of the nineteenth century, of albums and sets of drawings and paintings by Indian artists illustrating the appearance, dress, customs, and occupations of the Indians. These sets seem to have been one of the major items which the British collected in India, either commissioning Indian artists or buying them in the open market.[74]

The people of India most accessible to the Europeans were their domestic servants. Most newcomers to India commented on the large number of servants which even a modest European household contained. Captain Thomas Williamson, author of the first British guide book for India, *The East India Vade Mecum*, London, 1810, explained the large number of servants was largely due to "the division of Indians into sects, called by us casts." Williamson lists 31 kinds of servants that a gentleman would need for his home and office, depending on his occupation and status. The servants as described by Williamson were divisible into an upper and lower category. The upper servants, *naukeron*, held positions of trust or supervision and would not be expected to do menial work. The lower order of servants, or *chaukeron*, had their own hierarchy and were divided into those largely doing inside work, waiting on the table, cooking, acting as the wine cooler, the huka bearer, and the furniture keepers. The outside servants included a gardener, the palankeen bearers, a syace, a dhobi, poens, and the watchman and door keeper.

The household in many respects became the model which the British created for Indian society. The specificity of duties was assumed to be based on the caste system in which a member of one caste could not or would not do the work assigned to another caste. Functional positions appeared to reflect the hierarchy of the caste system, with the confidential servants being drawn from the upper castes of Indian society. A Muslim of some status was employed as a teacher and scribe. The table waiters were generally Muslim who had less scruples about handling foreign food. The cooks were generally low caste, untouchables or Portugese, as it was generally believed that upper caste Hindus would not touch beef. The *Khansman*, the butler, was usually Brahman or a high status Muslim; in some wealthy households he might be Portugese or Anglo-Indian. Ayahs were usually low caste, tailors Muslim; gardeners, washermen, and water carriers came from castes usually associated with these occupations. Those working in the stables as grooms and who also would take care of dogs and other household pets, were generally untouchable Chamars. Each occupational speciality with its assumed caste base, lived separately, usually in huts in back of the great house where their families lived and where they prepared and ate their food.

Throughout much of the nineteenth century the representation of servants and their duties was a major subject matter of paintings and drawings which were organized in sets, done by British and Indian artists, and sold as souvenirs to be brought back as one of the icons of the exile in India. Along with the servants, the depiction of the occupations, castes, and the varied dress of the Indians became extremely popular in India and in Great Britain.[75]

Typically in the paintings and drawings of the castes, trades, and occupations of India there is a total decontextualization of the subject. They are drawn without any background, and with an individual and perhaps his wife depicted with the tools of his or her trade or the products or goods produced for consumption and use by Europeans and Indians. Other popular forms of art which British collected were paintings of buildings, sometimes on ivory, religious ceremonies, usually the more bizarre the better, such as a hook swinging or the dragging of temple carts, and holy men. There was a counterpart in clay of the depictions of the typical household servants and the Indian craftsmen.

Given the difficulties of shipping, and the generally low evaluation by the British of the aesthetic qualities of Indian sculpture, it would appear that few major collections of Indian sculpture were made during the late eighteenth and the nineteenth centuries. Partha Mitter has extensively discussed the collections which Charles Townly and Richard Payne Knight had made, both these collectors being interested in the significance of the works for their studies and interest in the relationship between the erotic and ancient religions.[76]

Perhaps the most interesting of the collections made was that of Charles Stuart, generally known as "Hindoo" Stuart, who was in India from 1777 until his death in 1830. Stuart is best known for his tomb in Park Street Cemetery in Calcutta, which is in the form of a small temple which was decorated with representations of Indian gods and two miniature carvings of "Indo-Aryan temples," and has a doorway which "originally belonged to an ancient Brahmanic temple."[77] At his death in 1830 the bulk of Stuart's collection was shipped to London, where it was sold by Christie's and bought by James Bridge, who in turn offered the collection for sale in 1872, when it was bought for a "song" by Sir Woolston Franks of the British Museum. In all, the collection contained 115 specimens.[78]

Some idea of how Stuart made his collection was discussed by James Prinsep, who was trying to translate the inscription on a stone slab which was in the Asiatic Society of Bengal's collection, and about whose origin little was known. The script appeared the same as one known to have come from Orissa. Lt. Kittoe was at the time in Bhubaneswar copying inscriptions on the temples there. He found himself "impeded and foiled by the Brahmans of the spot." When he enquired about their opposition or as Prinsep put it, "the cause of so unusual a want of courtesy," Kittoe was informed by the priests that "their images and relics were carried off by former antiquaries" and mentioned in particular a "late Colonel Sahib." On checking the records of acquisitions of the society, Prinsep found that General Stuart was the donor of "two slabs with inscriptions in Orissa." Prinsep hoped that the society would return the slabs to the temple from which they were cut.[79] The following year this had been done, but Kittoe was not greeted with the cordiality and good will he had expected that the return of the slabs would have elicited. Rather the priests presented him with "a long list of purloined idols and impetuously urged him to procure their return as he had done with the Inscriptions."[80]

We have seen how surveys and exploration, conceived by individuals and by the Company for the amassing of practical knowledge as part of the agency of rule, led to the formation of important collections. In addition, objects obtained through direct commission and the patronage of artists led to extensive assemblages of text and albums. Many objects of everyday use or produced for a luxury market in India could be bought in the market place. Bribery, extortion, and outright theft also played a role in the amassing of significant collections.

Perhaps what was seen in Great Britain, and by the British in India, as the most significant objects which eventually found their way into public repositories of valued objects were the result of warfare. Individual and state-managed looting were the source of what, for the first half of the nineteenth century, were the most valuable and popular objects brought back from India. Pride of place in the establishment of the popular interest of the British relationship to India were objects looted from Tipu Sultan's palace in 1899 at the fall of Seringapatam.[81] Included in this loot were Tipu's tiger, his helmet and cuirass, a golden tiger's head from his throne, a howdah, and one of his "royal carpets." These had been presented to the Court of the Directors and members of the royal family, and within a few years were to go on display in a room set aside as a museum in the Company's headquarters on Leadenhall Street.

There was a great interest in the prints and drawings of the events connected with the British victory at Seringapatam. General Sir David Baird's "Discovering the Body of Tipu," "The Death of Tipu," and the surrender of "Two of Tipu's Sons" all circulated widely.[82] There were shows, popular plays, ballads, and broadsides, all of which presented aspects of events: the defeat of Tipu and the triumph of British arms over the arch villain and embodiment of evil, Tipu the Tiger.[83]

Popular guidebooks and books about the architecture of London, published between 1820 and 1860, all included discussion of the East India House as well as the contents of its small museum. Admission was by ticket and the museum was only open a few days a week; a tip to the doorman would guarantee the visitor being able to see as much as possible. Although Fergusson recalled seeing the Amaravati marbles in the museum, none of the contemporary descriptions mentioned the sculpture. All mentioned Tipu's tiger and the other memorabilia of the fall of Seringapatam.[84]

The following list drawn up by Britton and Pugin in 1838 gives some idea of the miscellaneous quality of the Company's collection.

> The Javanese Tapir, a quadruped with a hide like that of the Hog, having a lengthened proboscis, and its hoofs divided into three parts; exceeding greatly in size the South American Tapir. This newly discovered animal is described in Horsfield's Researches in Java.

A collection of quadrupeds, chiefly of the Cat and Monkey tribes, from Java.

Collections of birds from Java, distinguished by the beauty of their plumage; of aquatic birds, from the same island; of birds from India, Siam, and Cochin China; and a small collection of birds from the Cape of Good Hope.

A Lion's skin brought from India, where this animal is so seldom seen, that doubts have been raised as to its existence in the Asiatic quarter of the globe.

A collection of Javanese insects, principally of the Butterfly kind.

A marine production, called the Cup of Neptune; curious corals, &c., from the vicinity of Singapore.

Beautiful models of Chinese scenery, consisting of rock-work, executed in hard wood, bronzed; temples of ivory, with human figures, birds, trees, &c., formed of silver, embossed, and mother of pearl.

Chinese drawings, one of which, representing a Chinese festival, is executed with more attention to perspective than the artists of China usually display.

A complete Chinese Printing Press.

The Foot-stool for the Throne of Tippoo Saib, formed of solid gold, in the shape of a tiger's head, with the eyes and teeth of crystal. A magnificent throne, to which this appertained, was constructed by order of Tippoo, soon after he succeeded to the sovereignty of Mysore. It was composed of massy gold, the seat raised about three feet from the ground, under a canopy supported by pillars of gold, and adorned with jewellery and pendant crystals of great size and beauty. This throne was broken up and sold piecemeal, for the benefit of the captors, to whom the produce was distributed as prize-money.

A musical Tiger, found in the palace of Tippoo, at Seringapatam. It is a kind of hand-organ, enclosed in the body of the tiger; the whole represents a man lying prostrate in the power of that animal, of which the roar, together with the groans of the victim, are heard.

The armour of Tippoo Saib, consisting of a corselet and helmets, made of quilted cotton covered with green silk; of a texture sufficiently firm to resist a blow of a sabre.

Bricks brought from Hills, on the banks of the Euphrates, supposed to be the site of ancient Babylon. They have inscriptions indented in what has been termed the *nail-headed*, or Persepolitan character, forming lines or columns; for it is a subject of dispute among the learned, whether these characters are to be read perpendicularly, like those of the Chinese, or longitudinally, like those of European nations. Some of these bricks seem to have been baked on a matting of rushes, the impression left by which is still visible on the underside; as is also some of the bituminous cement, by which they were apparently united.[85]

Each of the major British wars and victories in the first half of the nineteenth century was brought home in the form of relics and trophies to be displayed by the Company in its museum or by the Crown in its armories in the Tower: a cannon cast like a dragon from Rangoon, swords, shields, daggers and other weapons from the Maratha wars. Of a more peaceful nature were Robert Gill's magnificent drawings of the frescoes of the caves at Ajanta. Most significant were those trophies marking the final triumph of the British over their most stubborn but respected enemy, the Sikhs. The most impressive of these trophies were on display in the Company's museum in 1853: the golden throne of Ranjit Singh, the unifier of the Sikh nation; the Koh-i-noor diamond, which became one of the great jewels of the British crown. A spear and arms belonging to Guru Gobind Singh and thought by the governor-general "impolitic to allow any Sikh institution to obtain possession," went to the Tower. The weapons captured from the Sikhs and shipped to England were the embodiment of the martial traditions of the Sikhs; they all had "genealogies" and marked the state-building successes of Ranjit Singh. The British were anxious to obtain not only the Sikh symbols of secular power, but also a "true copy of the Gurunth or Sacred Book of the Sikhs," so that it might be translated into English.[86] The establishment of British hegemony over India was also a conquest of knowledge.

The end of the Third Mysore War in 1799 marked the establishment of the collecting of what were to become the popular relics of the British conquest of India. It ended with an event which had an even greater impact on the public consciousness, the "Mutiny." This war generated an enormous public interest, fueled by mass literacy and an illustrated press, who could define a host of heroes and villains: the "Pandeys," the rebellious and mysterious brahmans, who along with other militarized peasantry were the backbone of the Bengal army, who had traitorously murdered their officers and spilled the blood of innocent Christian women and children; the rebel leaders, a decrepit but nonetheless dangerous Mughal emperor, and the debauched half-Europeanized Maratha brahman, Nana Sahib. The heroes were staunch Christian avengers and martyrs like Nicholson, the men of action like General Neil and Major Hodson, the careful but effective generals, Outram and Havelock. There was even an Anglo-Indian hero, an employee of the Post and Telegraph Department, Kavinaugh, the first civilian to be awarded a Victoria Cross, and then there was Jenny, the daughter of a common soldier whose dream of the relief of Lucknow was to be memorialized by a highly successful poem by Tennyson, and in paintings, drawings, and ceramics.

Once again loot poured into England to be treasured as memorabilia of families, symbolizing the privation and the sense of triumph generated by the war. Eventually these objects or relics found their way into public repositories. Some objects in the National Army Museum's catalogue of "Memorabilia of the Mutiny" include a dagger belonging to Bahadur Shah II, shamshirs and tulwars surrendered by the king of Delhi to Major W. S. R. Hodson on 21 September 1857; a brass betel nut box owned by Nana Sahib, taken by Lt. Claude Auchinleck; a wooden spatula found in the massacre well at Cawnpore by Sgt. C. Brooks, 9th Lancers; a table made from a section of tree near which Major W. S. R. Hodson shot the Mughal princes and was fatally wounded; a porcelain bucket from the service of the king of Oudh; a fragment of a dinner plate from the service used by Sir Henry Lawrence at the siege of Lucknow; a silver-mounted brick from Lucknow; a kurta worn by Tantia Topee; a snuffbox containing a lock of Tantia Topee's hair; a silver ring taken from a dead sepoy; a child's shoe found in the massacre well at Cawnpore; and a manicure set found in the massacre well at Cawnpore. This last item is currently on display at the National Army Museum.

Let an Indian have the final say on this period of collecting. Rakhal Das Halder, a student in London in 1862, recorded his reactions to reviewing the collections at Fife House:

> It was painful to see the State chair of gold of late lion of the Punjab . . . with a mere picture upon it; shawls without babes; musical instruments without a Hindu player; jezails and swords without sipahis and sowars; and above all hookahs without the fume of fantastic shapes.[87]

FIVE

CLOTH, CLOTHES, AND COLONIALISM:

INDIA IN THE NINETEENTH CENTURY

I N 1959, Mr. G. S. Sagar, a Sikh, applied for a position as a bus conductor with Manchester Transport. His application was rejected because he insisted that he wanted to wear his turban rather than the uniform cap prescribed by the municipality for all its transport workers. Sagar argued that the wearing of the turban was an essential part of his religious beliefs. He didn't understand why, if thousands of Sikhs who had fought and died for the empire in the two World Wars could wear their turbans, he couldn't do so. The transport authorities argued that "if an exception to the rules of wearing the proper uniform were allowed there was no telling where the process would end. The uniform could only be maintained if there were no exceptions."[1]

At its most obvious level, this was a dispute about an employer's power to impose rules concerning employee's dress and appearance, and the employee's right to follow the injunctions of his religion. Early in the dispute, which was to last seven years, a distinction was made between such items of attire as the kilt of a Scotsman, which were expressions of national identities—a "national costume" that could be legally pre-scribed for workers—and those items of dress that were worn as the result of a religous injunction. The advocates of allowing the Sikhs to wear their turbans on the job said that to prevent them from doing so was an act of religious discrimination. The transport worker's union sup-ported management in the dispute, on the grounds that an individual worker could not set the terms of his own employment, which they saw as a matter of union-management negotiation.

At another level the dispute was about working-class whites' resent-ment of dark-skinned, exotically dressed strangers, whom they saw as "cheap" labor allowed into their country, to drive down wages and take pay packets out of the hands of honest English workingmen. The fact that many of these British workers preferred easier, cleaner, or higher-paying jobs did not lessen their xenophobic reactions. Similarly, some of the middle class saw the immigrants from the "new" commonwealth as a threat to an assumed homogeneity of British culture. The turban, the dark skin, and the sari of Indian and Pakistani women were simply out-ward manifestations of this threat.

In short, the dispute over the Sikh's turban can be seen as a symbolic displacement of economic, political, and cultural issues, rooted in two hundred years of tangled relationships between Indians and their British conquerors. In order to understand this conflict, I will explore the meaning of clothes for Indians and British in the nineteenth century; the establishment of the categorical separation between dark subjects and fair-skinned rulers; the search for representations of the inherent and necessary differences between rulers and ruled as constructed by the British; and the creation of a uniform of rebellion by the Indians in the twentieth century.

Turbans of Identity

The dispute over Mr. Sagar's turban also echoed the growing sense of loss of power being felt by the British as they rapidly divested themselves of the empire in Asia and Africa, and heard their former subjects demanding their independence and some form of equity with their former rulers. The whole social order at home also appeared to the middle and upper classes to be changing, with the revolution being acted out in terms of clothes. The youth of the under class was setting the styles for their elders and betters, and mocking many former emblems of high status by turning them into kitsch and fads for an increasingly assertive new generation.

There is an irony that a Sikh's turban should be involved in the final act of a long-playing drama in which the costumes of the British rulers and their Indian subjects played a crucial role. For the British in nineteenth-century India had played a major part in making the turban into a salient feature of Sikh self-identity.

Sikhism was a religious movement that grew out of syncretic tendencies in theology and worship among Hindus and Muslims in north India in the fifteenth century. Guru Nanak, its founder, whose writings and sayings were codified in a holy book called the *Granth Sahib*, established a line of successors as leaders and interpreters of his creed. Through much of the sixteenth and seventeenth centuries, the Sikhs faced increasing persecution from their political overlords, the Mughals, as much for their strategic location across the traditional invasion route of India in the Punjab as for their growing religious militancy.

This militancy was codified and restructured by the tenth and last in succession of the Gurus, Gobind Singh. He created a series of distinctive emblems for those Sikhs who rallied into a reformed community of the pure, the Khalsa, from among the wider population, which continued to follow many Hindu and Muslim customs. In a dramatic series of

events in 1699, Guru Gobind Singh chose five of his followers as founding members of this new brotherhood. Those selected had shown their
willingness to have their heads cut off as an act of devotion to their guru.

Guru Gobind Singh issued a call for large-scale participation in the
celebration of the New Year in 1699. Those Sikh males attending were
enjoined to appear with their hair and beards uncut. As the festivities
developed, there was no sign of the Guru, who was waiting in a tent,
until he suddenly appeared brandishing a sword, and called upon the
assembled Sikhs to volunteer to have their heads cut off as a sign of their
devotion. One volunteered and accompanied his Guru back to the tent.
A thud was heard and the Guru reappeared with a bloody sword. The
apparent sacrifice was repeated with four other volunteers, and then the
side of the tent was folded back to reveal the five still alive and the
severed heads of goats on the ground.

These five were declared the nucleus of the Khalsa. They went
through an initiation ritual in which they all drank from the same bowl,
symbolizing their equality, and then the chosen five initiated the Guru.
Next, they promulgated rules: Sikh males would wear their hair unshorn; they would abstain from using alcohol and tobacco, eating meat
butchered in the Muslim fashion, and having sexual intercourse with
Muslim women. Henceforth they would all bear the surname Singh. In
addition to unshorn hair (*kes*), they would wear a comb in their hair
(*kangha*), knee-length breeches (*kach*), and a steel bracelet on their right
wrist (*kara*), and they would carry a sword (*kirpan*).[2]

J. P. Oberoi has analyzed these symbols as well as an unexpressed
sixth one, the injunction against circumcision, as establishing the total
separation of the Sikhs from Hindus and Muslims. In addition he sees
them as two opposed triple sets: the unshorn hair, sword, and uncircum-
cised penis representing "amoral," even dangerous power; the comb,
breeches, and bracelet expressing constraint. In the totality of the two
sets, he sees an affirmation of the power and constraint inherent in hu-
manness.[3]

Note that this excursus on the formation of the Sikhs and their sym-
bology does not mention the turban as part of their distinctive costume
and appearance. Most scholars who have written about the history of the
Sikhs and their religion are silent on the question of when and how the
turban became part of the representational canon of the community.
M. A. Macauliffe, translator of and commentator on the sacred writings
of the Gurus, noted in a footnote, "Although the Guru [Gobind Singh]
allowed his Sikhs to adopt the dress of every country they inhabited, yet
they must not wear hats but turbans to confine their long hair which
they are strictly enjoined to preserve."[4] W. H. MacLeod notes that the
turban is the one post-eighteenth-century symbol added to the "Khalsa

code of discipline." The wearing of turbans, though lacking "formal sanction . . . during the nineteenth and twentieth centuries has been accorded an increasing importance in the endless quest for self identification."[5]

Early nineteenth-century representations by European and Indian artists of the "distinctive" headdress of the Sikhs showed two different types. One was a tightly wrapped turban of plain cloth, which was either thin enough or loose enough on the crown to accommodate the topknot of the Sikh's hair. The second type of turban worn by the Sikhs in the early nineteenth century was associated with rulership. This turban was elaborately wrapped and had a *jigha*, a plume with a jewel attached, and a *sairpaich*, a cluster of jewels in a gold or silver setting. These ornamental devices were symbols of royalty, popularized in India by the Mughals.

In the eighteenth century, Mughal political and military power declined. The Punjab went through a period of invasions and the emergence of contending Sikh polities, which were combined under the leadership of Ranjit Singh by the early nineteenth century into a powerful state. With the death of Ranjit Singh in 1839, the state came under increasing pressure from the East India Company, which in a series of wars finally conquered and annexed the former Sikh state in 1849.

Although the Sikh state was fragmenting, the Sikh armies proved formidable; despite their defeat by the East India Company, Sikhs were treated more as worthy adversaries than as a defeated nation. Those British who fought against the Sikhs were highly impressed by their martial qualities. Unlike many of their conquered subjects, who struck the British as superstitious and effeminate, the Sikhs were considered manly and brave. Their religion prohibited "idolatry, hypocrisy, caste exclusiveness . . . the immurement of women" and immolation of widows, and infanticide.[6] Captain R. W. Falcon, author of a handbook for British officers in the Indian army, described the Sikh as "manly in his warlike creed, in his love of sports and in being a true son of the soil; a buffalo, not quick in understanding, but brave, strong and true."[7] In short the Sikhs, like a few other groups in South Asia (the hill peoples of Nepal, the Gurkhas, and the Pathans of the Northwest Frontier) who came close to defeating the British, were to become perfect recruits for the Indian army.

Within a year of their defeat, Sikhs were being actively recruited for the East India Company's army, and the officers who had just fought the Sikhs "insisted on the Sikh recruits being *kesadhari*, from among the Khalsa Sikhs who were unshorn. Only those Sikhs who looked like Sikhs—wearing those badges of wildness, the beard and unshorn hair—were to be enrolled. It was also official policy to provide every means for the Sikhs to keep their "freedom from the bigoted prejudices of caste . . . and to preserve intact the distinctive characteristics of their race and peculiar conventions and social customs."[8]

The effectiveness of the British decision made in 1850 to raise Sikh units for their army was borne out in 1857–1858. The bulk of their native army in north India rebelled. The Sikhs enthusiastically and effectively participated in the defeat of their hated enemies, the remnants of the Mughals and their despised Hindu neighbors of the Ganges valley.

With the reorganization of the British Army in India after 1860, the British came to rely increasingly on the Punjabis in general and Sikhs in particular to man their army. The Punjab, with 8 percent of the population of India, provided half of their army in 1911. The Sikhs, who were 1 percent of the Indian population, accounted for 20 percent of the total number of Indians in the military service.[9]

By the late nineteenth century a standardized Sikh turban, as distinct from the turban of the Punjabi Muslims and Hindu Dogras, had emerged and had become the hallmark of the Sikhs in the army. This turban, large and neatly wrapped to cover the whole head and ears, became the visible badge of those the British had recruited. The Sikh turban and neatly trimmed beard were to stand until 1947 as the outward sign of those qualities for which they were recruited and trained: their wildness, controlled by the turban, and their fierceness, translated into dogged courage and stolid "buffalo"-like willingess to obey and follow their British officers.

During World War I, the British army replaced the great variety of headgear of both their own troops and their colonials with steel helmets, but by now "the Sikhs had come to associate their uniform *pagri* (turban) with their religion," and the argument that the turban as such was not prescribed by their religious code was to no avail.[10]

Thus, the current significance of the distinctive turban of the Sikhs was constructed out of the colonial context, in which British rulers sought to objectify qualities they thought appropriate to roles that various groups in India were to play. The British sought to maintain the conditions that, they believed, produced the warrior qualities of the Sikhs' religion. In any post-eighteenth-century European army a uniform, in which each individual is dressed like every other one of the same rank and unit, symbolizes the discipline and obedience required for that unit to act on command. A distinctive style of turban, worn only by Sikhs and serving in companies made up of Sikhs, was the crucial item of their uniform, which represented and helped constitute the obedience that the British expected of their loyal Indian followers.

Over time the military-style turban became general, although far from universal, among the Sikhs. The Sikh has now come "home" to the British Isles, but the turban no longer symbolizes loyalty to an old military code identified with their former rulers. Instead, the turban now plays a part in the Sikhs' effort to maintain their unique identity in the face of hostility and pressure to conform to "normal" or expected dress in mass society.

The struggle to maintain the very difference that had been encouraged by their past rulers now is seen as a form of obstinacy. The pressure to conform to the rules of dress for bus conductors has been followed by a long legal struggle over whether Sikhs could ignore the law in England that motorcycle drivers and passengers had to wear crash helmets. The battleground has more recently shifted to the question of whether a Sikh boy could be barred from a private school because he and his father "insisted on his wearing uncut hair and a turban above his blazer." This case was settled in 1983, when the House of Lords reversed a lower court, which had found that the headmaster had "unlawfully discriminated against the Sikh . . . by requiring him to remove his turban and cut his hair."[11]

The British as They Wished to Be Seen

While the British established themselves as the new rulers of India, they constructed a system of codes of conduct which constantly distanced them—physically, socially, and culturally—from their Indian subjects. From the founding of their first trading station in Surat in the early seventeenth century, the employees of the East India Company lived a quasi-cloistered life. Although dependent on the Mughal and his local official for protection, on the knowledge and skills of Indian merchants for their profits, and on Indian servants for their health and well being, they lived as a society of sojourners. In their dress and demeanor they constantly symbolized their separateness from their Indian superiors, equals, and inferiors. Paintings by Indians of Europeans in the seventeenth and eighteenth centuries emphasized the differences in costume, which apparently made little concession to the Indian environment culturally or physically. At home, in the office, hunting in the field, or when representing the majesty and authority of power, the British dressed in their own fashion.

The one exception to the cultural imperative of wearing European dress was among those whose careers were spent up-country as British representatives in Muslim royal courts, where it was usual for some of them to live openly with Indian mistresses and to acknowledge their Indian children. These semi-Mughalized Europeans, although wearing European clothes in their public functions, affected Muslim dress in the privacy of their homes. The wearing of Indian dress in public functions by employees of the Company was officially banned in 1830. The regulation was directed against Frederick John Shore, a judge in upper India who wore Indian clothes while sitting in his court. Shore was a persistent critic of the systematic degradation of Indians, particularly local notables, intelligentsia, and Indians employed in responsible jobs in the revenue and judicial services. He argued strenuously not just for better understanding of the natives, but also for their full employment in the governance of their own country.[12]

The practice of maintaining their Englishness in dealing with Indians goes back to the royal embassy sent by King James the First to negotiate a treaty to "procure commodities of saftie and profit" in the Mughal's realm in 1615. The English ambassador, Sir Thomas Roe, was instructed by his ruler "to be careful of the preservation of our honor and dignity, both as wee are soverign prince, and a professed Christian, as well in your speeches and presentation of our letters as in all other circumstances as far as it standeth with the customs of these Countries."[13] Roe was not comfortable in conforming to the proper behavior expected of an ambassador at an Indian court. The Mughal, Jahangir, despised merchants as inferior to warriors and rulers. Although amused by Roe, and personally polite and accommodating to his peculiarities, he was sceptical about an ambassador representing a powerful European who seemed so interested in trade. Roe's explicit concern with establishing the means to increase "the utility and profits" of the subjects of King James was not shared by Jahangir.

The English effort to obtain a trade treaty was based on their own ideas about trade, which involved defining certain cultural objects as commodities. Increasingly in the seventeenth and eighteenth centuries, the commodities they sought in India were a wide variety of textiles, to be shipped to England or traded in Southeast Asia for spices and other valued objects to be sent to England. A major problem arose because the Indians were not much interested in the manufactured goods that the British had available—woolens, metal goods, and various "curiosities." What the Indians wanted was silver, copper, and gold. Another problem arose because the British persisted in viewing textiles as practical or utilitarian objects, suitable for providing profit for the shareholders and officials of the Company. The textiles and clothes made by Indians did indeed have a market and a practical value, but there were many other significations involved in the production and use of these objects, which the British defined as commodities.

Roe and his small party, which included the Reverend Terry as his chaplain, began to realize that the clothes worn—and particularly the use of cloth and clothes as prestations in the Mughal's court—had meaning far beyond any "practical use." Jahangir did allow Roe to follow his own customs of bowing and removing his hat, rather than using the various forms of prostration that were the usual means of offering respect to the Mughal. Through the three years that he traveled with Jahangir, Roe and his followers always wore English dress, "made light and cool as possibly we could have them; his waiters in Red Taffata cloakes." Terry, the chaplain, always wore "a long black cassock."[14]

Roe had brought with him to the Mughal court a considerable number of gifts, among which was a bolt of scarlet cloth that was perhaps more appropriate for the natives of North America than a sophisticated Indian ruler. Roe substituted for the cloth his own sword and sash. This gift was greatly appreciated by Jahangir, who asked Roe to send his servant to tie it on properly and then began to stride up and down, drawing the sword and waving it about. Roe reported that on a number of occasions Jahangir and some of his nobles, wishing to honor Roe, wanted to present him with clothes, jewels, and turbans. Although Roe, in his account, does not explain why he tried to avoid receiving these gifts, I can infer that he probably understood their significance. This kind of gift was the means by which authoritative relations were established and would, in the eyes of the Indians, make Roe into a subordinate or companion of the Mughals. In order to understand why Jahangir was pleased with Roe's sword and sash and why Roe was leery of accepting clothes and jewels, I will now explore the constitution of authority in Mughal India.

Clothes and the Constitution of Authority

By the fifteenth century, the idea that the king was the maintainer of a temporal as well as a sacred order was shared by Muslims and Hindus in India.[15] Royal functions were centered on the idea of protection and the increase of the prosperity of the ruled. "If royalty did not exist," wrote Abu'l Fazl, the chronicler of Akbar's greatness, "the storm of strife would never subside, nor selfish ambition disappear. Mankind being under the burden of lawlessness and lust would sink into the pit of destruction, the world, this great market place would lose its prosperity and the whole earth become a barren waste."[16]

The Mughals, who had established suzerainty over northern India in the early sixteenth century, were a Turkic-speaking people from Central Asia who traced their descent to Ghengiz Khan and Tammerlane. They based their authority on a divine relationship with God. The *padshah* (emperor), wrote Abu'l Fazl, was "a light emanating from God."[17] In constituting their authority, the Mughals also drew upon their descent from Ghengiz Khan as a world conqueror. Under the Mongols, the Mughals

were a ruling family that was part of a particular clan (*ulus*), which produced the legitimate ruler, or khan. Therefore, the Mughals claimed
authority on a historical basis as descendents of the Ghengiz Khan.[18]

Under Ghengiz Khan and his immediate successors, "the power of the
tribe over its members . . . was apparently transferred bodily to the
Khan."[19] Some of this sense of the embodiment of authority in the person of the ruler, not just of the tribe but of the state, was built upon by
Akbar and his successors. In this they were expressing a widespread and
older theory of kingship, found in Central Asia, Persia, and India, in
which "the king stands for a system of rule of which he is the incarna-
tion, incorporating into his own body by means of symbolic acts, the
person of those who share his rule. They are regarded as being parts of
his body, and in their district or their sphere of activity they are the
King himself."[20]

This substantial nature of authority in the Indic world is crucial for
any understanding of the widespread significance of cloth and clothes, as
they are a medium through which substances can be transferred.
Clothes are not just body coverings and matters of adornment, nor can
they be understood only as metaphors of power and authority, nor as
symbols; in many contexts, clothes literally *are* authority. The constitution of authoritative relationships, of rulership, of hierarchy in India cannot be reduced to the sociological construction of leaders and followers,
patrons and clients, subordination and superordination alone. Authority
is literally part of the body of those who possess it. It can be transferred
from person to person through acts of incorporation, which not only
create followers or subordinates, but a body of companions of the ruler
who have shared some of his substance.

The most literal representation of the act of incorporation into the
body of the Mughal padshah was through the offering of *nazr* (gold
coins) by a subordinate of the ruler and the ruler's presentation of a
khilat (clothes, weapons, horses, and elephants). Philologically, *khilat*
can be traced in both Persian and Arabic to an Aramaic and Hebrew root
halaf, "to be passed on," which is central to the Arabic idea of *khilafat*,
the succession to the title of the head of the Muslim community. Nar-
rowly, in Arabic, *khilat* derives from the word for "a garment cast off."
By the sixteenth century in India, the term *khilat* came to involve the
idea that a king, as a special honor, would take off his robe and put it on
a subject. F. W. Buckler suggests that there is a special significance involved in this act, as robes worn by the king could transmit his authority.[21] Buckler goes on to state: "Robes of Honour are symbols of some
idea of continuity or succession," which "rests on a physical basis, depending on the contact of the body of the recipient with the body of the
donor through the medium of the clothing. Or to put it rather differ-

ently, the donor includes the recipient within his own person through the medium of the wardrobe."[22]

The sets of clothes through which the substance of authority was transmitted became known as khilats, glossed in English as "robes of honor," in French *cap à pied*, "head to feet." In Mughal India the khilats were divided into classes consisting of three, five, or seven pieces. A seven-piece khilat might include, among other things, a turban, a long coat with full skirt (*jamah*), a long gown (*ka'bah*), a close-fitting coat (*alkhaliq*), one or more cummerbunds (*kamrband*), trousers, a shirt, and a scarf. Along with the actual clothes, other articles were included.

The most powerful khilat was a robe or garment that the Mughal himself had worn, and on occasion he would literally take off a robe and place it on one of his subjects, as a particular honor. Next to such a robe, the garment of most significance was a turban and its associated ornaments.

All forms of salutations in Indian society relate to the head, hands, and feet. In Akbar's court there were three major forms of salutation which entailed manifest acts of obeisance; these were termed the *kornish*, *taslim*, and *sijda*. Abu'l Fazl states: "Kings in their wisdom have made regulations for the manner in which people are to show their obedience . . . His Majesty [Akbar] has commanded the palm of the right hand to be placed on the forehead and the head to be bent downwards. . . . This is called the kornish, and signified that the saluter has placed his head [which is the seat of the senses and mind] into the hand of humility, giving it to the royal assembly as a present and has made himself in obedience ready for any service that may be required of him."[23]

The taslim "consists in placing the back of the right hand on the ground, and then raising it gently till the person stands erect, when he puts the palm of his hand upon the crown of his head, which pleasing manner of saluting signifies that he is ready to give himself as an offering."[24]

The sijda, or complete prostration, was objected to by the orthodox Muslims in Akbar's court as it is one of the positions of prayer. Akbar therefore ordered that it be done only in private, but it appears to have been used in subsequent rulers' courts.[25]

Abu'l Fazl makes it clear that in the context of the court, the person offering the salute is offering himself as a sacrifice; his head is being offered to the Mughal. In warfare, this sacrifice was literal. In a famous painting, the Emperor Akbar (1542–1605) is shown receiving the heads of his enemies, some being held by his warriors or piled up at the feet of his elephant. His defeated foe wears neither a helmet nor a turban as, head lowered, he is brought before the victor.[26]

In the eighteenth and nineteenth centuries, an Indian would place his turban at the feet of his conqueror as a sign of complete surrender. This was also used in a metaphoric sense to ask a great favor of someone, indicating a willingness to become their slave. Nineteenth-century guide books written for Englishmen traveling to India warned their readers never to touch a Hindu's or a Muslim's turban, as this was considered a grave insult.

The Sind in western India, conquered by the British in the 1840s, was a region of Muslim chieftains among whom the turban meant sovereignty. E. B. Eastwick, a company official with an excellent knowledge of Persian and Sindhi, writes of the turban "descending," "succeeded to" and being "aimed at." The governor-general, Lord Ellenborough, in writing to General Napier, commented about the need to support a particular ruler and underlined the substantial nature of the turban: "I have little doubt, that once established in the possession of the turban . . . Ali Murad will be able to establish the more natural and reasonable line of succession to the turban, and clothe the measure with the firms of legality."[27]

For the Mughal rulers of India, the turban and its associated ornaments had the powerful and mystical qualities that crowns had in medieval Europe. The jewels attached to the turban included the kalghi, an aigrete of peacock or heron feathers with a jewel attached to it. This was only conferred on the highest nobles. The jigha consisted of a cluster of jewels set in gold with a feather. The sarpech and sarband were strings of jewels or filigree work of gold or silver, stitched onto the turban. There was also a string or diadem of pearls worn as a garland around the turban, the sirha. Kings in the medieval Hindu tradition were the controllers of the earth and its products, and in cosmographic terms jewels were the essence of the earth, its most pure and concentrated substance. Thus the cloth turban with its associated jewels brought together all the powers of the earth.

Akbar, the Mughal emperor, delighted in innovative patterns or designs of clothes and created a new vocabulary for talking about them. Like all rulers of the period, he had special warehouses and treasuries for the maintenance and storage of clothes, arms, and jewels. He also decreed changes in the basic design of some articles of clothes. According to Abu'l Fazl, the author of the *Ain-i Akbari*, a general description of Mughal rule during the period of Akbar, the emperor took an inordinate interest in every aspect of the production of cloth. There were imperial workshops in major cities of the empire which could "turn out many master pieces of workmanship: and the figures and patterns, knots and variety of fashion which now prevail astonish experienced travelers."[28] Akbar collected cloth from other Asian countries and Europe, as well as India.

Cloth and clothes received as presents, or commissioned or bought in the open market, were carefully kept and classified by the day of the week and the day in the month on which they arrived at court, as well as by price, color, and weight. There was a rank order of clothes and cloth: those received on the first day of the month of Farwardin "provided they be of good quality, have a higher rank assigned to them than pieces arriving on other days; and if pieces are equal in value, their precedence or otherwise, is determined by the character of the day of their entry; and if pieces are equal as far as the character of the day is concerned, they put the lighter stuff higher in rank; and if pieces have the same weight, they arrange them according to colour."[29] The author lists thirty-nine colors, most of which refer to the colors of fruits, flowers, and birds. Given the variety of colors and fabrics, the almost infinite variations of design motifs in the textiles, and the great variation possible by folding, cutting, and sewing into garments, one can imagine the possibilities for originality and uniqueness. Some sense of this creativity and great variation was demonstrated in the exhibition of Indian textiles organized by Mattiebelle Gittinger.[30]

Akbar, like his successor, lived in a world of textiles, clothes, and jewels, and created elaborate rules restricting the wearing of some emblems, jewels, and types of clothes to certain ranks in Mughal society. As the British in the nineteenth century steadily extended their control over their subjects and their allied princes, they ordered and simplified those emblems of sovereignty and began to act as the sovereign in India.

From Robes of Honor to Mantles of Subordination

The significations entailed in the receipt of khilats were not lost on the British from the days of Sir Thomas Roe's visit. In the second half of the eighteenth century, as the Company's military power grew, the British transformed themselves from merchants dependent on the good will and protection of Indian monarchs into rulers of a territorially based state. As part of this process, the British officials of the Company sought to be honored with Mughal titles and khilats. In Bengal, as the Company's leaders gradually began to act as Indian sovereigns, they in turn began to grant khilats to their Indian subordinates and to use their influence with the Mughal emperor to obtain titles for their allies and employees. In the early decades of the nineteenth century, a visit to Delhi and the Mughal emperor and ennoblement at his hands had become a kind of tourist attraction for high-status Europeans. Captain Mundy, who accompanied Lord Combermere, the commander-in-chief of the army in India, on an inspection tour through north India from 1827 to 1829, visited Delhi. The offering of *nazr* (gold coins) and receipt of khilat was on the itinerary. Mundy describes the enrobement, and his reaction to it:

> On receiving Lord Combermere's offering, the King placed a turban, similar to his own, upon his head, and his lordship was conducted, retiring with his face sedulously turned towards the throne, to an outer apartment, to be invested with a khillât, or dress of honour. In about five minutes he returned to the presence, attired in a spangled muslin robe and tunic; salaamed, and presented another nuzzar. The staff were then led across the quadrangle by the "grooms of robes" to the "green room," where a quarter of an hour was sufficiently disagreeably employed by us in arraying ourselves, with the material tastily bound round our cocked-hats. Never did I behold a group so ludicrous as we presented when our toilette was accomplished; we wanted nothing but a "Jack i' the Green" to qualify us for a Mayday exhibition of the most exaggerated order. In my gravest moments, the recollection of the scene provokes an irresistible fit of laughter. As soon as we had been decked out in this satisfactory guise, we were marched back again through the Lâl Purdar and crowds of spectators, and re-conducted to the Dewânee Khâs, where we again separately approached His Majesty to receive from him a tiara of gold and false stones, which he placed with his own hands upon our hats.[31]

The officials of the East India Company exchanged what they defined as "presents" with Indian rulers and some of their subjects, but changed the nature and signification of this act. Company officials could not accept "gifts" and when protocol required officials to accept a khilat, weapons, or jewels, they had to deposit them in the Company's *toshakhana* (treasury). These gifts were recycled, given in turn to some Indian ruler at a durbar or other official meeting when it was deemed appropriate for the Company to exchange gifts with Indians. According to the rule that the Company followed, and which they imposed not only on their own subjects but on the allied princes when presents were exchanged, it was prearranged that the value offered by each party must be equal. In short, prestation and counter-prestation had become a contractual exchange. The British were aware of the contradiction inherent in the practice in terms of Indian theories of prestation. In India a superior always gives more than he receives, yet as an "economic man," the nineteenth-century Englishman was not about to enhance his honor by giving more than he received.

The basis of British authority in India in the first half of the nineteenth century was ambiguous. In their own eyes they ruled by right of conquest. Yet their own monarch was not the monarch of India; the agency of rule was a chartered Company, supervised by Parliament. In the wake of the Great Revolt of 1857–1858, the Company was abolished, their queen was declared ruler of India, and India became part of the empire in constitutional terms. The Crown of Great Britain became the ultimate source of authority for British and Indians. As part of the signalizing of this new legal arrangement, an order of knighthood, "The Star of India," was established.[32]

The intentions of the queen and her advisors in establishing this new order were spelled out in its "Letter Patent and Constitution" published July 6, 1861:

> It hath been the custom of Princes to distinguish merit, virtue and loyalty by public marks of honour in order that eminent services may be acknowledged and to create in others a laudable emulation, and we being desirous of affording public and signal testimony of our regard by the institution of an order of knighthood, whereby our resolution to take upon ourselves the government of our territories in India.[33]

Initially the order was restricted to twenty-five members, British and Indian, the highest British officials of government and the most important of the Indian princes being invested with the mantle and insignia of the order. Four years after its establishment, the order was reorganized into the three ranked classes of Knight Grand Commander (KGCSI), Knight Commander (KCSI), and Companion (CSI), and the numbers who would be awarded the honor were greatly increased.

The light blue mantle of the order was lined in white silk and fully covered the body. It fastened with a white silk cord decorated with blue and silver tassels. On the left side of the robe, over the heart, was embroidered in gold thread the rays of the sun, and superimposed in diamonds was the motto, "Heaven's light our guide" and a star. The collar was a large necklace made of a gold chain with palm fronds and lotuses; in its center was an emblem of the Crown of Great Britain, from which hung a pendant with a portrait of the queen of England.

The mantle, insignia, collar, and pendant were distinctly European in their form and content. The recipients of the knighthood had to sign a pledge that the mantle and its attachments would be returned at the death of the recipient, as the knighthood was not hereditary. This provision offended most Indian recipients, as Indians of all statuses stored gifts and emblems of honor that they received for their posterity. The *toshakhana* (treasure room) of a prince was an archive of objects whose origin and receipt embodied his status and honor. They could be taken out on occasion to be worn, used, or displayed, but they would be held from generation to generation to mark the constitutive events in the history of the family or the state. Shawls, robes, clothes, and pieces of cloth received in ritual contexts embodied those contexts. Even a peasant family will have several trunks full of cloth, saris, dhotis, and piece goods that have been received at weddings or in other ritual contexts, which are seldom worn but are displayed and discussed on solemn occasions. In a very direct way, these objects constitute the relationships between individuals, families, and groups.

The nizam of Hyderabad, the most important allied prince of the British, objected strenuously, not to the honor the knighthood bestowed on him by the queen, but to the mantle and the jeweled insignia. The nizam through his prime minister, Salar Jang, pointed out to the viceroy that the "people of this country have a particular antipathy to wearing costumes different from their own." This, Salar Jang stated, was especially true of princes, "who have always been tenacious of the costume of their ancestors," and he pointed out that "the wearing of the robe of the new order, would probably be ridiculed by his people." If the robe were made out of velvet or silk, it would be in contravention of Muslim law. The nizam also raised an issue about the wearing of the pendant which had a portrait of the queen, as proper Muslims were "prohibited from wearing the likeness of any created being on their person."[34] The viceroy sternly informed the Resident at Hyderabad, who had forwarded the objections of the nizam and his prime minister, that the statutes and constitution of the Star of India were not to be questioned. The nizam had to accept the regalia as is, or refuse to accept the honor.

In 1861, the British in India had yet to develop a formal investiture ceremony for the induction of knights into the order. Hence when the patent and regalia reached the nizam, although he made proper reverence both to the patent and to the insignia, he did not put the mantle on, and the whole matter was quietly dropped. But by the end of the nineteenth century, the nizams as well as all other recipients of knighthood seemed pleased enough to wear the robe and associated insignia.

By 1869, at the time of the first visit of a member of the royal family, the Duke of Edinburgh, the pages wore a seventeenth-century cavalier costume. At the Imperial Assemblage of 1877, a full-dress version of Victorian "feudal" was utilized for the design motif of the ceremony at which Queen Victoria was made empress of India. From 1870 to World War I, the number of occasions at which Indians, depending on their status, roles, and regional origins, had to appear in their assigned costumes, increased enormously.

With the advent of the railroad, the viceroy and his suite, the governors, and other high officials and their retinues traveled more and more frequently. The central government and each of the major provinces had a cool-season and hot-season capital. The seasonal trips between these capitals provided occasions for an increasing number of meetings between the top rulers and princes, landlords, rich merchants, and an army of lower Indian officials. The monarch's birthday, jubilees, the crowning of Edward VII and George V king-emperors of India, all provided occasions for the displaying of empire at home and in India.

With the opening of the Suez Canal in 1869, the trip to and from India was cut from months to a matter of weeks, facilitating the flow of royalty and aristocrats visiting India, and of Indian princes visiting the Continent and England. Indians as part of their tours would be presented at Victoria's court, at Windsor or at her "cottage," Osbourne House on the Isle of Wight. Here she had a "darbar room" built and decorated for receiving the homage of her loyal Indian feudatories. Indians were required on such occasions to appear in their "traditional" Indian royal dress rather than Western clothes.[35]

"Orientalizing" India

The establishment of the Star of India and its investiture evoked in its intent and regalia British Victorian conceptions of a feudal past. It was part of the general process of enhancing the image of the monarchy and the aristocracy to symbolize a simpler past, in contrast to the rapid social, economic, and political change that characterized contemporary reality. This past was seen as the source of Britain's liberties, its legal system, and its natural order, which grew from an organic relationship between rulers and ruled. This was more than mere nostalgia for a past that might have never been. It was a powerful symbolic statement by the ruling classes (who themselves were not necessarily aristocratic) about order, deference, and hierarchy as the prerequisites for maintaining political and social stability during a period of economic and technological change.[36]

As Britain had a feudal past, so did India, particularly the India of the princes and the great mass of the Indian peasantry. The application of social evolutionary theories to India by a wide range of British officials and scholars yielded a crucial ruling paradigm: the Indian present was the European past.[37] This construction of a universal history enabled the British to control the Indian past, as they too had been feudal but were now advanced out of this stage. But since the British were still in a position through their own history to direct the future course for India, it made the British part of India in their role as rulers.

India was seen as being capable of being changed through British beneficence. They had created the conditions for the Indians' advance up the social evolutionary ladder by introducing the ideas of private property and modern education, the English language and its thought and literature, railroads, irrigation systems, modern sanitation and medicine, and authoritarian yet rational bureaucratic government, and the form of British justice. The British also knew the dangers of too rapid a move out of the feudal stage—the unleashing of disorder, dislocation, and potentially dangerous revolutionary forces that, if not controlled and checked, could lead to anarchy. To prevent this dangerous outcome, Indians had to be controlled, made to conform to the British conception of appropriate thought and action, for their own future good. India had a future, but its present had to be an "oriental" one to prevent a too rapid and hence disruptive entry into the modern world. What might be thought of as the orientalization of the clothes of British rule in India began, as did the westernization of clothing in the army.

During the Great Uprising, the British quickly shed their heavy, tight, redcoated uniforms. W. H. Russell, who was sent by the *Times* to report on the war, wrote in one of his letters:

I have often thought how astonished, and something more, the Horse-guards, or the authorities, or the clothing departments, or whatever or whoever it may be that is interested in the weighty matters of uniform, and decides on the breadth of cuffs, the size of lace, the nature of trowser-straps, and the cut of buttons, would be at the aspect of this British army in India! How good Sir George Brown, for instance, would stand aghast at the sight of these sunburnt "bashi-bazouks," who, from heel to head and upwards, set at defiance the sacred injunctions of her majesty's regulations! Except the highlanders . . . not a corps that I have seen sport a morsel of pink, or show a fragment of English scarlet. The highlanders wear eccentric shades of gray linen over their bonnets; the kilt is discarded. . . . Lord Cardigan, in his most sagacious moments, would never light on the fact that those dark-faced, bearded horsemen, clad in snowy white, with flagless lances glittering in the sun, are the war-hardened troopers of her majesty's 9th lancers; or that yonder gray tunicked cavaliers, with ill-defined head-dresses, belong to the Queen's bays. . . . Among the officers, individual taste and phantasy have full play. The infantry regiments, for the most part, are dressed in linen frocks, dyed carky or gray slate colour—slate-blue trowsers, and shakoes protected by puggeries, or linen covers, from the sun. . . . It is really wonderful what fedundity or invention in dress there is, after all, in the British mind when its talents can be properly developed. To begin with the headdress. The favourite wear is a helmet of varying shape, but of uniform ugliness. In a moment of inspiration some Calcutta hatter conceived, after a close study of the antique models, the great idea of reviving, for every-day use, the awe-inspiring head-piece of Pallas Athene; and that remarkably unbecoming affair . . . became the prototype of the Indian tope in which the wisest and greatest of mankind looks simply ridiculous and ludicrous. Whatever it might be in polished steel or burnished metal, the helmet is a decided failure in felt or wickerwork, or pith, as far as external effect is concerned. It is variously fabricated, with many varieties of interior ducts and passages leading to escape-holes for imaginary hot air in the front or top, and around it are twisted infinite colours and forms of turbans with fringed ends and laced fringes. When a peacock's feather, with the iris end displayed, is inserted in the hole in the top of the helmet, or is stuck in the puggery around it, the effect of the covering is much enhanced. . . . I have seen more than one pistol in one of the cummerbunds, or long sashes, which some of our officers wear round the stomach in the oriental fashion.[38]

With the reestablishment of social order in upper India, the army was reorganized. What had been the Bengal Army was in effect dissolved. European soldiers who had enlisted in the Company service were pensioned and/or repatriated to Great Britain, and henceforth all of the European troops serving in the Indian army would be from regular royal battalions, which were rotated through India. The British officers of the Indian army were now commissioned by the king and would be permanently assigned to units made up of Indians, who were recruited from "the martial races"; Sikhs, who accounted for 20 percent of the army in 1912; Punjabi Muslims (16 percent); Gurkhas (12 percent); Rajputs, mainly from Rajasthan (8 percent); Dogras and Garhwalis (7.5 percent); Pathans (8 percent); Jats (6 percent). The remaining soldiers in the army were made up of Marathas, Brahmans, Hindustani Muslims, and "other Hindus," of whom the only significant number were Telugus and Tamils.[39]

In addition to the "class composition" of the new army, its dress was transformed as well, for both Indian soldiers and British officers. Over the second half of the nineteenth century, the service uniform for Europeans and Indians was much the same—cotton khaki trousers and shirt, with a jacket added in cold weather. Indians were given "exotic" headgear: the Sikh turban as previously discussed, and each of the other major martial races had their distinctive turban in terms of wrapping and color. The Gurkhas began to be recruited after the Gurkha wars of 1814–1815 and took readily to European-style uniforms, which they have continued to wear in the British and Indian army to the present. Their distinctive headdress in the second half of the nineteenth century was the Kilmarnock cap, a visorless, brimless pillbox. For service in the Boxer Rebellion they were issued broad-brimmed felt hats, which they wore up to World War I in the Australian style with one side turned up. Subsequently they have worn it with the brim down and at a "jaunty angle." Their uniforms, with jacket and trousers, have been dark blue or green.

Vansittart, the author of the handbook on the Gurkhas for use by their officers, described them as having a strong aversion to wearing a turban, as they associate it with the plainsmen whom they "despise." Vansittart goes on to eulogize the Gurkhas "as delighting in all manly sports, shooting, fishing . . . and as bold, enduring, faithful, frank, independent and self reliant . . . they look up to and fraternise with the British whom they admire for their superior knowledge, strength and courage, and whom they imitate in dress and habits."[40] The Gurkhas had a "traditional" weapon, the kukri, a twenty-inch curved knife carried in the waistband which became their trademark.

It was in designing the dress uniforms for the officers and men that the British exercised their fantasy of what an "oriental" warrior should look like. As was common in the second half of the nineteenth century, the cavalry units got the most colorful and dramatic uniforms. As was noted, during the Mutiny the British began to add cummerbunds and pagris—linen covers wrapped around their wicker helmets or cloth caps and hats. A few British went all the way and began to wear full turbans, which were recognized as having some protective function. A full turban could be made up of thirty or forty feet of cloth and, when thickly wrapped over the whole head and down the ears, could protect the head from a glancing sabre blow. General Hearsey, who commanded a division of the Bengal army, came from a family which had long provided officers, and many British thought he had Indian "blood." After the Mutiny, Hearsey had his portrait painted in a long black oriental-style robe, wearing a richly brocaded cummerbund and holding a scimitar. Could he have been seeking to appropriate part of his enemies' powers through using their clothes?

By the end of the nineteenth century, the dress uniform of the British officers of the cavalry had become fully "orientalized"; it included a knee-length tunic in bright colors, breeches and high boots, and a fully wrapped colorful turban. The Indian non-commissioned officers and troopers were similarly attired for dress parades and the increasing number of ceremonial functions.

The change in uniform for both European and Indian emphasized a basic conceptual change. One of the results of the Mutiny was to rigidify the already considerable differences between Indians and British. The Indians, seen by the British in the first half of the nineteenth century as misguided children, had been revealed by their actions in 1857–1859 to be treacherous and unchangeable. Outwardly they might conform to the sahib's expectation, but they could never be trusted. At any time their deep-seated, irrational superstitions could break forth in violence and overturn all the painful efforts of the conquerors to lead them in proper directions. Policies based on an assumption of change were proven wrong, so what was required was a strong hand capable of smashing any "sedition" or disloyalty, combined with an acceptance of Indians. Henceforth, the British should rule in an "oriental manner," with strength and with the expectation of instant obedience.

For this reason, Indians more than ever should look like Indians; those the British most depended on to provide the strength to keep India, the soldiers, should appear as the British idea of what Mughal troopers looked like, with their officers dressed as Mughal grandees. Another characteristic believed to be quintessentially Indian or oriental was a love of show, of pageantry, of occasions to dress up in beautiful or gaudy clothes. Indians, it was believed, were susceptible to show and drama, and hence more occasions were found where rulers and subjects could play their appointed parts and could act their "traditions" through costume. Hence the insistence that the chiefs and their retinues should always appear in their most colorful (if outmoded) clothes. The first major demonstration of this new ruling paradigm was during the visit of the Prince of Wales to India in 1876.

The prince and his large suite traveled widely throughout India, arriving in Bombay, then proceeding to Ceylon and Madras, and reaching Calcutta in November of 1876. There he was treated to a month-long round of entertainments, balls, and levees, culminating in a large investiture ceremony for the Star of India. The trip was well reported in England, with correspondents from the local newspapers. *The Graphic* and the *Illustrated London Weekly* sent artists who recorded all the events for the home audience. In their drawings, the artists dwelt upon the exotic quality of Indian life and dress, such as the "wild" Naga tribesmen and women brought down to Calcutta to entertain the prince and British high society with their barbarous dances. The prince was also treated to a nautch—a dance by young women which was a popular entertainment for eighteenth-century nabobs. The dancers' beautiful and colorful dresses and their sensuous movements were anything but Victorian.

At center stage throughout the Prince of Wales' visit were the princes of India, in all their splendor. Neither the pen of the journalists nor the black-and-white line drawings of the artists could adequately capture the variety and color of the clothes, nor the extraordinary display of precious stones and jewelry with which the figures of the Indian rulers were decked. The intent of the whole visit was to inspire the princes' loyalty by the presence of the eldest son of their English queen, and to affirm their central role in the maintenance of the empire.

Everywhere he went, the Prince of Wales was showered with valuable gifts by his mother's loyal Indian feudatories. Princes vied to outdo their competitors with the value, ingenuity, and brilliance of the jewels, paintings, antique weapons, live animals, richly embroidered brocades, and other art works which they presented to him. What he collected in six months of touring in India literally filled the large converted troop ship, the *Serapis*. When he returned, his trophies and gifts went on traveling exhibition throughout England and eventually wound up in a quasi museum in London at the Lambeth Palace. In return for their gifts, the Prince of Wales presented the princes with copies of Max Müller's English translation of the *Rig-Veda*.

It was not only the princes themselves who enthralled the prince and his suite as they traveled, but also their exotic retainers, dressed in a dazzling variety of costumes. The editors of *The Graphic* pulled out all stops in trying to describe for their readers the impression that these "military fossils" made on the Europeans.

> One of the chief features of the Maharajah of Cashmere's reception of the Prince of Wales was the wonderfully heterogeneous character of the troops who lined the route from the river to the Palace. Never on record has such a miscellaneous army been collected together. The troops wore uniforms of all countries and all ages, and carried as many different weapons, ranging from chain armour and Saracenic javelins to the scarlet uniforms and muskets of British soldiers half a century ago, the 12th and the 19th centuries being thus, as our artist remarks, face to face. There were troops in veritable native costume, turbaned, and carrying blunderbusses or flint-and-steel muskets; next to them would be a red-coated company, with white, blue, or black knickerbockers, and striped worsted stockings; then would come a detachment in chain-mail and breastplates, and steel caps with high tufts; while others again wore brass helmets, and were clad in brass breast and back-plates, not unlike our own Household Cavalry. One corporal particularly attracted our artist's attention, being clad in a new tunic of cloth, on which the mark "superfine" had been left, a badge of distinction of which the wearer appeared highly proud. He bore an old trigger gun, with a bayonet with a broad-leaved blade. Notwithstanding the semi-European clothing and armament of many of the troops, however, very little of European discipline, or drill, apparently existed, and our sketch of "Charge!" will give an idea of the helter-skelter ruck—so characteristic of Eastern warfare—with which a squadron of cavalry obeyed the word of command. Our artist writes: "This regiment wore a green uniform with red facings—some were shod and others barefoot—their trousers were reefed up to their knees, while their sleeves were exceedingly lengthy. As for the horses, they had ropes for bridles, and in appearance were veritable descendants of Rozinants.[41]

Through the first half of the nineteenth century, the British seemed to eschew competing with the splendors of Indian royal clothes. Unlike their eighteenth-century counterparts who wore vividly colored silks and satins, they wore fairly informal coats, dark or muted in color, straight and at times baggy trousers, and plain shirtwaists and vests. Until the middle of the nineteenth century, when the *sola topi* (pith helmet) became ubiquitous, their headgear was a beaver stovepipe hat or a cap. The white ruling elite must have appeared dowdy in comparison with their Indian underlings, who dressed in a version of Mughal court dress while carrying out their official functions. The British appeared to have given up the sartorial struggle of trying to outdress the pageant of oriental splendor they sought to control.

It was Queen Victoria herself who suggested that the civil servants in India should have an official dress uniform, as did their counterparts in the Colonial Service. The administration of India was completely separate from the ruling of the other colonies, one being run through the India Office and the other through the Colonial Office. Although the question of a special uniform was raised several times after the queen expressed interest, the Council of India decided that prescribing a dress uniform would be an undue expense for their officials.[42]

Lord Lytton, viceroy from 1876 to 1880 and a great believer in the power of ceremony and display as an integral part of ruling India, complained to his queen that "official functions" in India looked like "fancy dress balls," because there was no check on the "sartorial fancies of the civil service."[43] Although no uniform was prescribed for the Indian Civil Service until the early twentieth century, "some civil officers had provided themselves with one which was similar . . . to the levee dress of the 3rd and 5th class civil servants at home and in the colonies."[44] The only civilians allowed a "dress uniform" by regulations were those who had "distinct duties of a political kind to perform, and who are thereby brought into frequent and direct personal intercourse with native princes." This uniform included a blue coat with gold embroidery, a black velvet lining, collar and cuffs, blue cloth trousers with gold and lace two inches wide, a beaver cocked hat with black silk cockade and ostrich feathers, and a sword.[45]

The Gaekwar and the King

An incident occurred during the imperial darbar of 1911 that illustrates the official British concern with conformity of dress and manners expected of the Indian princes. In 1911, King George V and his queen traveled to India for his formal crowning as the king-emperor of India. This was to be the only time that a reigning monarch of Great Britain was to visit India before Independence. All three imperial darbars took place at the same site. In the first two, the structure marking the ritual center was a dais on which the viceroy proclaimed the new titles of the emperor. In 1911 the focal point of the event was a large platform, covered by velvet awnings and drapery and dubbed the "homage pavilion," on which the king and his princess sat on thrones. In previous darbars, the Indian royalty and nobles had been more or less passive bystanders; this time, it was decided that the leading princes would individually offer "homage" as an expression of fealty and respect to their imperial majesties.

The Gaekwar of Baroda was highly westernized, and generally considered by the British to be a "progressive" ruler, but too friendly with a number of prominent Indian nationalists. Baroda was ranked second behind Hyderabad in the official order of precedence at the imperial darbar established by the Government of India for Indian states. Therefore, the gaekwar was to follow the nizam in offering homage. The day before the actual ceremony a rehearsal was held to instruct the princes in the proper form of offering homage to the king-emperor and his consort. They were told to walk up the steps of the platform, bow low before each of their majesties, and then walk backwards down the steps in such a fashion as never to show their back to the royal couple. The Gaekwar of Baroda was unable to attend the rehearsal and sent his brother to take notes for him.

On the day of the offering of homage, the gaekwar was dressed in a plain white knee-length jacket and his "traditional" red turban. He wore white European trousers and carried an English-style walking stick. He did not wear, as was expected, the sash of the Order of the Star of India. The gaekwar approached the king, bowed once, omitting any obeisance to the princess, took several steps backward, then turned and walked down the steps swinging his cane. It appears that at the time nothing was said about his behavior; subsequently however, led by the *Times* reporter, his behavior was interpreted as seditious. A major row ensued in the English-language press of India as well as in England itself over what was defined as a studied, purposeful, and seditious insult. The storm was revived three weeks after the event, when the newsreels taken at the darbar reached England. The *Illustrated London News* of January 29 reproduced a page of sequential stills from the film showing "very clearly the way in which the Gaekwar of Baroda, carrying a stick, entered the Presence, bowed curtly, and walked off with his back to the King-Emperor."[46] In addition to the pictures of the gaekwar they printed pictures of two other ruling chiefs paying homage with deep bows of reverence. The gaekwar and members of his court protested that, for personal reasons, the gaekwar was distressed on the day of the ritual, was confused as to what was proper behavior, and intended no insult or lack of manners by what had happened.[47]

The intentions of the gaekwar are less relevant than his failure to maintain the dress code expected of Indian princes. The most seditious touch of all would seem to have been the gaekwar's use of a walking stick, an accouterment of the white sahibs, military and civilian, which marked the insouciance they displayed in the presence of the Indian masses. It was also used on occasion to thrash Indians whose actions, manners, or appearance irritated them.

In India, the military "orientalized" to overawe the Indian princes and the heathen masses; at home, the ruling classes archaized their ceremonial dress to overawe the new middle classes and the potentially dangerous lower orders of society. From the middle of the nineteenth century, the British at home increasingly invented or reinvented civic rituals at all levels of the polity. These rituals called for the creation of costumes, regalia, and accouterments to mark them as special and hallowed by tradition. They were designed to evoke in participants and audience, from the lord mayors of small cities to wealthy merchants and bankers in London, to the royal family, to union officials, a collective conception of the past.[48] The use of costumes and accouterments developed for such civic rituals were transported to India by the British to hierarchize the grandeur of their Indian princes. As a writer in the *Illustrated London News*, summing up what for him was the success of the imperial darbar of 1911, explained:

> Despite the oft-repeated statement that this age is a very drab one sartorially so far as the West is concerned, there are various occasions on which Europe is able to show the Orient that it, too, can display itself in brilliant plumage. Such instances as the Coronation of King George and Queen Mary and that of King Edward VII and Queen Alexandra jump to the mind at once: and to these memories of glittering kaleidoscopic state pageantry must now be added those of the Great Durbar held so recently at Delhi. There Europeans vied with Asiatics with excellent effect.[49]

Indians in Everyday Clothes

One of the first impressions formed by British travelers to India in the nineteenth century was of the nakedness of most of the Indians whom they encountered on their arrival. Most British travelers to India from the eighteenth century to the early nineteenth century arrived either in Madras or at Diamond Harbour, down river from Calcutta. Madras was an open roadstead where British passengers had to disembark from their ships into open row boats manned by Indian boatmen. At Diamond Harbour many travelers transferred to barges or small sailing boats for the remainder of the trip to Calcutta. The boatman was usually the first Indian they were able to observe closely. James Johnson, a surgeon in the Royal Navy who was in India in the late eighteenth century, records his impressions of the dress of the Bengali boatmen (*dandi*):

> The habilment of the Bengal *dandy*, or waterman who rows or drags our *budjrow* (barge), up the Ganges, consists in a small narrow piece of cloth (*doty*), passed between the thighs, and fastened before and behind to a piece of stout packthread, that encircles the waist. In this dress, or undress, corresponding pretty nearly to the figleaf of our great progenitor, he exposes his skin to the action of the tropical sun, a deluge of rain, or a piercing northwester, with equal indifference![50]

British women newly arrived in India recorded their shock not only at the seminakedness of lower-status Indian household servants, who seemed constantly underfoot, dusting, sweeping, lounging about, or playing with the *babalog* (white children), but also at their free access to the bedrooms of the memsahibs as if they were non-males. The traveler or sojourner in India quickly adjusted to the near nakedness of the Indian males, which after a while did not shock British sensibilities "owing to the dark colour of the skin, which as it is unusual to European eyes has the effect of dress."[51] They then began to discern great variation, based on region, caste, sect, and wealth, in Indian dress.

Indian Hindu male dress consists of three large pieces of cloth. One, the dhoti, is wrapped and folded in various ways, and covers the lower half of the body. A second piece, worn in cooler weather, is a cotton shawl, or chadar. The third piece, a long, narrow strip of cloth which is wrapped around the head, is the turban or pagri. The usual textile for these cloths was cotton, but on occasion silk would be worn. There is, however, enormous variation in how parts of the dhoti are tucked into the waist and in the length of draping. Such details frequently indicate the occupation or status of the wearer. Most Hindu dhotis were white and without seams. Even Hindus whose work required them to wear Muslim-style stitched clothes, and later European jackets or coats of various kinds, would change into a dhoti when arriving home.

The basic difference between Hindu and Muslim clothes was that Muslim clothes were tailored, which involved the cutting and sewing of cloth, but Hindu clothes were of uncut pieces, formed into garments by folding, tucking, and draping. Although it was frequently asserted that in ritual and domestic contexts in the nineteenth century, uncut and unsewn clothing was invariably worn, I have found no adequate explanation of this injunction to use only uncut cloth when performing puja worship. This is certainly a common habit today among more orthodox

Hindu males, who will bathe and then put on a fresh dhoti; on most auspicious ritual occasions such a dhoti will be of silk.

My speculation is that the use of unsewn cloth or a dhoti for males performing puja, or the use of sets of specified cloth and clothes as prestations, reflects an underlying concept of the necessity of completeness, or unpenetratedness, of totality, which is congruent with Hindu ideas of cosmogony. Parallel to the male wearing only an unsewn garment during puja were women who, by the late nineteenth century, had taken to wearing a choli, a sewn blouse, or a petticoat, which they removed while cooking food. Cooking had to be done in a specially designated and ritually cleansed area of the house.

N. C. Chaudhuri has described how males who worked in Mughal courts or in British offices would wear Muslim dress, but followed the rule that such garments were "worn for work only, and never in personal life. . . . Hindus who put on Muslim costume for public appearance scrupulously put them off when going into the inner house, and for religious observances, and they would never dream of wearing anything but orthodox Hindu clothes." The mansions of wealthy Calcutta Hindus in the late nineteenth century frequently had a western-style dressing room, complete with a wardrobe made in England, adjacent to the master's bedroom in the outer apartment of the house. There the master would change into Hindu clothes before entering the inner apartment and courtyard, the province of the women and the deities of the house.[52]

The exception to the rule of eschewing sewn clothing at home in pre-nineteenth-century India was in the Punjab and Rajasthan. The Rajputs appear to have taken to wearing a *jama* (sewn coat) before the advent of the Mughals.[53] What was conventionally thought of as Mughal court dress adapted major elements of Rajput dress during the time of Akbar.[54] It was also during this period that marking features were established to differentiate Hindu from Muslim attire, even when they were wearing the same type of coat (a jama or angarakha). The jama has ties that fix the flap of the upper half of the garment under the armpit and across the chest; Muslims wear their jama tied to the right, Hindus to the left. The jama became reduced to a shirt-like garment for cold weather among peasants of upper India in the nineteenth and twentieth centuries, but the custom of tieing continued to follow the old pattern of left for Hindus, right for Muslims.[55]

The Mughal rulers prescribed a form of their own dress for Hindus associated with them or employed in their offices and as officials. However, the British tried to have Hindus who worked for them—whether as domestic servants or as clerks, writers, and revenue and judicial officials—continue to wear the Mughal-style dress appropriate to their functions. Writing about British attitudes toward Indians wearing European clothes, N. C. Chaudhuri trenchantly sums up the situation: "They, the British, were violently repelled by English in our mouths and even more violently by English clothes on our backs."[56]

By the mid-nineteenth century, increasing numbers of urban Indians, particularly in Calcutta and Bombay, began to wear articles of European clothing. In Bombay the lead was taken by the Parsis, a group descended from the Zoroastrians, who had fled from Persia when the Islamic rulers began to persecute them for maintaining their religion. The Parsis settled in coastal areas of Gujarat, and by the eighteenth century were an important component of the population of Bombay, as carpenters, builders, and boat builders. By the early nineteenth century, some had become successful merchants, bankers, and European-style businessmen. Although they maintained a distinctive style of dress, particularly in the caps they wore, trousers, shoes, and an adaptation of a long English frock coat became new elements of their distinctive costume.

By the 1880s many successful, wealthy Indians and Western-educated Indian males had taken to wearing European clothes in public. Even those who normally wore a complete Western outfit, however, did not take to Western headgear. Many Indians continued to wear a turban with European clothes, particularly in the cold season. They also took to wearing a great variety of caps, from military forage caps to a wide range of brimless skull caps. The one type of hat that Indians did not wear was the pith helmet.

By the eighteenth century, the Europeans were aware of rules governing where Indians could wear footcoverings, and before whom they could appear in slippers. During a visit in 1804 to the peshwa in Poona, the head of the Maratha Confederacy, Lord Valentia, who was touring India collecting botanical specimens, observed the expected behavior. Accompanied by the long-time British Resident Colonel Close and his retinue, he entered the courtyard of the palace in a palanquin, but from there had to continue on foot. He entered the darbar room, and before stepping on the white cloth covering of the floor, took off his slippers. Lord Valentia was met by the peshwa's *dewan* (prime minister), and after a few minutes the peshwa entered and remained standing by his throne (*gaddi*, literally a cushion). Valentia approached, flanked by the dewan and the Resident, and was lightly embraced by the peshwa. Then, after the peshwa seated himself, Valentia had to sit on the floor crosslegged as "we had no chairs or cushions, and were not permitted to put out our feet, as showing the sole of the foot is considered disrespectful."[57] After formal conversation, done through an interpreter who spoke only to the dewan, who in turn spoke to the peshwa, Valentia was invited to have a private conversation with the peshwa in a small room adjacent to the darbar. Here, seated on a small "Turkey" rug next to the peshwa, they spoke more informally for over an hour before returning to the darbar room for dismissal. Valentia recorded, "I was extremely tired with my position, that it was with some difficulty that I could rise, and for a few minutes was obliged to rest against the wall."[58]

In portraits, successful and rich Europeans in India frequently are portrayed in their offices with several of their Indian employees or associates. The crucial Indians for the Europeans were their banians, a title minimally translated as "cash keeper." These were men who ran both official and commercial activities of the British. They secured credit, dealt with most Indians on the sahibs' behalf, kept their books, and were their factotums in all their public dealings. Another employee of high status was the munshi, inadequately described as a "scribe." The munshis frequently were highly educated Muslims who acted in the initial phases of a European's career as his teacher of Persian and Urdu, and later as a confidential secretary responsible for his correspondence with Indian officials and rulers. In eighteenth-century paintings, the munshi and banian have their slippers on while the bearer or hukkah bardar is barefoot. This is obviously a concession on the part of the European to the high status of these employees. Captain Thomas Williamson spent upwards of twenty years in India in the 1780s and 1790s. His *East India Vade Mecum* (1810), the first guidebook for Europeans to provide detailed instructions on managing a household and observing proper manners, observed that:

> A Banian invariably rides in his palanquin attended by several underlings. . . . He, to a certain degree, rules the office, entering it generally with little ceremony, making a slight obeisance, and never divesting himself of his slippers: a privilege which, in the eyes of the natives, at once places him on a footing of equality with his employer.[59]

In the 1830s F. J. Shore, a judge in upper India, complained that "natives of rank" walk into the rooms of Englishmen with their shoes on. He attributed this practice to a combination of the bad manners of the natives of Calcutta "who are of an inferior order" and the ignorance and carelessness of Europeans who do not know eastern etiquette.[60] Shore, who was highly critical of his countrymen's lack of knowledge and their disdain for the people of India, explained to his European readers they should not allow Indians in their presence with shoes. If Indians did so, the sahib should explain to them that:

> "Nations have different customs; ours is to uncover the head—yours to uncover the feet, as a token of respect. You would not presume to walk into the sitting-room of another native with your shoes on; why then do you

treat me with a disrespect which you would not show to one of your own countrymen? I am not prejudiced, and it is quite immaterial to me which practice you choose to adopt. You can either take off your shoes or your turban, but I must insist on one or the other mark of civility if you wish me to receive your visits." This is unanswerable by the native; and those English who have acted in this manner, have been decidedly more respected by the people.[61]

By 1854, so many Indians in Bengal, particularly in Calcutta, had taken to wearing European shoes and stockings that the Governor-General in Council passed a resolution allowing native gentlemen "on official and semi-official occasions . . . to appear in the presence of the servants of the British government" wearing European boots or shoes.[62] Twenty years later, the rule was made general throughout India and now included government courts, as the practice of wearing European dress had spread up-country, among "educated native gentlemen accustomed to European habits." The rule was to apply only to the public parts of courts, and not the chambers of the judge. His rooms were "private" and hence he could there enforce whatever rules he wished.

There were several issues lurking beneath the seemingly trivial question of which Indians of what status could wear what kinds of shoes, and where. Indian Christians always were allowed to wear their shoes wherever Europeans would normally wear their shoes. Europeans had long objected to removing their shoes when entering an Indian temple or when appearing in the darbar of an Indian ruler. The British construction of the rules governing the wearing or non-wearing of shoes was that Europeans did not have to conform to Indian custom, but Indians had to conform to European ideas of what was proper Indian behavior. The Europeans could also decide when an Indian practice had changed sufficiently to allow their subjects to follow new rules. The "victory" of the Bengalis, in getting rules regarding the wearing of shoes changed, encouraged some of them to try to have changed the rule that they must wear turbans while they were in government offices.

A group of Bengali officials in the 1870s petitioned the lieutenant-governor of Bengal to allow them "to adopt the European custom of uncovering the head in token of respect in durbars and courts of justice, and on all other official occasions and places."[63] The petitioners pointed out that the "wearing of the pagri [turban] is at present not a national custom of the Bengalis." Many Bengalis, they wrote, think the pagri an unreasonable headdress, as "it does not act as sufficient protection from the glare and heat of the sun," and is inappropriate to "active occupations." As a result of the decline in the use of the pagri, they claimed that Indians who work in government offices are forced to keep two headdresses: A pagri, which they carry in boxes or store in their offices, and a "light cap" which they actually wear. When a European superior approaches them while they are working in the office, they remove their caps and put on the pagri.

The Indians suggested a simple solution to the question: "We think that the best course is to wear caps and to uncover the head as token of respect." They pointed out that this would not prevent those Indians who continued to wear pagris from doing so, but those who by inference were more progressive in their dress and manners should not be forced to continue a custom they thought old-fashioned. In making their request, the petitioners felt they were acting in concert with the rulings about shoes, as that question was settled by the acceptance of the fact that Indians could wear shoes while the rest of their dress was "oriental," and did not require Indians to adopt fully European dress. Hence, substituting the wearing of a cap indoors rather than going bareheaded in the European fashion could seem appropriate. To continue to be forced to wear a pagri in the presence of Europeans rather than wearing brimless caps could act "as a cause of moral depression on the people."

The lieutenant-governor was strongly opposed to the suggested innovation. He did not think the petitioners represented "even the middle class of the natives of Bengal." It was proper for native gentlemen to wear whatever they wanted in private life, he wrote, but the use of the cap "was a very slovenly and unbecoming style of dress for public occasions." The lieutenant-governor declared that "no European of respectability would appear in such caps." They were not "western" nor were they "oriental," and hence by application they were some kind of bastard concoction, which furthered a tendency he abhorred toward laxity in dress and manners—and dress and manners were the means by which Indians showed proper respect in the office and on public occasions. Sir Ashley Eden then went on to lecture those Indians seeking to change current dress codes:

> If any change in the rules is to be made it should not in the Lieutenant-Governor's opinion, take the shape of further relaxation of existing customs. Indeed, the Lieutenant-Governor thinks that the chief change required, is that some of the Native gentlemen, especially native officials, who attend levees and durbars should pay greater attention than heretofore to their customs, and should in this way imitate the European custom of showing respect by not appearing on such occasions in the ordinary clothes in which they have just left their desks or court-houses. The new prevailing laxity in this matter may possibly have some bearing on the want of cordiality in the relations between Europeans and Natives, of which such frequent complaint is made by those who remember a different state of things. Attention to

costume was a form of respect in which the forefathers of the present generation were never deficient. In giving up the customs of appearing with the
head covered on public occasions, Native gentlemen are adopting neither
the customs of the West nor of the East, and the movement is one which
the Lieutenant-Governor deprecates and which he is certainly in no way
prepared to encourage.[64]

Indian Women's Dress and European Conceptions of Modesty

In the iconography of colonial India, the two most enduring representations of Indians are of "naked fakirs" and of graceful sari-clad women,
carrying water pots on their heads as they return from the village well.
Nineteenth-century British males, whose female counterparts at home
and in India went to great lengths to obscure or rearrange the natural
shape and outline of their bodies from the neck down, were obviously
highly admiring of the seemingly unfettered Indian women whom they
saw on the streets, or on the paths and in the fields of rural India.

Major Royal Sherer, who was posted to Madras in the early 1820s,
recorded his impression of "native women of a common class" carrying
water back to their houses with "erect carriage and admirable walk."
Their "simple dress" consisted of "one piece of cloth wrapped twice
around their loins in its breadth, and passing in its length over the
bosum is either disposed mantle-like to cover the head, or thrown
gracefully across the left shoulder. . . . Their shining hair rolled up into
a knot at the back of the head."[65]

Edward Balfour, author of the *Cyclopedia of India*, was even franker
in his enjoyment of the gait, appearance, and in his eyes the sensuality
of Indian women and their dress. For his mid-Victorian readers, he
painted a vibrant and exciting picture of a street scene in Bombay as it
appeared on the occasion of a festival: "The large and almost bovine
Banyan and Bhattia women roll heavily along, each plump foot and ankle
loaded with several pounds weight of silver. The slender, gold tinted
Purbhu with their hair tightly twisted, and a corona of mogra flowers,
have a shrinking grace and delicacy which is very attractive. The Marwari females, with skirts full of plaits . . . and sari dragged over the
brow . . . are very curious figures, seldom pretty. Surati girls, with their
drapery so tightly kilted as to show great sweeps of the round, brown
limbs, smooth and shapley." The Surati girls are Venuses of the "stable
and kitchen" and are frequently seen "with a child on their hips." Then
there were the "trim little Malwen girls," whose skin, from "confine-
ment" in the cotton factories, is getting "fairer and lighter," who "sling
quickly along with a saucy swing of their oscillant hips."[66]

British and Indian conceptions of the relationship between women's dress and appearance in public and female modesty were in marked contrast with one another. Upper-class Indian women in north India, both Hindu and Muslim, were rarely seen outside of their homes, and within their houses usually spent most of their time in their own quarters, the zanana. For these women there was an elaborate code of avoidances of certain male affines, and sharp separation of the domains of males and females. Modest behavior centered around the face and head; covering for the rest of the body could be more or less casual and to some extent revealing of the shape of the body. If a male entered the female quarters, usually announced by a servant or by a loud cough, women would quickly cover their faces with their sari or a scarf, unless the visitor was classified as a younger brother. If upper-class women were to go out, they would usually travel in a closed palanquin or a totally cloth-draped conveyance. If they had to move in public on foot, they would be covered from head to toe in a wrapper, or would wear their saris in such a way as to cover their heads and obscure their faces completely. In the north, lower-class or lower-caste women would be seen in public, at times working the fields, assisting males in their work, or moving about on errands. In the south, except in areas of Muslim settlement, women tended to be less restricted in their movements and their appearances in public.

British women in India similarly restricted their public appearances to areas defined as British space, and when seen outdoors were usually riding horses, in carriages, or being carried. They were, however, much concerned to be well covered both in terms of protecting their skin from the Indian sun and for modesty's sake. In the house, they shared the domestic space with their husbands and male Indian servants. Although British women would cover their heads with bonnets, caps, or shawls, and in the second half of the nineteenth century and the twentieth century with sun helmets, they would make no effort to obscure their faces. In fact, their faces, lips, and complexion were lovingly painted or chronicled by European men, and admired or denigrated by other women.

Unlike their European counterparts, Indian women of all statuses did not wear undergarments that confined or constricted their breasts, stomachs, and/or hips. When Indian women wore bodices or blouses (*choli*), in the later nineteenth century, they were made to be form-fitting and to accentuate the shape of their breasts. Mrs. Meer Hassan Ali, an Englishwoman married to an upper-class Muslim in Lucknow in the early nineteenth century, who lived for a number of years happily in a zanana, described for her British readers the *angiya* (bodice) worn by her Muslim relatives. The garment was made of gauze or net or muslin, "the more transparent in texture the more agreeable to taste. . . . It is made to fit the bust with great exactness, and to fasten behind with strong cotton threads; the sleeves are very short and tight and finished with some fanciful embroidery or silver riband."[67]

Until quite recently, Indian women have shown little inclination to adopt items of Western women's attire, except for adding petticoats under their saris, and the choli. Even in households in which the men wore Western clothes, women usually continued to wear versions of the sari. Since the late nineteenth century, prepubescent girls have been wearing European-style frocks, or a cameeze (kamis)—a word and a garment presumably modeled on the European shirt.

S. C. Bose, who roundly condemned the Bengali babus in late nineteenth-century Calcutta for their imitation of European dress, thought their wives, sisters, and daughters could be more decently attired if they "adopted a stouter fabric for their garment in place of the present, thin, flimsey, loose, sari." He highly approved of the fact "that a few respectable Hindoo ladies have of late years begun to put an unghia or a corset over their bodies," but their "under vestments are shamefully indelicate." Bose went on to lecture "the Baboos of Bengal" that they should strive to introduce a salutary change "in the dress of their women folk, which private decency and public morality most urgently demand." Bose recommended changes in female dress that were less revealing, and averred that well-corseted bodies had to "go hand in hand with religious, moral and intellectual improvement. The one is essential to the elevation and dignity of female character as the other is to the advancement of the nation in the scale of civilization."[68]

Official India did not concern themselves with women's attire as they did with that of their Indian employees and allied princes. Until the later part of the nineteenth century, women did not often appear on those public occasions when the Raj was on display. The Begum of Bhopal, her face entirely veiled and her body fully draped in her mantle of the Star of India, was a curiosity much commented on and a mainstay of the illustrated periodicals of the later nineteenth century. When women did appear in public, as at the visit of the Prince of Wales to Gwalior in 1876, the British artist sketching the scene depicted many of the women with head bowed and hands covering their faces.

Although officially the Raj was little concerned with the "decency" or indecency of women's attire, there were Europeans who were very much concerned with how Indian women were dressed—the Protestant missionaries. During the first half of the nineteenth century in Travancore, a princely state on the southwest coast of India, Protestant missionaries had been successful in converting a substantial number of low-caste Shanars, or Nadars as they came to term themselves. The southwest coast is sociologically and culturally one of the most complex regions in the subcontinent, with a significant population of Muslims, Moplahs (Muslims), a community of Syrian Christians, and even Jews who date from the first or second century C.E. In addition, there was a large and highly stratified Hindu community. European observers of the nineteenth century regarded the caste system of Malabar in general and Travancore in particular as the most rigid in the subcontinent.

The nineteenth-century historian of the Travancore state, P. Shungoony Menon, described his homeland with pride and some hyperbole as "perhaps the only kingdom in India which preserves its original caste, religion, customs, manners and institutions etc."[69] He went on to quote with approval the comments of the compiler of the Travancore records "that Travancore is one of the very few remaining specimens of a pure Hindu government, the institutions of which have never been affected by the Mohammedan conquest."

The Nadars, among whom the missionaries were to have so much success, are usually described as palmyra tappers, the sap being used to make jaggary, a form of sugar which when distilled becomes toddy. Some Nadars were also carters and semi-nomadic; others were agricultural laborers and tenants of Nair landlords. They were concentrated in the southwestern tip of India, some in the Tinnevelly district of Madras, and others across the border in the southernmost part of Travancore. The Nadars were ranked below shudra Nairs, who were the military and landholding caste in the state, and the untouchable "slave castes," who were bound to upper-caste landholders and the state. The highest ranking caste, the Nambudri brahmans, were priests, landlords, and state officials.

There was a highly specified code of respect and avoidance behavior enforced by the state. Caste status was marked by fixed distances to which a low-caste person could approach a brahman: the Nadars were supposed to remain thirty-six paces from the person of a Nambudri brahman. They were also prohibited from carrying umbrellas, and wearing shoes or golden ornaments. Their houses had to be only one story high, and they could not milk cows. Nadar women could not carry pots on their hips nor could they cover the upper part of their bodies.[70] Nair women were allowed to wear a light scarf around their shoulders, which at times would be draped over their breasts. However, they were expected to be bare-breasted in the presence of brahmans and other high-status people, as a sign of respect. In addition, all castes below the rank of Nair could wear only a single cloth of rough texture, which was worn by both men and women and which could come no lower than the knee nor higher than the waist.[71]

Syrian Christian and Moplah women were permitted to wear a short, tight-fitting jacket, the *kuppayam*.[72] The Syrian Christians were in a relatively privileged position in the state and were, like the Nairs, warriors and landholders. The Moplahs also supplied troops and were merchants.

The conversion to Christianity of the Nadars began in the Company's Tinnevelly district. Here the Nadar women began wearing "long clothes" at the request of the missionaries; as conversion spread across the border into Travancore, the Nadar women began to wear the Nair breast cloth. Colonel John Munro, who was both the British Resident and dewan (prime minister) at the Travancore court in 1813, issued an order granting permission to "women converted to Christianity to cover their bosoms as obtain among Christians in other countries." This order was quickly rescinded when the pidakakars, members of the raja's ruling council, complained that such an order would eliminate the differences among castes and everything would become polluted in the state. Munro modified his orders by forbidding the Nadar women to wear the Nair loose scarf, but allowing them to wear the *kuppayam*, the jacket worn by Syrian Christians and Moplahs.[73]

In the next ten years the missionaries followed a policy of vigorous proselytizing with an educational and economic program aimed at changing the economic and legal position of dependence of their low-caste followers. One of their first acts was to establish a school for Nadar girls in which they were trained in European-style lace making. Earnings from lace making and other cash-producing activities were used to buy their "freedom" from their landlords, who had extracted various forms of labor from them. The Nadars, somewhat ironically, also profited from their traditional trade of toddy tapping, as the Company's government here and everywhere in India controlled and encouraged the use of alcohol. Establishing a system of shops for its sale, the government taxed its use and collected fees from the licenses granted to the sellers.

The missionary agenda, in addition to conversion of the Nadars, was to free them from what they saw as the thraldom of "the heathen caste system." To do this meant establishing communities, centered on chapels, churches, and schools, and to enhance their sense of worth and separate them from other subjects of the Travancore kings. The missionaries, directly and through the British Resident, established a position of influence with the king and his immediate court as representatives of culture and political order whose power was clearly growing throughout India. In doing this they attempted to bypass the king's local and regional officials, usually drawn from or with close connection to the dominant landed caste of the Nairs and Nambudris, who resented what they took to be the pretentions to higher status within the caste system being demonstrated by their inferiors, the Nadars.

Although the wives of the missionaries had designed and were producing a loose jacket that met their criteria for modest clothing that befitted Christian women, the Nadar women continued, with or without the jacket, to prefer to wear the Nair-style breast cloth. In the 1820s there was an increasing number of incidents in markets and other public places, when Nadar women wearing the Nair breast cloth were attacked, stripped, and beaten; chapels and schools were also burned. The government of Travancore in 1828 acted to prevent further violence by restating the previous policy of forbidding the Nadar women to wear the Nair-style cloth, but allowing the jacket. The king reaffirmed the requirement that the Nadars, like other low castes, were still required to perform *ooliam* service—corvee labor—and that Nadars were enjoined to act in relation to upper castes according to "usage before conversion."[74]

In 1859, trouble broke out in Travancore. General Cullen, the British Resident, reported to the governor of Madras "that the wearing of the cloth by Shanar women, like that of the Shudras [Nairs] had led gradually to violent outrages and quarrels and almost to an insurrection."[75] Cullen explained that many of the Nairs had misinterpreted Queen Victoria's proclamation of 1858, which ended the Company's rule and established direct rule of India under the Crown of Great Britain. In the proclamation she stated that "we shall respect the rights, dignities and honour of Native Princes as our own" and then went on to state, "in framing and administering the law due regard" would "be paid to the ancient rights, usages and customs of India."[76] The proclamation was widely read and disseminated in all the languages of India. The Nairs and the officials interpreted the proclamation to mean that it not only prohibited all future interference with caste, "but annulled all previous interventions."[77]

Although Cullen leaned toward enforcing the right of the Travancore state to enforce rules forbidding the wearing of the Nair cloth by Nadar and other low-caste women, the government of Madras, under pressure from missionaries in England and in India, instructed Cullen in no uncertain terms that they were a Christian government and "the whole civilized world would cry shame on us, if we did not take a firm stand" against the king of Travancore.[78]

The maharaja did not completely yield to the pressure of the Madras government, but seemed to satisfy them that "he was desirous to put an end to the barbarous and indecent restrictions previously existing on the dress of Shanar women." In his proclamation of July 26, 1859, he agreed to extend the privileges previously granted to Nadar Christians to all Nadars, as he didn't want any of his subjects to "feel aggrieved"; all could wear jackets like Christian Nadars, and they all could dress in "coarse-cloth, and tying themselves round with it as the Mukkavattigal [low-caste fisherwomen] and they could cover their bosoms in any manner whatever; but not like the women of higher caste."[79] These "rights" were further extended to Iravars, another low caste that was rapidly being converted to Christianity.

The solution was far from satisfactory as far as the missionaries were concerned. The proclamation was seen as, if anything, retrograde. Christian Protestant women occupied a good position in Travancore life, "socially and morally," wrote the Reverend Samuel Mateer of the London Mission Society. They were educated and "trained in the habits of refinement and comfort"; they were accomplished in the work of producing "embroidery or beautiful lace, for which medals have been given at some of the great Exhibitions." Yet they were still forced to wear coarse cloth, which although tied across the breasts left the shoulders bare, as in the dress of fisherwomen, whom the Nadars considered beneath them. Mateer found this attempt to legislate dress counter to the spirit of "advancing civilization," and the prescribing of the coarse, that is, handwoven, cloth was a "suicidal policy in respect to the development of commerce and manufactures."[80]

It appears the Nadars continued to ignore the restrictions, and evolved a costume that imitated the costume "of the higher class Hindus." P. S. Menon, who was dewan, a peishcar (high revenue official), and who had been personally involved in the events of 1859, wrote "that this style of costume adopted by the Shanar converts was with the express object of annoying the Hindu section of the population." Menon believed that it was the missionaries who were directly behind what could only be thought of as a direct insult not only to Nairs, but to all Hindus. He conceived of the dress as part of a concerted plan on the part of the missionaries, who used their color and nationality to influence the Madras government, "to create in the Hindus a spirit antagonistic to the Christian religion," and by implication to draw the British government into supporting the Christian converts in Travancore.[81] He may have been right, as Mateer states, that not until "all classes of the community are allowed, as in Tinnevelly [a part of British India] full liberty to follow their own inclinations and tastes in matters of dress, personal adornment and comfort" would the issue be settled.[82]

The controversy over the breast cloth lives on in the works of the historian R. N. Yesudas.[83] The analysis and discourse which Yesudas adopts translates the battle into part of a wider class struggle, and the missionaries are credited with providing the conditions for a Marxist-style social revolution. T. K. Ravindran, in the Foreword to Yesudas' *People's Revolt*, considers the battle waged by the Nadar women as a victory in the march of progress against entrenched habits, customs, and privileges of orthodox Hindus, who are the representatives of a "licentious, degenerate, pleasure loving feudal caste-culture." These Hindus have dominated an "oozy, slavish and meek underprivileged class" until, through "the conscious and voluntary efforts" of the lower classes, they overthrew the outmoded social and political order and showed the way toward "the social regeneration of Travancore."[84]

Whether the breast-cloth controversy was part of an epic struggle to free the lower classes from feudal domination, as Yesudas and Ravindran would have it, or part of a wider movement within the caste order of south India for the Nadars to raise their status in the social hierarchy, as Hardgrave would have it, or the triumph of decency and Christian values, as Mateer would have it, would seem paradigmatic of the relationship between clothes and colonialism. Changes in dress become the tokens of much wider social, economic, and political changes that refracted in unpredictable ways, from the point of view of the principle actors in the events. For the missionaries, as part of their civilizing package, Indian women had to be modestly dressed, taught useful skills, and be freed from the domination of—in this case—brahmans and Nairs who were sexually as well as economically exploitative. A bare-breasted woman, by definition, was the object of male lust. Significantly, it was the wives of the missionaries who seemed to have taken the lead in designing a properly demure clothing style.

The Nadars utilized the position and influence of the missionaries to attack directly their superiors in the state hierarchy; throughout the controversy they were much more concerned with wearing the Nair woman's scarf or adopting the dress of upper-caste women than appearing to meet the missionaries' concern with decent dress *per se*. The controversies became crucial in the formation of a wider caste or group identity, which fit with the capacity to take advantage of new economic opportunities created by the conditions of foreign colonial rule, through the government's encouragement of the use of alcohol to increase revenue. As Hardgrave has traced, some of the Nadars moved from being toddy tappers and makers to being sellers and transporters of the toddy, and from these activities into other lucrative occupations. In the twentieth century, the Nadars in Madras utilized their religious, caste, and economic networks to become a political force. By trying to overthrow the prescriptive rules imposed by the Travancore state, a wider market for machine-manufactured cloth would be created, Mateer argued, so that decency and proper dress would be linked with the expansion of the markets for British industrialists, and all this could be done in the name of the advancement of civilization.

The Uniform of the Indian National Congress

By the last decades of the nineteenth century, there was increasing documentation of the declining production of fine cotton textiles in India.

Muslins of Dacca, printed cloths of the south of India, palampores, fine woolen shawls of Kashmir and the Punjab had all but disappeared.[85] While the demise of fine weaving and printing was being decried, it was also noted that cheaper and coarser cotton cloth, frequently woven out of imported thread, continued to be in demand as it was cheaper and sturdier than Lancashire-made dhotis and saris. The effects of European imports on the production of Indian textiles were highly differentiated on a regional basis, and reflected ritual imperatives, changing social statuses, and taste. E. B. Havell, superintendent of the School of Arts in Madras and subsequently of the Government Art School in Calcutta, who was the most influential of the Europeans concerned with the restoration of Indian fine arts and crafts, described the complexities of the situation in regard to Indian textiles in Madras:

> The European goods have their great advantage in point of cheapness, and consequently the native manufacturer who supplies the wants of the low caste and poorer classes has suffered most.
>
> *White Cloths—for Male Wear.* Two kinds of white cloth for personal wear are produced by the native weaver: first, a plain white cloth with a narrow border of coloured cotton, and sometimes with a broader band woven across each end, which are worn by the low caste poor; and, secondly, superior cloths of fine texture in which the borders are broader and of silk, and generally embroidered with a simple pattern, and the bands at each end either of silk or of silver lace. These cloths, originally intended for Brahmins only, are now indiscriminately worn by the wealthier classes of every caste. The first of these has been almost entirely superseded for general wear by English long cloth, which is cheaper than the native cloth by about one half. Still, the manufacture is carried on throughout the districts on a very small scale, for the native cloth is always worn, by those who can afford it, on occasions of ceremony, and by some it is preferred on account of its superior durability and thicker texture. The manufacture of the finer cloths still occupies a very large proportion of the weavers, and is extensively carried on in and around about Madura and Salem. The prosperity of this industry has also been affected to a less extent by the cheapness of European goods, in a similar way, that whereas a well-to-do native would formerly have four to six country cloths in constant wear, many now reserve the more expensive costume for the religious and domestic ceremonies at which a Hindu would expose himself to ridicule if he appeared in other than this traditional dress. But as these cloths are only within the reach of the wealthier classes, it is probable that the spread of Western ideas and mode of dress has had more prejudicial effect on the industry than the mere cheapness of European goods. Both in the fine, but more especially in the inferior cloths, the profits of the weaver seem to be reduced to a very low margin.

Cloths for Female Wear. The manufacture of cloths for female wear is carried on on a very extensive scale, and has not declined to such an extent as the other, for though the industry has suffered considerably in the inferior kinds by the competition of English and French cheap printed cotton goods, European manufacturers have not hitherto produced anything which can at all compete with the finer cloths of Tanjore, Kuttálam and Kuranád, and other places. While the more gorgeous beauties of the textile manufactures of the north, such as those of Benares, Surat and Gujerat, have been fully recognised, it is a pity that the more sober, though none the less remarkable, artistic qualities of these fine cloths and their adaptability in many ways to decorative purposes have not been better appreciated. Artistically speaking, a decline is only noticeable in the cotton cloths, most of which have lost their characteristic beauty by the use of European dyed thread. The Madura cloths, however, are an exception.[86]

The decline of the craft production of Indian cloth, used for dress, decoration, and rituals, was caused by a combination of price and the changing of taste of Indian consumers. In the 1860s European manufacturers had not yet developed an adequate knowledge of the varied tastes of Indians or the functions of cloth in India. James Forbes Watson, reporter of economic products at the India Office in London and director of the India Museum, was a lifetime student of Indian textiles who produced eighteen volumes containing seven hundred samples of Indian textiles. Twenty sets of what Watson thought of as portable "textile museums" were distributed in Great Britain and India. His goal was to acquaint manufacturers with the "tastes and needs of their Indian customers." In addition to his sample books, he wrote what remains today the most extensive single-volume study of Indian dress and textiles, *The Textile Manufactures and the Costumes of the People of India.* In this work he explained that to be successful, the manufacturer producing cloth for the Indian market had to know "how the garment was worn, by which sex and for what purpose." Above all, he had to grasp "the relationship between the size of cloth, its decoration and use, if he were to be sucessful in selling textiles in India." The European manufacturer might produce a cloth that was correct in size, length, and breadth for a turban or *lungi* (loincloth) but it might prove "unsaleable because its decoration is unsuitable . . . or because it is not in good taste from an Indian point of view."[87]

Watson cheerfully stated that increased consumption of European cloth in India would be good for both the Manchester manufacturers and the people of India. Indians were underclothed and hence cheap textiles would be a boon for them. If the Indian weavers couldn't compete, it wouldn't necessarily be a bad thing as:

In a great productive country like India it is certain that *she* will gain; for if supplies from Britain set labour free there, it will only be to divert it at once into other and perhaps more profitable channels. It might be otherwise if India were not a country whose strength in raw products is great and far from developed; but as it is, her resources in this direction are known to be capable of a vast expansion and to be sufficient to occupy the energies of her whole people.[88]

As can be seen by the exchange between the lieutenant-governor of Bengal and his Bengali underlings, Indian tastes in clothes were rapidly changing. The thousands of clerks and functionaries who worked in the government and commercial offices of Calcutta and Bombay had by the late nineteenth century developed a distinctive form of dress, a mixture of Indian and European. They wore an unironed white European shirt with tails out, covering the top of their finely draped white dhoti; their legs were bare to mid-calf, showing white socks held up by garters, and their feet were shod in patent leather pumps or short boots produced by Chinese bootmakers in Calcutta.[89]

Some of the wealthier and more flashily dressed Bengalis were described by S. C. Bose as thinking that an adaptation of the European style of dress could bring them the benefit of "modern civilization" by "wearing tight pantaloons, tight shirts and black coats of alpaca or broadcloth." They would top this costume with "a coquettish embossed cap or a thin folded shawl turban."[90]

The wealthy of Calcutta sought to modernize not only their dress, but their home furnishings as well. I noted above the separation of the large Calcutta mansions into two sections: a domestic one of the women which was private, and a public set of rooms used by males for entertaining their Indian and occasional European guests. The drawing rooms were furnished in a mixed "oriental" and "western" style.

A Canadian visitor, Anna Leonowens, described a visit to the home of a wealthy gentleman, Ram Chunder, in Bombay. She described him as "educated in all the learning of the East as well as in English, but never the less a pure Hindoo in mind and character." The occasion was for an evening of Indian dance, drama, and music. Her host was dressed in a "rich and strikingly picturesque" manner. He wore deep crimson satin trousers, a white muslin angaraka or tunic, a purple vest with gold embroidery, a fine Cashmere cummerbund, white European stockings, and embroidered antique Indian slippers. The entertainment took place in a large room, furnished in the oriental style, with *kincob* (brocade) wall hangings decorated with peacock feathers. The floors were a fine tile mosaic, and around the walls on tables and shelves were a "melange of European ornaments, clocks, antique pictures, statues, celestial and terrestrial globes and a profusion of common glass wear of the most brilliant colors."[91]

It was not only the wealthy, Western-educated, or urban middle classes whose dress was beginning to change, but more common folk as well. Tribesmen recruited from the hills of southern India as labor on tea and coffee plantations spent some of their wages on turbans and caps (innovations for them) and woven coats "of English cut" for festival clothes.[92] An Indian working for Edgar Thurston, superintendent of the Madras Government Museum and head of the Ethnographic Survey of Madras, appeared wearing a white patchwork shirt, adorned "with no less than six individual and distinct trademarks representing the King-Emperor, Brittania and an elephant, etc." The inclusion of the printed trademarks was generally popular; soldiers of the maharaja of Kashmir wore jackets blazoned with the manufacturer's identification of "superfine."[93] European manufacturers were supplying cloth with all sorts of designs, which according to Thurston met the "Indians' love of the grotesque," a taste nurtured by exposure to the "carvings on Hindu temples and mythological paintings." One of the most popular patterns in cloth manufactured for use in women's petticoats had a border "composed of an endless procession of white bicycles of ancient pattern with green gearing and treadles, separated from each other by upright stems with green and gold fronts."[94]

While a few Europeans were proselytizing for better taste and seeking to "direct progress in a right groove and to prevent the decline of Indian art," some early Indian nationalist writers were developing a critique of the Government of India's policies furthering the destruction of Indian "manufactures," which they claimed advantaged British manufacturers to the detriment of incipient Indian efforts to establish modern industry. The early nationalists also argued that government revenue policies were contributing to the continued misery of the mass of Indian cultivators.[95]

Thus there were two streams of thought: the aesthetic and moral concern of Europeans influenced by the arts and crafts movement in Great Britain and their Indian experience, and the early Indian nationalist critique of government policies leading to the continued impoverishment of India. These two streams of thought provided a major part of the ideology of the swadeshi movement in Bengal, 1903–1908. The movement's goals were complex, but one aim was to encourage the development and use of indigenously produced goods through a boycott of European manufactures. As the movement developed, there was increasing discussion and propaganda to encourage Indian weavers and to revive the hand spinning of cotton thread.[96] These ideas were taken up and formalized by Mahatma Gandhi through the next decade. Gandhi had been much influenced by Ruskin's and Morris's critiques of modern industrial society and its destructive and alienating effects on the bodies, minds, and morals of the European working classes.[97] Gandhi continually articulated and elaborated on the theme that the Indian people would only be free from European domination, both politically and economically, when the masses took to spinning, weaving, and wearing homespun cotton cloth, khadi. To give substance to these theories, he created the enduring symbols of the Indian nationalist movement: the *chakra* (spinning wheel), which appeared on the Indian National Congress flag and continues to be ambiguously represented on the Republic of India's flag, and the wearing of a khadi "uniform," a white handspun cotton dhoti, sari, or pajama, kurta and a small white cap.

In 1908, when he was still in South Africa, Gandhi began to advocate handspinning and weaving as the panacea for the growing pauperization of India. (Decades later, Gandhi could not recall ever having seen a spinning wheel when he began to advocate their use).[98] In 1916, after his return to India, he established an ashram where a small group of his followers were to begin practicing what Gandhi had been preaching. The first order of business was to find or develop a chakra to implement his call, not only to boycott foreign-made cloth and thread, but to make and wear their own khadi. At first they had to make do with cloth that was handwoven, but made of mill-made thread produced by Indian mills. It was not until 1917 or 1918 that one of his loyal followers, Gangabehn Majumdar, located some spinning wheels in Baroda and encouraged some weavers to spin and weave cloth for the ashram. The next step was to try to produce their own cloth at the ashram; the first result was a cloth thirty inches wide, which was too narrow for an adequate dhoti. The first piece of cloth produced cost seventeen annas per yard, grossly expensive for the time. Finally Gangabehn was successful in getting cloth of adequate width, forty-five inches, made so that Gandhi was not "forced to wear a coarse short dhoti."[99]

I have been unable to find out when and how Gandhi created the uniform of the Indian National Congress, but it was clearly between 1918 and 1920. During the first Non-Cooperative Movement of 1920–1921, the wearing of khadi and especially the cap, by now dubbed a "Gandhi cap," was widespread and became the symbolic focus, once again, of the British-Indian battle over headdress. In March of 1921, Gandhi reported that some European employers were ordering that the white khadi caps not be worn in the office. Gandhi commented that "under the rule of Ravana," the villain in the Ramayana, "keeping a picture of Vishnu in one's house was an offence, [so] it should not be surprising if in this Ravanarajya [Raj of Ravana] wearing a white cap . . . not using foreign cloth, or plying the spinning wheel came to be considered offences."[100]

A month later, the collector of Allahabad in eastern Uttar Pradesh forbade government employees from wearing "the beautiful, light inoffensive caps." A few months later in Simla, Indians in government service said they risked dismissal if they wore khadi dress and caps. A lawyer in Gujarat was fined two hundred rupees and ordered out of court for wearing the cap; when he returned an hour later still wearing the cap, another two hundred rupees were added to his fine.[101] The campaign, as far as Gandhi was concerned, was highly successful. When an English businessman dismissed a young clerk for wearing the offending hat, he declared "the manager by his simple act of dismissal of a poor Indian employee had given political color to the transaction." The British were falling for Gandhi's symbolic transformation of the khadi cap into a sign of rebellion. He urged Indians everywhere, by the simple act of wearing a hat, to bring the Raj to its knees.[102] The British, Gandhi argued, were confusing Non-Cooperation with the use of khadi, thereby reinforcing the power of the movement. If they were so frightened by the mere wearing of a khadi cap, which was a "convenience and symbol of swadeshi," what might happen if he, Gandhi, asked government employees to stop working, and not just wear khadi?

The chief justice of the High Court of Bombay issued a letter to all judges under his jurisdiction to bar pleaders in their courts from wearing the Gandhi cap; if they continued to do so, he said, they were to be charged with contempt of court for having been disrespectful to the judge. The chief justice went on to state, "No pleader should appear in Court if he wears any headdress *except* a turban." Gandhi also reported that a Muslim youth was shot by a European youth for selling or wearing a Gandhi cap."[103]

Mad Dogs and Englishmen Go Out in the Midday Sun

Aside from the questions of power, status, and respect reflected in clothing, the British were also concerned about how their clothing might protect them from heat and disease. For the majority of English men and women the adaptation to life in India began on shipboard. The length and nature of the trip was to change from the eighteenth century, when the trip around the Cape of Good Hope to Madras or Calcutta could take upwards of seven or eight months. In the 1840s it was down to 100–120 days, with voyages sometimes beginning in England or in one of the Mediterranean ports going to Alexandria, then over land to Suez, and then catching another ship for Bombay or the east coast of India. With steamships and the opening of the Suez Canal in 1867, the voyage could be done in a month or six weeks; by the time of the First World War it was down to a little over three weeks.

The form of the trip, its symbolic significance, and the preparations for the trip and life aboard ship maintained a constancy through all these changes. Comforts aboard ship increased but the meaning of the voyage remained the same. The outward-bound voyage for most meant a new life and separation from family, friends, and the green fields, gardens, and cool damp climate of England. On ship the "griffin" (newcomer) or "spin" (unmarried woman or spinster) mingled with the old hands, who began their socialization to the codes of conduct expected of pakka sahibs and memsahibs.

The first set of questions the voyager faced, no matter what his or her purpose for going to India, was about collecting a proper kit for the voyage and for life in India. The voyagers in the early nineteenth century were advised to bring with them enough clothes to last through the voyage, as there were no laundry facilities aboard ship. Captain Williamson suggested no fewer than four dozen shirts of a very fine "stout calico, such as may be used in a hot climate, where linen is particularly prejudicial to health due to its feeling cold when moist with perspiration."[104] About a dozen of the shirts should be of superior quality and with frills. He advised an equal number of undershirts, some of which should reach to the hips to serve as sleeping garments.

The male voyager would require four pairs of pantaloons, two of heavy and two of light cloth, in addition to an unspecified number to wear when he would get to India. He needed woven cotton underwear, about six dozen pairs of stockings of varying length and material, two or three velvet stocks, four dozen linen neck handkerchiefs, and an equal number made of some inferior material for underwear, plus two or three woolen waistcoats and two dozen white Irish linen waistcoats. Our voyager should be equipped with a warm greatcoat, presumably for the Atlantic portion of the voyage, and two or three other coats or jackets for the voyage, along with several pairs of boots and shoes. Young men in the Company's military service, as they wouldn't know which regiment they were going to be assigned to, were warned not to have their uniforms made up in England, since they would not have the proper facings, collars, and cuffs. They should, however, take along a bolt of superfine scarlet broadcloth of good quality, which could be made up into uniform coats after arrival in India.

Captain Williamson was silent on the question of the necessary kit for a lady traveling to India. Rather he thought it necessary to instruct his readers on the costs and benefits of acquiring an Asian *chère amie*. Forty rupees a month or about forty pounds a year would provide our English sojourner not only with a bed companion but someone who could manage his household. Nine out of ten women, he advised his readers, "domiciled by gentlemen are Mussulmans, Hindus being far more scrupulous."[105] The other possibility was a Portuguese lady, as they made far better housekeepers than their Muhammadan counterparts, but Williamson had found them too full of pride about their ancestry, and vindictive. Williamson provided his reader with ten pages of description of the jewelry which Indian ladies preferred and which made up part of their pay.

Fifteen years after Williamson's first edition of *India Vade Mecum*, a digest of this work, with additions, was produced by J. B. Gilchrist, the pioneer linguist who had written while still in India a series of grammars, dictionaries, and class books on Hindustani for the aid of Englishmen who had to learn the language. On his return from about twenty years in India in 1803, he opened up a language school in London. Times had changed and the reader would get no instructions from Gilchrist on hiring an Asian *chère amie*, but we are told about the kite-flying capacities of Muslim ladies and get an abridged version of Williamson's directory to Indian jewelry.

He did, though, provide a list of "Necessaries for a Lady Proceeding to India":

72	Chemises
36	Night Gowns
36	Night Caps
3	Flannel Petticoats
12	Middle ditto, without bodies
12	Slips
36	Pr. Cotton Stockings
24	Pr. Silk ditto
2	Pr. Black Silk ditto
18	White Dresses
6	Coloured ditto
6	Evening ditto
60	Pocket Handkerchiefs
4	Dressing Gowns
	Silk Pelisse
3	Bonnets
12	Morning Caps
24	Pr. Long Gloves
24	Pr. Short Gloves
4	Corsets
6	Pr. of Sheets
6	Pillow Cases
36	Towels
	Riding Habit. . . .[106]

The quantities of clothes suggested for both men and women going to live in India did not vary much through the first half of the nineteenth century, but the nature of the materials thought best fitted for the Indian climate did. Gilchrist advised ladies going to India to take fifteen flannel petticoats, and for civilian employees of the Company he advised taking about twelve yards of flannel for waistcoats. There is indeed a cold season in India when flannel and woolen clothes are desirable, particularly in the evening. But Gilchrist does not discuss the use of various kinds of cloth for clothes, nor does he comment on the objections of Dr. James Johnson to the use of flannel clothes in India.

Johnson, a naval surgeon who served in India and the West Indies, was the author of an extensive discussion of the diseases of India in relation to the climate and its effects on Europeans, published in 1813. The European, when he enters the tropics, said Johnson, "must bid adieu to the luxury of linen," linen being the common textile used for underwear by Europeans of the eighteenth and early nineteenth centuries. The danger of linen in the tropics was its retention of perspiration, for if there was a breeze the wet linen "would often occasion a shiver and be followed by dangerous consequences." Johnson went on to explain that flannel was inconvenient for three reasons: it was too heavy, it was a much too slow conductor of heat from the body, and most importantly it was too irritating to the skin, and would "increase the action of the perspiratory vessels on the surface, where our great object is to moderate that process."[107] Nevertheless, for many decades thereafter flannel next to the skin was recommended to the European living in the tropics.

From the time of the Greeks down to the early nineteenth century, there was a cluster of ideas about the internal heat of the body, "the vital flame innate in heart," which had to be cooled by breathing and by the production of fluids and vapors, bile, urine, phlegm, and sweat. Not only was respiration necessary to cool the body but the skin itself was thought to breathe through the pores as well. The pores of the skin were involved therefore in a double function of bringing cool air in and allowing waste to leave in the form of sweat and vapors. It was long believed by medical practitioners and scientists that there were two forms of perspiration: the visible one and an invisible one, termed insensible perspiration. This insensible perspiration was the means by which "the denser excrement is eliminated." If this necessary body function was blocked, sickness and disease would follow. Hence the use of heavy bed clothes, heated rooms, hot baths, and hot drinks for the treatment of disease and to "release obstructions of the pores."[108]

Associated with the theories about perspiration, visible and insensible, was the doctrine of the "consent of parts" or "sympathies." Dr.

Johnson explained: "There exists between different and often distant parts of the body, a certain connexion or relation, that is, when *one* is affected by particular impressions, the *other*, sympathises, as it were, and takes on a kind of analogous action." The most widely noted of these sympathies is between the external surface, the skin of the body, and "the internal surface of the alimentary canal." Johnson went on to explain this relationship by an example. There is a man who has been out in the hot sun and his body temperature has risen to 100 degrees. When he comes in, he takes a glass of cold water and his body cools to 99, at this point "the external surface of the body immediately sympathising with the internal surface of the stomach relaxes, and a *mild* perspiration breaks out, which reduces the temperature to its natural standard, 98 degrees."[109]

Theories about the role of perspiration in "the consent of parts" were to continue to be standard assumptions in medical practice until the twentieth century, and were to have a determining effect on the clothes which Europeans wore in India and other tropical areas. Physicians, old India hands, tropical outfitters, and the writers of guide books and manuals of instruction were unanimous and constant in advising the traveler or sojourner in India to wear flannel next to the skin at all times. For example: "Most people wear flannel under their clothes, and a very proper practice it is, and an excellent protection against sudden alterations of weather."[110] And: "whatever may be said upon the subject of wearing flannel in India, I am quite certain that no one thing is more essential to health in warm climates than the continual use of flannel."[111]

W. J. Moore, deputy surgeon general of the Indian Medical Service, wrote *A Manual of Family Medicine for India*, which won a prize offered by the Government of India in 1873 for the production of a manual suitable for use for all those British scattered about India, "more or less remote from medical and surgical aid." In its various editions this was to be the standard work on health and hygiene for Europeans in "unhealthy localities" until the 1920s. Moore advised equestrians, even in the hottest weather, to wear "cord breeches and flannel, with overcoat of flannel or cotton" when out riding.[112]

Dr. Julius Jefferies, inventor of the *sola topi*, wrote extensively on the relationship between clothes and health in the European military in India. He argued that the campaigner's skin required a protective partition between it and the atmosphere as a barrier "against the passage of heat and gaseous particles either way." The physical properties of flannel made it the ideal textile for this important function, as it was "slow conducting, porous and spongy." This enabled flannel to "husband the resources of the skin"; it blocked the entrance of heat from the air into the body and prevented the too rapid cooling off of the body as it husbanded "all sensible perspiration."[113] He recommended wearing flannel underwear that covered the whole body and the arms and legs. Having worn such an outfit himself for seven years, he completely escaped from cholera, dysentery, and fever.

By the 1880s the injunction to wear flannel next to the skin had become reduced to the wearing of a flannel or woolen cummerbund at all times around the waist; this was referred to as a "cholera belt."[114] When I went to India by sea in July of 1952, as soon as we entered the Suez Canal I was warned by fellow passengers never to sleep without something covering my middle, particularly if I were under a fan. This advice was reinforced by my edition of Murray's guide, published in 1949, which strongly recommended a flannel cummerbund, a belt of flannel 8 inches to 12 inches wide around the waist with tapes over the shoulder, to be worn at all times.[115]

The redoubtable Flora Annie Steel, who spent twenty years in India in small district towns in the Punjab as the wife of a collector and magistrate, and who was an educational officer and novelist, was one of the few who cast doubt on the desirability of heavy clothing and flannel next to the skin during the hot season. Although she stated that "flannel next to the skin day and night is of course the shibboleth of doctors, and doubtless they are right," in the next sentence she cited her own experience of having spent many hot seasons on the plains, comfortably wearing silk, discarding her stays, and dressing in nun's veiling and serge. The key to health, she said, was proper food and "avoiding chills and heats."[116]

Even after cholera was established to be a water-borne disease, the cummerbund continued to be regular issue in the British, French, and German armies in the tropics. The American army of occupation in the Philippines was issued flannel shirts. Periodic unannounced inspections were ordered for the Bengal army as late as 1888 to insure that the men continued to wear their cholera belts.[117] Although by 1900 the flannel cummerbund was no longer worn to prevent cholera, it continued to be worn as protection against dysentery, diarrhea, and liver disorders, and was widely believed to maintain the bowels in good working order. The concerns of the British in India with their colons is neatly summed up in the statement of "an ex-civilian" offering advice to a newcomer. "If I were asked what is necessary for a man going to India in any department? I should say good bowels and Hindustani; failing either he will not succeed."[118]

The insistence on the use of flannel and the cummerbund, rooted in a theory of disease, had highly charged symbolic significance. In the cultural construction of the body, Europeans saw the body as having two halves: the half above the waist was the locus of the higher functions, thought, and conscience; the heart and head were the centers of the senses, feelings, and passions. The top half of the body was thus positively valued and was pure. The lower half of the body was seen as impure, the site of basic instincts that had to be controlled. Renbourn noted that "the flannel belt has become symbolic of duty, of a tight rein over basic instincts and of protection from a hostile environment."[119]

From the earliest days to the present, Europeans have viewed the Indian environment as dangerous. The heat, the direct rays of the sun, the heavy moisture in the air during the rainy season, the dust and hot winds of the dry season, the odors of the extensive marshes, the sudden drops of temperature in the evenings and dew of early morning, the odor of urine, feces, of rotting fruit and vegetables of the crowded cities and towns—these meant danger, pestilence, and disease, sudden death or lingering maladies, enervation and ultimately the degeneration of the vigorous European constitution.

Learned arguments developed that reflected changes in biological and social theory throughout the nineteenth and twentieth centuries as to whether white men could ever adapt to life in the tropics. One school held that with adequate precautions and through the process of "seasoning,"—changing diet, adjusting one's clothes, mode of life and accepting an initial period of fevers and fluxes—the body could adjust to a radically different climate. This process could be made more effective if proper personal hygiene and adequate sanitary measures were followed, relating to water, preparation of food, and disposal of body wastes. Attention had also to be paid to the location and construction of proper housing for Europeans to ensure free circulation of air to carry off as quickly as possible disease-inducing miasmas. A requisite for the health of the white man in the tropics was the prohibition, particularly in the heat of the sun, of any strenuous physical exercise. An army of dark-skinned servants was required to relieve the sahib of strenuous work. Even the enlisted white man in the tropics required personal servants to carry his pack during marches by day, and needed "coolies" for the necessary constructions accompanying military actions. There was an opposing school which argued that even with all these precautions white men could not adjust to the tropics.

To the late-twentieth-century reader, there would seem to be a contradiction between the concerns of Europeans to ensure for fresh, easily circulating, clean air, and their clothes, which prevented the circulation of air. The men wore tight-fitting jackets and well-buttoned shirts bound round the middle with a cummerbund, and long flannel underwear. The women were layered with tight-fitting blouses or bodices, heavy skirts, multiple flannel chemise and underdrawers, and tightly laced stays. But whatever else their function and meaning to the British in nineteenth-century India, clothes were a protective device against the manifest dangers of foul air emenating from marshes, swamps, rice fields, and the animal exhalations of humans. The air was so saturated with miasmata, Emma Roberts cautioned her readers, that even in the warm weather they should not dispense with their mosquito nets, under the mistaken impression that they "prevent the free circulation of the air." In addition to the protection they afford from the bite of insects, they also protect "from the miasma with which the atmosphere is frequently loaded. The moisture which is often found on the outside of these curtains showing how much they tend to preserve the party sleeping within from actual contact with baleful influences." Malaria, cholera, bowel disorders, chills, fevers, and croup were believed to be caused by the atmosphere. There was a perpetual and never-ending battle fought against the effects of chills, which appeared to be more dangerous than heat. To sleep in a draught could expose one to be awakened with a "stroke of the land wind," which in some instances "will deprive the individual so attacked, of the use of the limbs, and will at any rate be productive of severe pain."[120]

How was it that Indians could live and work in an atmosphere so highly dangerous to Europeans? It turns out that Indian anatomy, skin, and physiology are different from that of the Europeans. Dr. Johnson observed that boatmen could row for hours in the "scorching noontime heat," and when a boat would become stranded on a sand bar would jump into the water to free it. If a European would subject his body to such sudden changes in the surface temperature of the skin, he did so at "the risk of his life" or the destruction of his health. Nature fortunately has provided the poor Indian who has to labor in such a fashion with protection in the "color and texture of his skin." It was lucky for the Europeans who had to depend on the Indian's labor that the "extreme vessels" (pores) of the Indian's skin "are neither so violently stimulated by the heat, nor so easily struck torpid by sudden transitions to cold." The Indian's skin and the whole process of perspiring are different from that of the Europeans. Indian skins "secrete a very different kind of fluid being more of an oily and tenacious nature than the sweat of the European."[121] Not only did visible perspiration and insensible perspiration pass through the skin, disease-causing miasmas could enter the European's body through the same means, with pain and death following in short order.

As if the miasmata-laden atmosphere of India was not enough of a threat, another killer lay in wait for the unsuspecting European—the sun. Dr. Johnson had noted that the two indispensible items of Indian clothing were the cummerbund and the turban: the one to protect the viscera of the abdomen from the deleterious impressions of cold, the "other to defend the head from the direct rays of a powerful sun."[122] Johnson recommended not that Europeans adopt turbans as their headgear in India, rather that they place a wet handkerchief folded in their tall beaver hats to keep their heads cool.

The British in India did not develop and widely use any special hat as protection from the sun until the 1840s. Europeans had long feared direct exposure during the hot season to "the blows or strokes" of the sun, which it was believed caused apoplexy or sunstroke.[123] Indians and other dark-skinned peoples were believed by Europeans to be immune from these blows or strokes because they had a denser scalp or a thicker cranium. If a European man had to be out in the sun in the late eighteenth or early nineteenth century, he made sure his head was covered, usually with a tall stovepipe hat, and if he was walking he was frequently accompanied by a servant carrying a chatta, an umbrella or sun shade. Dr. Julius Jefferies, who was nothing if not inventive, stated that when he was in the Himalayas in 1824, "where the power of the sun is very great," he had made for himself a gothic-shaped hat with a wicker frame, over which he placed layers of cotton wadding, lined inside and out with white silk, and with ventilating space for free movement of air. He followed this hat with another: "the next which I used for several years had a cylindrical crown of large dimensions and a very broad brim. It was formed of two layers of pith *sola*, one-third inch thick, nearly one inch apart all around the top, with very free exits for the currents of air."[124] Jefferies was referring to pith of the sola plant, a light, easily shaped material. Sometimes the helmets made from sola were referred to by the British as "solar" topis. *Topi* is the Hindi term for hat, the Hindi *sola* being changed into the English "solar" by borrowing and a reanalysis through a folk etymology into a "solar topi" (sun hat).

During the siege of Delhi and the defense of the Residency in Lucknow in 1857, which took place during part of the hot season and during the monsoon, the formality of British military dress broke down. Large numbers of European and Indian troops had to march and maneuver in what were defined as terrible conditions. This was reflected in the protective headgear. While some troops fresh from Britain continued to wear their bearskin buskins, shakos, and forage caps, others, particularly officers, took to wearing helmets they thought more fitted to the exigencies of having to fight in the sun. Most popular were a wicker helmet that was vaguely modeled on Roman military headgear, with a pagri wrapped around the lower part of the crown; sola topis, with broad brims; and the "Napier topi," a brimless hat that featured a pagri acting as a neck curtain to keep the rays of the sun from the back of the neck. British officers who led irregular cavalry units frequently wore turbans, as did their men. The ever-inventive Dr. Jefferies, who by now had retired to England, actively proselytized for several of his own inventions in a book, *The British Army in India: Its Preservation by an Appropriate Clothing*, and in his extensive testimony before the Royal Sanitary Commission on the Army in India in 1863.

Jefferies assumed that very few natives of Britain "can long endure exposure to the sun without serious damage to the constitution unless . . . scientifically protected." He further assumed that to protect the British soldier in India effectively one had to proceed in a "scientific manner, and neither experience or usages of the Indians as far as clothes are concerned can provide a guide in developing the correct solutions to the problem." After explaining the processes by which heat is increased or decreased in its effects on the body, he criticized existing clothes and hats to show that they accummulate and fix heat, particularly on the head. The direct rays of the sun and high atmospheric temperatures in India excite the nervous skin, he said, especially that of the head, and the brain then acts on the impression from the overly excited skin "so acutely as to rule its own destruction by apoplectic congestion. The man falls struck by the sun. But much more frequently the brain, *the fountain of vital influence*, impresses its infirmity upon all the other organs, especially the liver, intestines and skin."[125] Having analyzed the causes of sunstroke in relation to the "killer clothing" which the British soldier had to wear, Jefferies turned to the question of the design of a scientifically produced helmet and body covering that would protect the soldier from the effects of the sun and atmosphere and his human enemies as well.

He designed helmets with an internal suspension system fitted to the actual head shape of the wearer, which allowed for several inches of air space between the top of the head and crown of the helmet. They were also designed to have a ventilating system based on convection, so that air would freely circulate and thereby keep the head cool through the evaporation of perspiration, and curtains of cloth to protect the back of the neck.[126] Jefferies then went on to develop a design of "body dress for British soldiers in India." He criticized the current practice of the army which encased men in heavy, tight-fitting jackets and trousers that were far "too retentive of the animal heat." Some had argued that the least and lightest clothing was best, as it allowed the freest action of evaporation. However, light cotton clothing without flannel underwear did not protect "the spine and trunk of the body" from the rays of the sun and radiations from walls and the ground. The back of a marching soldier exposed for many successive hours to the fierce "impulses of a tropical sun" needed more protection than a few layers of clothing. Jefferies advocated a kind of fore-and-aft curtain of metalized cloth, which would be layered on the front and back of the soldier, reflecting the sun and also allowing for convection to occur to carry off some of the heat.

As far as I know no one took seriously Jefferies' elaborate designs for headgear and "sun screen tunic" for soldiers or civilians. The sola topi in its military version of canvas, pith and later cork became standard summer dress for the European troops. To meet Jefferies' and others' concern for protection of the neck and especially the spine, neck curtains could be added to the rear brim of the sola topi, or a long strip of cloth could be wrapped around the crown, with a long end dangling down to provide a neck curtain.

Many physicians, though, felt that simple cloth was not enough protection for so vital a part of the body as the spine, and the spine pad or protector was designed. Dr. Moore graphically described the perils to which the spine was exposed, and offered this prescription:

> What is required is a permanent and immovable protection for the spine; a protection which may be put on and off with the clothing. And this is to be obtained by placing a pad about seven inches long and three wide from the collar of the coat to about the lower angle of the blade-bone. This pad should be constructed of cork shavings, a material which, while acting as a non-conductor of heat, is light, and sufficiently soft not to occasion inconvenience even if lain upon. The shavings should be stitched, so that the position of the pad cannot alter. The thickness of the pad should be about three inches.[127]

The sahibs had by 1870 generally adopted a "uniform," the distinctive components of which were sola topi with pugri, spinal pad, and cholera belt or flannel cummerbund. The topi was the most obvious mark of the ruling caste. British were rarely, from this time until the final demise of the empire, bare-headed. Men, women, and children each had their versions of the topi. The military, police, civilians, and political officers each had distinctive types of protection from the common enemy, the Indian sun. In the hills or during the cool season the topi might be replaced with the felt terai hat, which originated with the Gurkhas and subsequently spread into other parts of the empire, particularly South and East Africa, where the double terai with its distinctive red silk lining was to be popular until the 1960s—its name, terai (the wooded swampy sub-Himalayan tract), indicating its origins.

Medical research and theory continued to explore the effects of the sun's rays and heat on the European heads and bodies in India. By the end of the nineteenth century, the term "sun stroke" tended to be replaced by the term "heat stroke," and physicians began to argue that it might not be the direct rays of the sun beating on the cranium which were the direct cause of sun stroke. The experience of white-skinned troops, American, Australian, and British, who worked and fought in the southwest Pacific and in the China, Burma, and India theaters of World War

II, finally put to rest the strongly held beliefs that white men couldn't survive in the tropics if they worked in the noonday sun without their pith helmets and specially designed heavy protective clothing. It was found that minimally dressed, bare-headed soldiers could toil all day in the tropical sun, as long as they had plenty of water and could retreat into the shade occasionally. Today the pith helmet is all but gone in India; it is occasionally seen in a kind of scaled-down cheap version of a khaki canvas-covered pith helmet on the head of an officious stationmaster or whistle-blowing conductor, a last heritage of the Eurasians who provided many of the crews for the Indian railways in the pre-Independence days.

Heads and Feet: Turbans and Shoes

From the eighteenth to the twentieth century, the British and Indians fought out a battle about the proper forms of respectful behavior, centered on heads and feet. But to say that turbans, caps, and shoes were symbolically charged for both groups tells us little. What were the underlying meanings of this battle?

Europeans explained the nature of Indian headdress in functionalist and materialist terms: the turban was for the protection of the head. Watson described the Indian turban as providing "protection from the heat of the sun, it is usually of a fine muslin-like texture, which when folded, is at once bulky and porous—this admirably fulfilling its main purpose . . . [the light cloth] is a good non-conductor" and "allows the free escape of perspiration."[128] Indians clearly did not share the idea that the turban or other headdresses were primarily for protection from the sun. The elaborate decoration of the caps, the jewel-bedecked turbans of the rulers, and the choice of a hat as a major symbol of the Nationalist movement all indicate that hats are much more than a form of protection from the heat or the rays of the sun.

I can only sketch some of the possibilities that might help explain the significance of head coverings for Indians. Clearly, there is no simple answer to the question of the significance of the head for Indians. Abu'l Fazl wrote that for Muslims the head is the seat of the senses.[129] For Hindus the head is the locus of the eyes, including the third or inner eye in the center of the forehead. Lawrence Babb has persuasively argued that sight is the crucial sense cosmographically for Hindus. "Hindus wish to see their deities."[130] Today, Hindus live in constant sight of the deities, in the form of ubiquitous colored lithographs, which emphasize and accentuate the face and eyes of the deities. Indians wish to see and be seen, to be in the sight of, to have the glance of, not only their deities, but persons of power. The concept of darshan, to see and be seen, includes going to a temple, visiting a holy man or guru, or waiting for a glimpse of a movie star or the prime minister.

Babb stresses that the Hindu conception of "seeing" is not "just a passive product" of "sensory data originating in the outer world"; it involves the observer directly with the person or deity seen. Hindus live in a substantive world in which there are constant flows of various forms of matter, among them emanations from "the inner person, outward through eyes to engage directly with objects seen, and to bring something of these objects back to the seer."[131] Not only is the head the seat of sight, but it is also the part of the body that concentrates positive flows of substances and powers within the body. In the practice of raj yoga, for example, one seeks to concentrate through exercise and meditation the power of the whole body in the head.

As the head is the locus of power and superior forms of knowledge, the feet become the opposite. The feet are "the sources of downward and outward currents of inferior matter." When a Hindu visits a guru, a parent, a patron, a landlord, a government official, or a god, he or she will touch their feet. This is an "act of submission or surrender" but it is also a reciprocal act, as one is obliged to offer "shelter and protection to the one who has surrendered." By touching the feet one is taking what is ostensibly base and "impure" from a superior being and treating it as valuable and "pure."[132]

I think Babb's exegesis and analysis, which draws on the work of Wadley and Marriott in their discussions of power and substantive flows, provides an explanation for the significance of the head and feet, and hence their coverings. It explains why Lord Valentia was correct in surmising that his feet, if pointed toward the peshwa, would have defiled him; they were the source of impurity. Shoes and slippers were dirty, not just from being used to walk around in, but as the repositories of base substances flowing from the wearer's body. This is why it was an Indian custom not only to take off one's dirty shoes or slippers when entering the space of a superior, but more importantly, to sit so that the feet would not imperil the well-being of others.

The solution worked out in Indian courts to accommodate the inability of Europeans to sit for long periods on a rug or a cushion with their feet tucked under them was to allow them to sit on chairs; thus their feet, covered or uncovered, would be facing downward. Today, or at least yesterday—thirty-five years ago when I was doing field work in a village—the few villagers who had chairs would sit on them, particularly if they had provided me with a chair, but with their feet off the ground and tucked up under them.

A painting by Thomas Daniel, based on sketches by James Wales, shows Sir Charles Malet delivering a ratified treaty to the peshwa in Poona in 1792; we see almost all the Indians and Europeans sitting or kneeling on a large rug, while the peshaw sits on a slightly raised platform, supported by large cushions. Of the fifty-odd figures depicted, all but two have their feet placed so that they cannot be seen. Some of the English appear to have lap cloths or cummerbunds covering their feet; one English military officer is wearing boots, but the sole of his boot is on the ground. One Indian soldier is kneeling in such a fashion that one bare foot can be seen, but he too has the sole of his foot firmly on the rug.[133]

The writers of guide books who advised British travelers never to touch an Indian on his turban or head were correct, but this was not merely politeness in observing yet another peculiar Indian custom; because the hands, like the feet and mouth, are sources of impurities, touching the head would threaten the well-being of the Indian being touched.

In the conceptual scheme which the British created to understand and to act in India, they constantly followed the same logic; they reduced vastly complex codes and their associated meanings to a few metonyms. If Indians wore shoes in the presence of sahibs, they were being disrespectful in the early nineteenth century. But to Indians, the proper wearing of slippers or shoes stood for a whole difference in cosmology.

The European concepts of custom and superstition were a means to encompass and explain behavior and thought, and allowed the British to save themselves the effort of understanding or adequately explaining the subtle or not-too-subtle meanings attached to the actions of their subjects. Once the British had defined something as an Indian custom, or traditional dress, or the proper form of salutation, any deviation from it was defined as rebellion and an act to be punished. India was redefined by the British to be a place of rules and orders; once the British had defined to their own satisfaction what they construed as Indian rules and customs, then the Indians had to conform to these constructions. Wearing the Gandhi cap thus was a metonym for disorder. To the Indian this cap was indeed a symbol, but a highly complex one. Involving a cosmological system which set the meaning of the head and its covering, it had as well an ideological referent as a critique of British rule in India, and embodied to its wearer a protest against the insults and deprivations of 150 years of colonial rule.

NOTES

FOREWORD

1. "The British and the Mughal Court in the Seventeenth Century," unpublished paper written in the 1970s; not printed here, but planned for publication in a revised form.

2. It would be beyond the scope of this brief foreword to document this claim, though I quote another of Cohn's students, Paul Rabinow, who wrote in the preface to his own book, *French Modern* (Cambridge: MIT Press, 1989): "Bernard Cohn, at the University of Chicago, was teaching us about the relations of knowledge and power, spaces and colonies, long before I ever heard of Foucault" (p. x).

CHAPTER ONE
INTRODUCTION

1. Some of the material in this chapter has appeared in "Beyond the Fringe: The Nation State, Colonialism, and the Technologies of Power," by Bernard S. Cohn and Nicholas B. Dirks, in *Journal of Historical Sociology* 1:2 (June 1988), 224–29.

2. Benedict Anderson has established the parallel growth of "imagined communities," based upon mystical notions of the common origins of nations, of shared blood, descent from mythical heroes, or membership in nations which have fathers and mothers, whose male descendants are constituted as "brothers." *Imagined Communities* (London, 1983). In their book *The Great Arch*, Peter Corrigan and Derek Sayer (Oxford, 1985) described and analyzed how the British state was constructed as a repertoire of rituals and routines of rule that legitimized the state's powers to control its subjects' activities.

3. It is ironic that the twentieth century, which has seen so many radical breaks with the past, has been marked by the production of innumerable new histories. With the establishment of each "new" nation out of the old European colonial order, each has to be equipped with an official history of its precolonial past and its freedom struggle.

4. J. R. Mangan, *The Games Ethic and Imperialism* (Middlesex, 1985); Richard Symonds, *Oxford and Empire* (New York, 1986).

5. Bernard Cohn, "Representing Authority in Victorian England," and David Cannadine, "The Context, Performance and Meaning of Ritual: The British Monarchy and the Invention of Tradition," both in Eric Hobsbawm and Terence Ranger, eds., *The Invention of Traditions* (Cambridge, 1983).

6. Anthony D. Smith, *The Revival of the Modern World* (Cambridge, 1981), pp. 153–54.

7. See Bernard S. Cohn, "The Census, Social Structure and Objectification in South Asia," first published in the 1960s, frequently reprinted, including Ber-

nard Cohn, *An Anthropologist among the Historians and Other Essays* (Delhi, 1990), pp. 224–54.

8. George Peter Murdock, "Introduction" to *Social Structure* (New York, 1949), p. 476.

9. Ibid., p. 478.

10. Clellan Ford, "On the Analysis of Behaviour for Cross Cultural Comparisons," in *Cross-Cultural Approaches: Readings in Comparative Research* (New Haven, Conn., 1967).

11. Urbana, Illinois, 1967.

12. Ibid., p. 2.

13. Ibid., pp. vii, x.

CHAPTER TWO
THE COMMAND OF LANGUAGE AND THE LANGUAGE OF COMMAND

1. Sir Richard Temple, ed., *The Diaries of Streynsham Master, 1675–1680* (London, 1911), 1:446–47.

2. D. V. Kale, ed., *English Records on Shivaji* (Poona, 1931), pp. 195–96, 205, 266; Sir Charles Fawcett, ed., *The English Factories in India*, new series (London, 1936) 1:29, 69, 106.

3. Sir William Foster, ed., *The Embassy of Sir Thomas Roe to India, 1615–19* (London, 1926), p. 129.

4. Ibid., p. 100.

5. Ibid., p. 130.

6. Mohiuddin Momin, *The Chancellery and Persian Epistolography under the Mughals, from Babur to Shah Jahan* (Calcutta, 1971); Riazul Islam, *A Calendar of Documents on Indo-Persian Relations, 1500–1750* (Karachi, 1979), 1:1–53.

7. William Foster, ed., *English Factories in India* 12 (Oxford, 1925):14.

8. G. W. Forrest, ed., *Selections from the Bombay Records* (1887), 1:169–71; Madras Presidency, *Records of Fort St. George, Diary and Consultation Book, 1740* (Madras, 1931), pp. 224–26; Peter Marshall, *East Indian Fortunes* (Oxford, 1976), p. 11.

9. Forrest, *Selections* (1887), 2:202–9; Madras Presidency, *Records, 1740*, 85:209–303; S. C. Hill, ed., *Bengal in 1756–57* (London, 1905), pp. 411–13.

10. James Fraser, *The History of Nadir Shah* (London, 1742), pp. iii–vi; William Irvine, "Notes on James Fraser," *Journal of the Royal Asiatic Society*, 1899, pp. 214–20; L. Lockhart, *Nadir Shah* (London, 1938), pp. 304–6.

11. For Hastings's language skills see Peter Marshall, "Hastings as Scholar and Patron," in Anne Whiteman et al., eds., *Statesmen, Scholars and Merchants*, (Oxford, 1923), p. 243.

12. Mark Bence Jones, *Clive of India* (London, 1974), p. 225.

13. Some of the leading texts of the period are: Alexander Dow, *The History of Hindostan*, 1770; Sir William Jones, *A Grammar of the Persian Language*, 1771; George Hadley, *The Practical and Vulgar Dialect of the Indostan Language Commonly Called Moors*, 1772; N. B. Halhed, *A Code of Gentoo Laws, or, Ordinations of the Pundits*, 1776, and *A Grammar of the Bengal Language*, 1778; John Richardson, *A Dictionary of English, Persian and Arabic*, 1780; Wil-

liam Davy, *Institutes Political and Military of Timour*, 1783; Francis Balfour, *The Forms of the Herkern*, 1781; Charles Wilkins, *The Bhagvet Geeta*, 1785; William Kirkpatrick, *A Vocabulary, Persian, Arabic and English, Containing such Words as Have Been Adopted from the Two Former Languages and Incorporated into the Hindvi*, 1785; Francis Gladwin, *Ayeen i Akberry or the Institutes of the Emperor Akbar*, 1783–1786; and John A. Gilchrist, *A Dictionary English and Hindustanee, Part I*, 1787.

14. Great Britain, Parliament, *Third Report from the Committee appointed to Enquire into the Nature, State and Condition of the East India Company* (London, 1803), 3:379; originally published in 1773.

15. William Davy, *Institutes Political and Military of Timour* (Oxford, 1783), pp. li–liii.

16. Letter from William Davy to John Richardson, dated 8 March 1780, in John Richardson, *A Dictionary, English, Persian and Arabic* (Oxford, 1780), 2:xv.

17. Sir William Jones, *A Grammar of the Persian Language* (London, 1771), pp. i, viii, ix.

18. Ibid., p. x.

19. K. D. Bhargava, ed., *Fort William—India House Correspondence* (Delhi, 1969), 6:110–11.

20. Garland Cannon, *Oriental Jones* (Bombay, 1964), p. 24; see also idem, "Sir William Jones' Persian Linguistics," *Journal of the American Oriental Society* 78 (1958):262–73.

21. Jones, *Grammar*, pp. xiv–xv.

22. Ibid., pp. xiv, xvi–xix.

23. Marshall, "Hastings as Scholar," p. 245.

24. W. H. Hutton, ed., "A Letter of Warren Hastings on the Civil Service of the East India Company," *English Historical Review* 44 (1929):635.

25. Alexander Dow, "A Dissertation Concerning the Customs, Manners, Language, Religion and Philosophy of the Hindoos," in *The History of Hindostan*, 3rd ed. (London, 1792), 1:xxvii; reprinted with a commentary in Peter Marshall, ed., *The British Discovery of Hinduism in the Eighteenth Century* (Cambridge, 1970), pp. 107–39.

26. In John Z. Howell, *Interesting Historical Events Relative to the Province of Bengal and the Empire of Indostan* (London, 1767).

27. Marshall, *British Discovery*, p. 46 notes a and b.

28. Howell, reprinted ibid., pp. 48–50.

29. Letter from the Governor-General and Council to Court of Directors, Fort William, 3 November 1772, printed in Great Britain, House of Commons, *Reports from Committees of the House of Commons, 4: East Indies, 1772–3* (reprinted London, 1804):345–46.

30. George R. Gleig, comp., *Memoirs of the Life of the Right Honourable Warren Hastings* (London, 1841), 1:400.

31. *Reports from Committees of the House of Commons . . . 1772–3* 4:348–50.

32. Ibid., p. 348.

33. J. D. M. Derrett, "Sanskrit Legal Treatises Compiled at the Instance of the British," *Zeitschrift für Vergleichende Rechtswissenschaft* 63 (1961):72–117;

idem, "The Administration of Hindu Law by the British," *Comparative Studies in Society and History* 4 (1961):10–52; idem, *Religion, Law and the State in India* (London, 1968); Marc Galanter, "The Displacement of Traditional Law in Modern India," *Journal of Social Issues* 24 (1968):65–91; Lloyd and Susanne Rudolph, "Barristers and Brahmans in India: Legal Cultures and Social Change," *Comparative Studies in Society and History* 8 (1965):24–49; Ludo Rocher, "Indian Reactions to Anglo-Indian Law," *Journal of the American Oriental Society* 92 (1972):419–24.

34. Rosane Rocher, *Orientalism, Poetry, and the Millennium: The Checkered Life of Nathaniel Brassey Halhed, 1751–1830* (Delhi, 1983), pp. 48–73.

35. N. B. Halhed, *A Code of Gentoo Laws; or, Ordinations of the Pundits* (London, 1776), p. x.

36. R. Rocher, *Orientalism*, p. 51.

37. Jones to Cornwallis, 19 March 1788, in Garland Cannon, ed., *The Letters of Sir William Jones* (Oxford, 1970), 797.

38. Jones to Wilkins, 24 April 1784, ibid., p. 646.

39. Sir William Jones, " 'Preface,' Institutes of Hindu Law . . ." in *The Works of Sir William Jones* (London, 1807), 7:37.

40. Jones to Pitt, 5 February 1785, in Cannon, *Letters*, p. 664.

41. Jones to Wilkins, March 1785, ibid., p. 666.

42. Jones to Russell, 8 September 1785, ibid., p. 680.

43. Jones to Macpherson, October 1785, ibid., p. 687.

44. Jones to Hastings, 23 October 1786, ibid., p. 718.

45. Murray B. Emmenau, "India and Linguistics," *Journal of the American Oriental Society* 75 (1955):148.

46. Cannon, ed., *Letters*, pp. 643–44; and Garland Cannon, "Sir William Jones and Edmund Burke," *Modern Philology* 54 (1956/7):165–86; and see my "Law and the Colonial State in India," printed in this volume.

47. Jones to Cornwallis, 19 March 1788, Cannon, *Letters*, p. 795.

48. Jones to Chapman, 28 September 1785, ibid., p. 684.

49. Jones to Rouse, 24 October 1786, ibid., p. 721.

50. Jones to Cornwallis, 19 March 1788, ibid., p. 799.

51. George Lewis Smyth, *Monuments and Gennii of St. Paul's Cathedral and Westminster Abbey* (London, 1839), 2:631.

52. Nathaniel Halhed, *A Grammar of the Bengali Language* (Hooghly, 1778; facsimile reprint, 1969), pp. i–ii.

53. H. P. Foster, *A Vocabulary in Two Parts, English Bongalee and Vice a Versa, Part I* (Calcutta, 1799; reprinted Calcutta, 1830), p. iv.

54. Ibid., p. i.

55. William Carey, *Dialogues Intended to Facilitate the Acquireing of the Bengali Language* (Serampur, 1801), p. v.

56. William Carey, *Grammar of the Bengali Language* (Serampur, 1805), p. iv.

57. Halhed, *Grammar*, pp. xxi, xxii.

58. Ibid., pp. x–xi. See also Muhammad Abdul Qayyam, *A Critical Study of the Early Bengali Grammars: Halhed to Houghton* (Dhaka, 1982), for a highly sophisticated analysis of the linguistic and historical context of Halhed's *Grammar*.

59. Halhed, *Grammar*, p. xii.
60. Ibid., p. iii.
61. Ibid., p. ix.
62. Ibid., pp. xi–xii.
63. For early British ideas about Indian languages see: John Fryer, *A New Account of East India and Persia* (London, 1909), 1:95, 2:41–42, 103; J. Ovington, *A Voyage to Surat in the Year 1689* (London, 1929), p. 147; Thomas Bowrey, *A Geographical Account of the Countries Around the Bay of Bengal* (Cambridge, 1903), 18:6; H. D. Love, *Vestiges of Old Madras* (London, 1913), 2:147, 3:128; Temple, *Diaries*, 2:192.
64. Edward Terry, *A Voyage to East India* (London, 1655), p. 232.
65. G. A. Grierson, "On the Early Study of Indian Vernaculars in Europe," *Journal of the Asiatic Society of Bengal* 62 (1893):41–50; see also idem, "Bibliography of Western Hindi, Including Hindostani," *Indian Antiquary* (January 1903), pp. 16–25; (February 1903), pp. 59–76; (April 1903), pp. 160–79.
66. George Hadley, *Grammatical Remarks on the Practical and Vulgar Dialect of the Indostan Language Commonly Called Moors* (London, 1772), pp. vi, xii–xiii.
67. For Gilchrist's biography and selections from his works see M. Atique Siddiqi, *Origins of Modern Hindustani Literature: Source Materials: Gilchrist Letters* (Aligarh, 1963), and Sadiq-ur-Rahman Kidwai, *Gilchrist and the "Language of Hindoostan"* (New Delhi, 1972).
68. Siddiqi, *Origins of Modern Hindustani*, p. 21.
69. John B. Gilchrist, "Preface" to *A Dictionary English and Hindoostanee*, 2 parts (Calcutta, 1786, 1790). The preface was reprinted as an appendix to the *Grammar and Dictionary* (Calcutta, 1798). References here are to the 1790 edition.
70. Ibid., pp. vii, xiv.
71. Ibid.
72. Ibid., p. xxvi.
73. Ibid., p. v.
74. Ibid., p. xli.
75. Ibid.
76. Ibid., pp. xix–xx.
77. Ibid., p. xx.
78. Ibid., p. iv.
79. Ibid., p. xxiii.
80. Ibid., p. xxii.
81. Ibid, pp. xxii–xiv,
82. India Office Records and Library, Board's Collection, #1981, vol. 97.
83. For the history of the College of Fort William see Sisir Kumar Das, *Sahibs and Munshis: An Account of the College of Fort William* (Calcutta, 1978); and David Kopf, *British Orientalism and the Bengal Renaissance* (Berkeley and Los Angeles, 1969).
84. There is no agreement on the exact number of books published in Hindustani, Braj, and Urdu under the auspices of the college. Kidwai, *Gilchrist*, p.

25, lists sixty Urdu books published between 1800 and 1804; Das, *Sahibs and Munshis*, lists forty-four books in Hindustani produced at the college between 1802 and 1804. A. Locket, secretary of the college, listed twenty-eight works in Braj, Urdu, and Hindustani published at the expense of the government between 1800 and 1812. India Office Library and Records, Board's Collection, #10708, vol. 446.

85. William Carey, *Dialogues*. For discussion of the significance and a partial linguistic analysis of these dialogues, see Sisir Kumar Das, *Early Bengali Prose: Carey to Vidyasagar* (Calcutta, 1966), pp. 68–75, and Das, *Sahibs and Munshis*, pp. 74–75.

86. Das, *Sahibs and Munshis*, p. 74.

87. John Borthwick Gilchrist, *English and Hindostanee calculated to promote the Colloquial intercourse of Europeans in the most useful and familiar subjects, with Natives of India Upon their arrival in That Country*, 2nd ed. (London, 1809).

88. Quoted in Gilchrist's *Dialogues*, p. lxxx.

89. Ibid., p. lxxi.

90. J. B. Gilchrist, *The General East India Guide and Vade Mecum . . . Being a Digest of the work of the Late Cap' Williamson with Many Improvements and Additions* (London, 1825), pp. 536–37.

91. John Briggs, *Letters Addressed to a Young Person in India* (London, 1828).

92. "Instructions by Major General Sir John Malcolm, To Officers Acting under His Orders in Central India, in 1821," in Sir John Malcolm, *The Political History of India, from 1784–1823* (London, 1826): 2, appendix 7, pp. cclxiii–cclxiv.

93. Briggs, *Letters*, pp. 9, 50.

94. Gilchrist, *East India Guide*, pp. 536–39; *Dialogues*, pp. 174–81.

95. Gilchrist, *East India Guide*, p. 546.

96. V. C. P. Chaudhary, "Imperial Honeymoon with Indian Aristocracy," *Kashi Prasad Jayaswal Research Institute, Historical Research Series* (Poona), no. 18 (1980), appendix 13, pp. 425–36.

97. Gilchrist, *East India Guide*, p. 551.

98. Ibid., pp. 564–65.

99. Frederick John Shore, *Notes on Indian Affairs* (1837), 1:27.

100. Christopher King, "The Nagari Prachaini Sabha . . . ," Ph.D. dissertation, University of Wisconsin, 1974; Rajendralal Mitra, "On the Origin of the Hindvi Language and Its Relation to the Urdu Dialect," *Journal of the Asiatic Society* 33 (1864):489–515; John Beames, "Outline for the Plea for the Arabic Element in Official Hindustani," ibid. 35 (1866):1–13; F. S. Growse, "Some Objections to the Modern Style of Hindustani," ibid., pp. 172–81.

101. W. C. Taylor, "On the Present State and Future Prospect of Oriental Literature Viewed in Connection with the Royal Asiatic Society," *Journal of the Royal Asiatic Society of Great Britain and Ireland* 2 (1835):4, 9. Capitals in original.

102. Letter printed as part of the introduction to Charles Wilkins, ed., *The Bhagvet-Geeta or Dialogues of Kreeshna and Arjoon* (London, 1785), p. 13.

103. Ibid., p. 15.

104. Sir James Mackintosh, "A Discourse at the Opening of the Literary Society of Bombay, 26 November 1804," *Transactions of the Literary Society of Bombay* 1 (1819, reprinted 1877):xiv, xi.

105. H. T. Colebrooke, *Miscellaneous Essays*, edited by Sir T. E. Colebrooke (London, 1873), 1:61, letter dated April 18, 1794.

106. "Minute by Governor General Warren Hastings, 17 April 1781," in H. Sharp, ed., *Selections from the Educational Records*, part 1: *1781–1839* (Calcutta, 1920), p. 8.

107. Ruth Gabriel, "Learned Communities and British Educational Experiments in North India: 1780–1830," Ph.D. dissertation, University of Virginia, 1979, p. 109.

108. Glieg, *Memoirs of Warren Hastings*, 3:159.

109. Gabriel, "Learned Communities," pp. 112–20.

110. Letter from Jonathan Duncan to Lord Cornwallis, 1 January 1792, in Sharp, ed., *Selections*, pp. 9–11.

111. Sharp, ed., *Selections*, pp. 33–36.

112. "Minute by Lord Minto, 6 March 1811," ibid., p. 19.

113. Lord Wellesley, "Notes with Respect to the Foundation of a College at Fort William," in Montgomery Martin, ed., *Despatches and Minutes . . . of the Marquis of Wellesley . . . In India* (London, 1836), 2:329–30.

114. Sisir Kumar Das, *Sahibs and Munshis*, pp. 7–21.

115. Bernard S. Cohn, "Recruitment and Training of British Civil Servants in India 1600–1800," in Ralph Braibanti, ed., *Asian Bureaucratic Systems Emergent from the British Imperial Tradition* (Durham, 1966), pp. 116–40.

116. India Office Library and Records, Board's Collection, vol. 465, #110708, for the list of books subsidized, and #11252 for the Court's remarks. For publications in the entire period of the College, see Das, *Sahibs and Munshis*, appendix E, pp. 155–66.

117. Mathew Lumsden, *A Grammar of the Persian Language* (Calcutta, 1810), p. xxviii.

118. Das, *Sahibs and Munshis*, p. 107.

119. "Some Account of the Literary Life of Charles Philip Brown, Written by Himself," in C. P. Brown, *English-Telugu Dictionary* (1866; 2nd ed., Madras, 1895), p. xiv.

120. Robert Caldwell, *A Comparative Grammar of South Indian Family of Languages* (1896; 3rd ed., reprinted New Delhi, 1974), pp. xii–xiii.

121. "Report of A. D. Campbell, 17 August 1823," in House of Commons, *Committee on the Affairs of the East India Company*, 1832–1833, appendix, Public I.2, vol. 12, p. 353.

122. William Adam, *Reports on Vernacular Education in Bengal and Behar*, edited by J. Long (Calcutta, 1868), p. 20.

123. F. W. Ellis, "Note to the Introduction" in A. D. Campbell, *A Grammar of the Telagu Language* (Madras, 1820), pp. 1–2; for a discussion of Ellis's work and significance see Walter Eliot in *Indian Antiquary* 4 (July 1875):219–21 and 7 (November 1878):274–75; R. E. Asher, "Notes on F. W. Ellis and an Un-

published Fragment of His Commentary on the Tirukkural," *Proceedings of the First International Conference Seminar of Tamil Studies* (April 1966), pp. 513–22.

124. India Office Library and Records, Board's Collection, vol. 12, #549, letter dated 12 May 1814, pp. 19, 47.

125. Ibid., pp. 47, 49–51.

126. Thomas R. Trautman, "The Study of Dravidian Kinship," in Madhav M. Deshpande and Peter Edwin Hook, eds., *Aryan and Non Aryan in India*, Michigan Papers on South and Southeast Asian Studies, no. 14 (Ann Arbor, 1979), pp. 153–54.

127. Caldwell, *Comparative Grammar*, pp. xi–xii.

128. Brown, *Dictionary*, p. xv.

129. Kamil Zvelbil, "Tamil Literature," in Jan Gonda, ed., *A History of Indian Literature*, vol. 10, fasc. 1 (Wiesbaden, 1974), p. 3.

130. Ibid., pp. 3–4.

CHAPTER THREE
LAW AND THE COLONIAL STATE IN INDIA

1. C. S. Srinivasachari, ed., *Fort William—India House Correspondence* (Delhi, 1962), p. 184.

2. Ranajit Guha, *A Rule of Property for Bengal* (Paris, 1963), p. 13.

3. A. M. Davies, *Strange Destiny: A Biography of Warren Hastings* (New York, 1935), pp. 65–72; Keith Feiling, *Warren Hastings* (London, 1966), pp. 92–107; Peter Marshall, "Warren Hastings as Scholar and Patron," in Ann Whiterman et al., eds., *Statesmen, Scholars and Merchants* (Oxford, 1973), pp. 242–62; H. Blochmann, *The Aini Akbari* (translation) (Calcutta, 1865; reprinted New Delhi, 1965), pp. v–ix.

4. Davies, *Strange Destiny*, p. 71.

5. R. Koebner, "Despots and Despotism: Vicissitudes of a Political Term," *Journal of the Warburg and Courtald Institutes* 14 (1951):276.

6. Alexander Dow, *The History of Hindustan*, 3 vols. (London, 1772), 1:xi.

7. Ibid., 2:xxxiii, 3:xxxv.

8. Robert Orme, "General Idea of the Government and People of Indostan," in *Historical Fragments of the Mogul Empire* (1792; London, 1805), p. 437.

9. Ibid., pp. 443–46.

10. Ragahavan Iyer, "Utilitarianism and All That," in Ragahavan Iyer, ed., *South Asian Affairs*, St. Antony's Papers 1 (London, 1960); Lewis D. Wurgaft, *The Imperial Imagination* (Middletown, Conn., 1983), pp. 17–53; Francis G. Hutchins, *The Illusion of Permanence* (Princeton, 1967), pp. 17–153.

11. G. R. Gleig, *Memoirs of the Life of Warren Hastings, First Governor-General of Bengal*, 3 vols. (London, 1841), 1:273, 401.

12. Ibid., p. 400.

13. Great Britain, House of Commons, *Reports from the Committees of the House of Commons*, 4: *East Indies 1772–3* (reprinted London, 1804):348.

14. Rosane Rocher, *Orientalism, Poetry, and the Millennium: The Checkered Life of Nathaniel Brassey Halhed, 1751–1830* (Delhi, 1983), p. 51.

15. N. B. Halhed, *A Code of Gentoo Laws; or, Ordinations of the Pundits* (London, 1776), p. x.

16. J. D. M. Derrett, *Religion, Law, and the State in India* (London, 1968), pp. 240–41.

17. Rocher, *Orientalism*, p. 51.

18. Ibid., p. 65 n.20.

19. Halhed, *Code of Gentoo Laws*, p. ix.

20. S. N. Mukherjee, *Sir William Jones: A Study in Eighteenth-Century British Attitudes to India* (Cambridge, 1968); Garland Cannon, *Oriental Jones* (Bombay, 1964).

21. See Cannon, *Oriental Jones*, 2:797.

22. Ibid., pp. 666–80, 718.

23. Ibid., pp. 643–44.

24. Ibid., p. 795.

25. Ibid., p. 684.

26. Ibid., p. 699.

27. Ibid., Jones to Rouse, ibid., p. 720–22.

28. Ibid., pp. 795, 798.

29. Ibid., pp. 801–6; Raghuber Sinha, ed., *Fort William—India House Correspondence* (Delhi, 1972), 5:626, 660–61.

30. Amales Tripathi, ed., *Fort William—India House Correspondence* (Delhi, 1978), p. 349.

31. George Lewis Smyth, *The Monuments and Gennii of St. Paul's Cathedral and Westminster Abbey* (London, 1839), 2:631.

32. Sir William Jones, "Preface" to *The Digest of Hindu Law on Contracts and Successions* (Calcutta, 1798), p. 75.

33. H. T. Colebrooke, *Miscellaneous Essays*, 3 vols. (London, 1873), 2:465.

34. Jones, "Preface," p. 76.

35. Ibid., pp. 89–90.

36. Colebrooke, *Miscellaneous Essays*, 1:53.

37. V. A. Narain, *Jonathan Duncan and Varanasi* (Calcutta, 1959), p. 171.

38. Colebrooke, *Miscellaneous Essays*, 1:666; Thomas Strange, *Elements of Hindu Law*, vol. 1 (Madras, 1825).

39. Colebrooke, *Miscellaneous Essays*, 1:95.

40. J. D. M. Derrett, *Dharmashastra and Juridical Literature* (Wiesbaden, 1973), pp. 51–52.

41. Colebrooke, *Miscellaneous Essays*, 1:95, 96.

42. Ludo Rocher, "Schools of Hindu Law," in J. Ensink and P. Gaeffke, eds., *Maior: Congratulatory Volume Presented to J. Gonda* (Leiden, 1972), pp. 168, 170.

43. Colebrooke, *Miscellaneous Essays*, 2:479.

44. Ibid., p. 978

45. Ibid., p. 487.

CHAPTER FOUR

THE TRANSFORMATION OF OBJECTS INTO ARTIFACTS, ANTIQUITIES, AND ART IN NINETEENTH-CENTURY INDIA

1. In writing this paper I have relied heavily on the works of Mildred Archer, Pramod Chandra, and Partha Mitter, who have made accessible through their

researches to an outsider, such as myself, the history of European interpretations of Indian art, architecture, and antiquities in the nineteenth century.

2. Chandra Mukherji, *From Graven Images: Patterns of Modern Materialism* (New York, 1983), pp. 166–209; John Irwin, *Studies in Indo-European Textile History* (Ahmedabad, 1966); John Irwin and Margaret Hall, *Indian Painted and Printed Fabrics* (Ahmedabad, 1971).

3. Donald F. Lach, *Asia in the Making of Europe*, vol. 2, book 1: *The Visual Arts* (Chicago, 1970), pp. 7–55.

4. De La Crequinière, *The Agreement of the Customs of the East-Indians, with those of the Jews, and other Ancient People* (London, 1705), p. 216.

5. Jean de Thevenot, *Travels into the Levant* (London, 1687), p. 65; Thomas Bowrey, *A Geographical Account of the Countries around the Bay of Bengal* (Cambridge, 1905), p. 25.

6. Thomas Herbert, *Some Years Travels into Africa and Asia Major* (London, 1638), p. 443, illust. 1.

7. Michael Ryan, "Assimilating New Worlds in the 18th and 17th Centuries," *Comparative Studies in Society and History*, 1981, p. 525.

8. Ibid., p. 527.

9. Thomas Hahn, "The Indian Tradition in Western Medieval Intellectual History," *Viator* 9 (1978):214.

10. Montgomery Martin, ed., *Despatches and Minutes . . . of the Marquess of Wellesley . . . in India* (London, 1836), 2:329–30.

11. R. H. Phillmore, comp., *Historical Records of the Survey of India* (Dehra Dun, 1950), 2:91.

12. Francis Buchanan (Hamilton), *Journey from Madras through the Countries of Mysore, Canara and Malabar . . .* (London, 1807), 1:vii; Benjamin Heyne, *Tracts, Historical and Statistical on India* (London, 1814); Phillmore, *Historical Records*, 2:405–6.

13. William Cook Mackenzie, *Colonel Colin Mackenzie: First Surveyor General of India* (Edinburgh, 1952), pp. 1–10; H. H. Wilson, *A Descriptive Catalogue of the Mackenzie Collection*, 2nd ed. (1828; reprinted Madras, 1882).

14. Colin Mackenzie, "Biographical Sketch . . . Contained in a Letter Addressed by Him to the Right Honourable Sir Alexander Johnson," *Journal of the Royal Asiatic Society* 1 (1834):335.

15. Ibid.

16. Cavelly Venkata Ramaswami, "Biographical Sketches of Dekkan Poets," *Journal of the Royal Asiatic Society* 1 (1834):140–4.

17. Mackenzie, "Biographical Sketch," pp. 339–40.

18. T. V. Mahalingam, ed., *Mackenzie Manuscripts: Summaries of the Historical Manuscripts in the Mackenzie Collection* (Madras, 1972), 1:xiv–xv; India Office Library and Records, Catalogue, European Manuscripts, vol. 1, part 1 (London, 1916).

19. India Office Library and Records, Board's Collection, vol. 761, #20670, p. 15.

20. Extract, Public Letter to Fort St. George, 9 February 1810, ibid., vol. 867, #22924, p. 29.

21. Ibid., p. 33.

22. Ibid., p. 8.

23. William Taylor, *Catalogue Raisonnée of Oriental Manuscripts in the Library of the (Late) College, Fort Saint George*, 3 vols. (Madras, 1857–1862), 1:x.

24. Wilson, *Descriptive Catalogue*, pp. 14–15.

25. India Office Library and Records, Mackenzie Collection, Unbound Translations, Class XII, Letters and Reports #9:39–99.

26. Ibid.

27. Wilson, *Descriptive Catalogue*, p. 600.

28. Ibid., p. 602.

29. Ibid., p. 615.

30. Ibid., p. 617.

31. India Office Library and Records, Board's Collection, vol. 867, #22924.

32. Wilson, *Descriptive Catalogue*, pp. 594–99.

33. Taylor, *Catalogue Raisonnée*, 1:xvi.

34. India Office Library and Records, Board's Collection, vol. 1766, #72386, pp. 3–5.

35. James Prinsep, "Report of the Committee on Papers on Cavelly Venkata Lachmia's Proposed Renewal of Colonel Mackenzie's Investigations," *Journal of the Royal Asiatic Society* 5 (1836):512.

36. Taylor, *Catalogue Raisonnée*, 1:iv, x.

37. Ibid., 1:xii, xx.

38. Mahalingam, *Mackenzie Manuscripts*, 1:xxiv.

39. Mackenzie 1803, p. 273.

40. Ibid., p. 278.

41. Phillmore, *Historical Records* 2:340–52.

42. James Fergusson, *Tree and Serpent Worship* (London, 1873; reprinted Delhi, 1971), p. 150.

43. Colin Mackenzie, "Ruins of Amravutty, Depauldina, and Durnacotta," *Asiatic Journal* (1823), pp. 464–78.

44. Ibid., p. 469.

45. Ibid., pp. 469, 471.

46. Robert Sewell, *Report on the Amaravati Tope: and Excavations on Its Site in 1877* (London, 1880; reprinted Delhi, 1973), p. 19; James Burgess, *The Buddhist Stupas of Amaravati and Jaggayapeta* (London, 1888), p. 117; Douglas Barrett, *Sculpture from Amaravati in the British Museum* (London, 1954), p. 23; Ray Desmond, *The India Museum, 1801–1879* (London, 1982), p. 93.

47. Burgess, *Buddhist Stupas*, p. 17.

48. James Prinsep, "Translation of an Inscription on a Stone in the Asiatic Society's Museum, Marked No. 2," *Journal of the Asiatic Society of Bengal* 6:1 (1837):88–97, 218–23, 278–80.

49. Fergusson, *Tree and Serpent Worship*, p. 2; Desmond, *The India Museum*, pp. 115–16; Barrett, *Sculptures from Amaravati*, pp. 23–24.

50. Fergusson, *Tree and Serpent Worship*, p. 165.

51. James Fergusson, "On the Study of Indian Architecture," *Journal of the Society of Arts* 15 (1866):71–76.

52. Ibid., pp. 72–73.

53. Ibid., p. 73.

54. James Fergusson, "Description of the Amaravati Tope in Guntur," *Journal of the Royal Asiatic Society* NS 3 (1868):132–65.

55. Ibid., p. 163.

56. Fergusson, *Tree and Serpent Worship*, p. 157.

57. Ibid., p. 161.

58. Warren Gunderson, "The World of Rajendralal Mitra and Social and Cultural Change in Nineteenth-Century Calcutta," PhD Dissertation, University of Chicago, 1966, pp. 249–57.

59. James Fergusson, *Archaeology in India with Especial Reference to the Works of Babu Rajendralal Mitra* (London, 1884; reprinted Delhi, 1974).

60. Ibid., pp. 1, 3.

61. Ibid., p. iv.

62. Ibid., p. 5.

63. Ibid., p. 7.

64. Ibid., p. vii.

65. C. Sivaramamurti, "Amaravati Sculptures in the Madras Government Museum," *Bulletin of the Madras Government Museum, NS, General Section* 4 (1942).

66. Basil Grey, Introduction to Douglas E. Barrett, *Sculptures from Aravati in the British Museum* (London, 1954), p. vii.

67. Bernard S. Cohn, "The Command of Language and the Language of Command," 1985, reprinted in this volume.; Sisir Kumar Das, *Sahibs and Munshis: An Account of the College at Fort William* (Calcutta, 1978).

68. Bernard S. Cohn, "Recruitment and Training of British Civil Servants in India 1600–1860," in *Asian Bureaucratic Systems Emergent from the British Imperial Tradition*, edited by Ralph Braibanti (Durham, N.C., 1966), pp. 116–40.

69. James Fraser, *The History of Nadir Shah*, 2nd ed. (London, 1742).

70. Toby Falk and Mildred Archer, *Indian Miniatures in the India Office Library* (London, 1981), p. 15.

71. Ibid., p. 27.

72. Ibid., p. 31.

73. Robert Cran, "The Manley Ragamala: An Album of Indian Illustrated Musical Modes," *The British Museum Yearbook* 4: *Music and Civilization* (London, 1980), pp. 187 ff.

74. Mildred Archer, *Patna Painting* (London, 1947), and especially idem, *Company Drawings in the India Office Library* (London, 1972); and M. and W. G. Archer, *Indian Painting for the British, 1770–1880* (London, 1955).

75. Bernard S. Cohn, "The Census Social Structure and Objectification in South Asia," *Folk* 26 (1984). The quotation is from Thomas Williamson, *The East-India Vade-Mecum; or, Complete guide for gentlemen intended for the civil, military, or naval service of the honorable East India Company*, 2 vols. (London, 1910), 1:181.

76. Partha Mitter, *Much Maligned Monsters: History of European Reactions of Indian Art* (Oxford, 1977), pp. 84–106.

77. Ramprasad Chanda, *Medieval Indian Sculpture in the British Museum*

(London, 1936), p. iv; Evan Cotton, " 'Hindoo' Stuart," *Bengal Past and Present* 46:1 (1927):31–33.

78. Chanda, *Medieval Indian Sculpture*, p. xii.

79. Prinsep, "Translation of . . . No. 2," pp. 278–80.

80. Prinsep, "Translation of Inscription in Societies' Museum: Brahmeswar Inscription from Cuttack," *Journal of the Asiatic Society of Bengal* 7:1 (1938):558.

81. Mildred Archer, *Tipoo's Tiger* (London, 1959).

82. Ibid., Plates 15, 16, 17.

83. Denys Forrest, *The Tiger of Mysore: The Life and Death of Tipu Sultan* (London, 1970); Richard Altick, *Shows of London* (Cambridge, Mass., 1978).

84. Anonymous, *The Pictures of London* (London, 1820), 164–65; Augustus Charles Pugin and John Britton, *Illustrations of the Public Buildings of London*, 2 vols., 2nd ed. (London, 1838), 2:35–41; Thomas Miller, *Picturesque Sketches of London* (London, 1852); for a full discussion of the history of the museum see Desmond, *The India Museum*.

85. Pugin and Britton, *Public Buildings*, 2:40–41.

86. Ibid., p. 33.

87. Quoted in Desmond, *The India Museum*, p. 91.

CHAPTER FIVE
CLOTH, CLOTHES, AND COLONIALISM

1. David Beetham, *Transport and Turbans: A Comparative Study in Local Politics* (London, 1970), pp. 19, 20.

2. W. H. MacLeod, *The Evolution of the Sikh Community* (Oxford, 1976), pp. 14–15; Khushwant Singh, *A History of the Sikhs* 1 (Princeton, 1963):83–84.

3. J. P. Singh Oberoi, "On Being Unshorn," *Transactions of the Indian Institute of Advanced Study* 4 (Simla, 1967):97.

4. M. A. Macauliffe, *The Sikh Religion: Its Gurus, Sacred Writings, and Authors*, 6 vols. (Oxford, 1909), 5:215.

5. MacLeod, *Evolution*, p. 53.

6. Macauliffe, *Sikh Religion*, 1:xxiii.

7. R. W. Falcon, *Handbook on the Sikhs for the Use of Regimental Officers* (Allahabad, 1896), Preface.

8. Khushwant Singh, *The Sikhs* (London, 1953), p. 83; and idem, *A History of the Sikhs* (Princeton, 1966), 2:111–15.

9. Government of India, *Proceedings of the Committee on the Obligations Devolving on the Army in India, Its Strength and Cost I–A: Minority Report* (Simla, 1913), p. 156.

10. T. A. Heathcote, *The Indian Army: The Garrison of British Imperial India, 1822–1922* (New York, 1975), p. 103.

11. Sandra Wallman, "Turbans, Identities, and Racial Categories," *Royal Anthropological Institute Newsletter* 52 (October 1982):2; ibid. 56 (1983):16.

12. F. J. Shore, *Notes on Indian Affairs* (London, 1837), vol. 1.

13. William Foster, ed., *The Embassy of Sir Thomas Roe to the Court of the Great Mughal, 1615–19* (London, 1899), 1:552.

14. Ibid., p. 106.

15. Ibn Hasan, *The Central Structure of the Moghul Empire and Its Practical Working up to the Year 1657* (London, 1936), pp. 55–57.

16. Abu'l Fazl, *The Ain-i-Akbari* (Calcutta, 1927), 1:2.

17. Ibid.

18. I. A. Khan, "The Turko-Mongol Theory of Kingship," in *Medieval India: A Miscellany* (1972), 2:11–12; R. P. Tripathi, *Some Aspects of Muslim Administration* (Allahabad, 1959), pp. 105–6.

19. Khan, "Turko-Mongol Theory," p. 12.

20. F. W. Buckler, "The Oriental Despot," *Anglican Theological Review* 10:3 (1927–1928):239.

21. F. W. Buckler, "Two Instances of Khilat in the Bible," *Journal of Theological Studies* 23 (1922):197; idem, "Oriental Despot," p. 240.

22. Buckler, "Oriental Despot," p. 24.

23. Abu'l Fazl, *Ain-i-Akbari*, pp. 166–67.

24. Ibid.

25. Riazul Islam, *Indo-Persian Relations: A Study of the Political and Diplomatic Relations between the Mughal Empire and Iran* (Tehran, 1970), pp. 321–22.

26. Bamber Gascoigne, *The Great Mughals* (London, 1971), pp. 71–72.

27. E. B. Eastwick, *A Glance at Sind before Napier or Dry Leaves from Young Egypt* (Karachi, 1849), p. 277.

28. Abu'l Fazl, *Ain-i-Akbari*, 1:94.

29. Ibid., p. 97.

30. Mattiebelle Gittinger, *Master Dyers to the World* (Washington, D.C., 1982).

31. Godfrey Charles Mundy, *Pen and Pencil Sketches, Being the journal of a tour in India* (London, 1832), p. 172.

32. Bernard S. Cohn, "Representing Authority in Victorian England," in *The Invention of Tradition*, edited by Eric Hobsbawm and Terence Ranger (Cambridge, 1983), pp. 165–209.

33. India Office Library and Records, L/P & S/15/1:215.

34. Ibid., 3:80–82.

35. V. C. Chaudhuri, *Imperial Honeymoon with Indian Aristocracy* (Patna, 1980), p. 344.

36. J. W. Burrow, *A Liberal Descent: Victorian Historians and the English Past* (Cambridge, 1981); Roy C. Strong, *Recreating the Past: British History and the Victorian Painter* (New York, 1978); Eric Hobsbawm and Terence Ranger, *The Invention of Tradition* (Cambridge, 1983).

37. See, for example, Sir Henry Sumner Maine's influential *Village Communities in the East and West* (London, 1890).

38. W. H. Russell, quoted in Charles Ball, *The History of the Indian Mutiny*, 2 vols. (London, 1859), 2:325–27.

39. Government of India, *Proceedings 1913*, I-A:156.

40. Vansittart, quoted in Francis Tucker, *Gorkha: The Story of the Gurkhas of Nepal* (London, 1957), pp. 92–93; see also David Bolt, *Gurkhas* (London, 1975).

41. *The Graphic*, March 4, 1876, p. 222.

42. C. C. Davies, "India and Queen Victoria," *Asiatic Review* NS 33 (1937): 487.

43. Ibid., p. 488.

44. Earle, India Office Library and Records Memo 1876, Euro MSS F86/163.

45. N. C. Chaudhuri, *Imperial Honeymoon*, p. 373.

46. *Illustrated London News*, January 29, 1912, p. 67.

47. Stanley Rice, *The Life of Sayaji Rao III, Maharaja of Baroda* (London, 1931), 2:16–22; Philip W. Sergeant, *The Ruler of Baroda: An Account of the Life and Work of the Maharaja Gaekwar Sayajirao III* (London, 1928), pp. 127–41.

48. David Cannadine, "The Context, Performance and Meaning of Ritual: The British Monarchy and the 'Invention of Tradition' c. 1820–1977," in Hobsbawm and Ranger, eds., *The Invention of Tradition*, pp. 101–64.

49. *Illustrated London News*, January 27, 1912, p. 11.

50. James Johnson, *The Influence of Tropical Climates more especially the Climate of India on European Constitutions; and the Principal Effects and Diseases thereby Induced, their Prevention or Removal and the Means of Preserving Health in Hot Countries, Rendered Obvious to Europeans of Every Capacity* (London, 1813), pp. 420–21.

51. Maria Graham Calcott, *Journal of a Residence in India* (Edinburgh, 1812), p. 2.

52. N. C. Chaudhuri, *Culture in a Vanity Bag* (Bombay, 1976), pp. 53, 57.

53. Som Prakash Verma, *Art and Material Culture in the Paintings of Akbar's Court* (New Delhi, 1978), p. 47.

54. J. B. Bushan, *The Costumes and Textiles of India* (Bombay, 1958), p. 30.

55. G. S. Ghurye, *Indian Costume* (Bombay, 1966), p. 129.

56. N. C. Chaudhuri, *Culture*, p. 58.

57. George Annesley Mountnorris, Lord Valentia, *Voyages and Travels in India, Ceylon* . . . (London, 1809), 2:120–21.

58. Ibid., p. 122.

59. Thomas Williamson, *The East-India Vade Mecum*, 2 vols. (London, 1810), 1:189–90.

60. Shore, *Notes*, 1:79–80.

61. Ibid., p. 80.

62. V. C. Chaudhuri, *Imperial Honeymoon*, p. 425.

63. Ibid., p. 429.

64. Ibid., p. 436.

65. Royal Sherer, *Sketches of India, Written by an Officer for Fireside Travellers at Home* (London, 1894), p. 12.

66. Edward Balfour, *Cyclopedia of India* (1885), p. 745.

67. Mrs. Meer Hasan Ali, *Observations on the Mussulmauns of India*, edited by W. Crooke (Lucknow, 1832; reprint London, 1974), pp. 60–61.

68. S. C. Bose, *The Hindoos as They Are: A description of the manners, customs, and inner life of Hindoo society in Bengal* (Calcutta, 1881), pp. 194, 195.

69. P. Shungoony Menon, *A History of Travancore* (Madras, 1878), p. vii.

70. Robert Hardgrave, "The Breast Cloth Controversy: Caste Consciousness and Social Change in Southern Travancore," *Indian Economic and Social History Review* 5 (1968):173.

71. R. N. Yesudas, *The History of the London Missionary Society in Travancore, 1806–1908* (Trivandrum, 1980), p. 172.

72. R. N. Yesudas, *A People's Revolt in Travancore: A Backward Class Movement for Social Freedom* (Trivandrum, 1975), p. 73.

73. Ibid., pp. 72, 73.

74. Hardgrave, "Breast Cloth Controversy," pp. 78–79.

75. Cullen to Pycroft, letter dated 13 January 1859, Great Britain, Parliament, *House of Commons Session II 1859*, vol. 25, paper 158, p. 357.

76. C. H. Philips, H. L. Singh, and B. N. Pandey, *The Evolution of India and Pakistan, 1858–1947: Select Documents* (London, 1962), pp. 10–11.

77. Great Britain, House of Commons Session II, 1859, *Proceedings*, vol. 25, paper 158, p. 357.

78. Governor of Madras to Cullen, in Hardgrave, "Breast Cloth Controversy," p. 185.

79. Samuel Mateer, *The Land of Charity: An Account of Travancore and Its Devil Worship* (New York, 1871), p. 305.

80. Ibid., p. 306.

81. Menon, *History*, pp. 506, 507.

82. Mateer, *Land of Charity*, p. 306.

83. Yesudas, *London Missionary Society* and *People's Revolt*.

84. *People's Revolt*, pp. x–xi.

85. E. B. Havell, "The Printed Cotton Industry of India," *Journal of Indian Art* 2:19 (1888):18–20; idem, "The Industries of Madras," *Journal of Indian Art* 3:26 (1890):9–16; George Birdwood, *The Industrial Arts of India* (London, 1880), pp. 244–58; John Irwin, *The Kashmir Shawl* (London, 1973).

86. Havell, "Printed Cotton Industry."

87. J. Forbes Watson, *The Textile Manufactures and the Costumes of the People of India* (London, 1866), p. 5.

88. Ibid., p. 8.

89. Edgar Thurston, *Ethnographic Notes in Southern India* (Madras, 1906), p. 519.

90. S. C. Bose, *The Hindoos as They Are*, p. 192.

91. Anna H. Leonowens, *Life and Travel in India* (Philadelphia, 1884), pp. 174, 175.

92. Thurston, *Ethnographic Notes*, p. 520.

93. *The Graphic*, March 4, 1876, p. 229.

94. Thurston, *Ethnographic Notes*, p. 522.

95. E. C. Buck, "Preface," *Journal of Indian Arts* 1:1 (1886):i–iv; Mahrukh Tarapor, "India and the Arts and Crafts Movement," paper read at the Victorian Studies Conference, Birmingham, 1978; idem, "John Lockwood, Kipling, and British Art Education in India," *Victorian Studies* 23:21 (1980):53–81; idem, "Art Education in Imperial India: The Indian Schools of Art," paper read at the Seventh European Conference on Modern South Asia Studies, SOAS, London, July 1981; Bipan Chandra, *The Rise and Growth of Economic Nationalism in India* (New Delhi, 1960); Sumit Sarkar, *The Swadeshi Movement in Bengal, 1903–08* (New Delhi, 1973), chapter 3. For a counter-argument, see Morris D. Morris,

"Towards a Representation of Nineteenth Century Indian Economic History," *Journal of Economic History* 23:3 (1963); and idem et al., "Reinterpretation of Nineteenth Century Indian Economic History," *Indian Economic and Social History Review* 5:1 (1968):1–15.

96. Sarkar, *Swadeshi Movement*, pp. 94–108.

97. Dilip Kumar Chatterjee, *Gandhi and Constitution Making in India* (New Delhi, 1984).

98. M. K. Gandhi, *An Autobiography: The Story of My Experiments with Truth*, vols. 1 and 2 of *The Selected Works of Mahatma Gandhi*, 6 vols. (Ahmedabad, 1968), 2:730.

99. Ibid., pp. 735–37.

100. M. K. Gandhi, *Collected Works* (Delhi, 1964–1965), 19:482.

101. Ibid., 20:105, 223, 204.

102. Ibid., 20:378–79, 487–88.

103. Ibid., 22:15, 175.

104. Thomas Williamson, *The East-India Vade Mecum*, 2 vols. (London, 1810), 1:9.

105. Ibid., p. 413.

106. J. B. Gilchrist, *The General East India Guide and Vade Mecum* (London, 1825), pp. 526–27.

107. James Johnson, *The Influence of Tropical Climates*, pp. 423–25.

108. E. T. Renbourn, "The Natural History of Insensible Perspiration: A Forgotten Doctrine of Health and Disease," *Medical History* 4 (1960): 135–37.

109. Johnson, *Influence of Tropical Climate*, pp. 13, 15.

110. John McCosh, *Medical Advice to the Indian Stranger* (London, 1841), p. 79.

111. J. H. Stocqueler, *The Oriental Interpreter* (London, c. 1850), p. 259.

112. W. J. Moore, *A Manual of Family Medicine for India* (London, 1883), p. 646.

113. Julius Jefferies, *The British Army in India: Its Preservation* (London, 1858), p. 102.

114. John Murray, *A Handbook for Travelers to India* 1st ed. (london, 1892), p. xvi.

115. Ibid., 16th ed. (1949), p. xx.

116. Flora Annie Steel, *The Complete Indian Housekeeper and Cook* (London, 1902), p. 172.

117. E. T. Renbourn, "The History of the Flannel Binder and the Cholera Belt," *Medical History* 1 (1957):211–25.

118. *Asiatic Journal* (1832), p. 189.

119. Renbourn, "The Flannel Binder," pp. 211, 223.

120. Emma Roberts, *The East India Voyager or the Outward Bound* (London, 1845), p. 38.

121. Johnson, *Influence of Tropical Climate*, pp. 421–22.

122. Ibid., p. 422.

123. E. T. Renbourn, "The Life and Death of the Solar Topi," *Journal of Tropical Medicine and Hygeine* 65 (1962):203.

124. Quoted ibid., p. 206.

125. Julian Jefferies, *The British Army in India: Its Preservation by an Appropriate Clothing, Housing, Locating, Recreative Employment and Hopeful Encouragement of the Troops* (London, 1858), pp. 9, 44–45. Enphasis in the original.

126. Ibid., pp. 55–101.

127. W. J. Moore, *A Manual of Family Medicine for India* (London, 1883), pp. 645–46.

128. Watson, *Textile Manufacturers*, p. 13.

129. Abu'l Fazl, *Ain-i-Akbari*, p. 167.

130. Lawrence Babb, "Glancing: Visual Interaction in Hinduism," *Journal of Anthropological Research* 37 (1981):387.

131. Ibid., p. 396.

132. Ibid., p. 395.

133. Mildred Archer, *India and British Portraiture, 1770–1825* (New York, 1979), plate 261.

INDEX

Note: Throughout, "Company" refers to the East India Company.

ABOUT THE AUTHOR

Bernard S. Cohn is Professor Emeritus of History and Anthropology at the University of Chicago. He is the author of *An Anthropologist among the Historians and Other Essays* and *India: The Social Anthropology of a Civilization*.

PRINCETON STUDIES IN CULTURE/POWER/HISTORY

SHERRY B. ORTNER, NICHOLAS B. DIRKS, AND GEOFF ELEY, EDS.

What Was Socialism, and What Comes Next? *by Katherine Verdery*

Citizen and Subject: Contemporary Africa and the Legacy of Late
Colonialism *by Mahmood Mamdani*

Colonialism and Its Forms of Knowledge: The British in India
by Bernard S. Cohn

Charred Lullabies: Chapters in an Anthropography of Violence
by E. Valentine Daniel

Theft of an Idol: Text and Context in the Representation of
Collective Violence *by Paul R. Brass*

Essays on the Anthropology of Reason *by Paul Rabinow*

Vision, Race, and Modernity: A Visual Economy of the Andean
Image World *by Deborah Poole*

Children in Moral Danger and the Problem of Government in Third
Republic France *by Sylvia Schafer*

Settling Accounts: Violence, Justice, and Accountability in Postsocialist
Europe *by John Borneman*

From Duty to Desire: Remaking Families in a Spanish Village
by June Fishburne Collier

Black Corona: Race and the Politics of Place in an Urban Community
by Steven Gregory

The Contradictions of Modernity and the Politics of Welfare Reform:
Welfare, Citizenship, and the Formation of the Weimar State, 1919-1933
by Young-Sun Hong

Remaking Women: Feminism and Modernity in the Middle East
edited by Lila Abu-Lughod